ISBN 978-1-332-33675-3
PIBN 10315795

1 MONTH OF
FREE
READING

at

www.ForgottenBooks.com

By purchasing this book you are eligible for one month membership to ForgottenBooks.com, giving you unlimited access to our entire collection of over 700,000 titles via our web site and mobile apps.

To claim your free month visit:
www.forgottenbooks.com/free315795

English
Français
Deutsche
Italiano
Español
Português

www.forgottenbooks.com

Mythology Photography **Fiction**
Fishing Christianity **Art** Cooking
Essays Buddhism Freemasonry
Medicine **Biology** Music **Ancient**
Egypt Evolution Carpentry Physics
Dance Geology **Mathematics** Fitness
Shakespeare **Folklore** Yoga Marketing
Confidence Immortality Biographies
Poetry **Psychology** Witchcraft
Electronics Chemistry History **Law**
Accounting **Philosophy** Anthropology
Alchemy Drama Quantum Mechanics
Atheism Sexual Health **Ancient History**
Entrepreneurship Languages Sport
Paleontology Needlework Islam
Metaphysics Investment Archaeology
Parenting Statistics Criminology
Motivational

THE NEW FORESTRY,

OR THE

CONTINENTAL SYSTEM ADAPTED TO BRITISH WOODLANDS AND GAME PRESERVATION.

ILLUSTRATED.

By JOHN SIMPSON,

Consulting Forester and Rural Estate Agent, Studfield House,
Wadsley, near Sheffield ;

**Expert to The Country Gentleman's Association, 16, Cockspur Street,
London, S.W.**

**Lately Head Forester, &c., to the Right Hon. the late Earl of Wharncliffe,
on the Wharncliffe Estates in Yorkshire.**

*Premier Medalist of the Société Nationale d'Acclimatation de France; Author of "Improved
Pruning and Training of Fruit Trees; Report on Horticulture (Fruit and
Vegetable Division) in " The Society of Arts Artizan Reports on the
Paris Universal Exhibition of 1878 ;" " The Wild Rabbit·
and Rabbit Warrens, &c."*

Assisted by his Son, J. J. SIMPSON, Estate Agent to Sir George Armytage, Bart., Kirklees,Yorks.

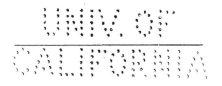

SHEFFIELD :

Published by Pawson & Brailsford, High Street and Norfolk Street,
1903.

TO THE MEMORY

OF

THE RIGHT HONOURABLE THE LATE EARL

OF WHARNCLIFFE,

THIS VOLUME IS GRATEFULLY INSCRIBED

BY

THE AUTHOR

(BY PERMISSION).

CONTENTS.

Contents—-Continued.

Contents—Continued.

ILLUSTRATIONS.

CUTS AND DIAGRAMS.

Plate No. 1.—Spruce Forest, not yet thinned, beginning of Rotation Period. Hartz Mountains, Germany. Pages 159—161.

Plate No. 2.—Fir Forest, once thinned and cleaned. 2300 feet elevation. Thuringer Wald, Germany. Page 161.

Plate No. 3.—Spruce Forest. Edge of a clear cut, end of Rotation Period. Page 161. Average height of Trees, 100 feet. Hartz Mountains.

Plate No. 4.—Dense Spruce Forest. Cylindrical Trunks. Hartz Mountains, Germany. Page 158.

Plate No. 5.—Beech and other Hard Woods. Page 155.

Thuringer Wald, Germany. The vegetation in the foreground consists of young Beech seedlings springing up on the ground from which the previous crop has been cleared.

Plate No. 6.—Young Beech and Hornbeam, &c.   1800 feet elevation   Hartz Mountains, Germany.   Page 155.

Plate No. 7.—Crop of Poles. Page 175.
From an Old Oak Stool, Wortley.

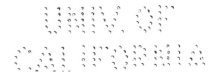

Plate No. 8.—Sylviculture. Page 97.

Plantation-grown Oak Tree,
Wortley.

About 50 feet high to the top of trunk. and containing 50 cubic feet of timber.

Plate 9.—Park Tree (Oak) same age as Plate 8, and showing the effects of too much top room.   Page 97.

Plate 10.—Nearly Full Crop of Douglas Fir on the Highland Railway, Perthshire, Scotland. Page 109.
41 years of age. Trees 70 to 80 feet high. 12 feet apart. Value per acre in 41 years, £225. Poor land.

From a Photo by J. J. Simpson, 1901.

Plate 11.—Dense Douglas Fir Plantation, Perthshire. Page 109.

Plate 12.—Beech Hedge, over 80 feet high, Meiklour, Perthshire. Page 117.

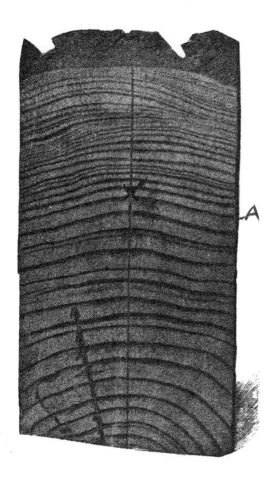

Plate 13.—Section of Larch showing how increment
is reduced by injudicious thinning.   Page 171.

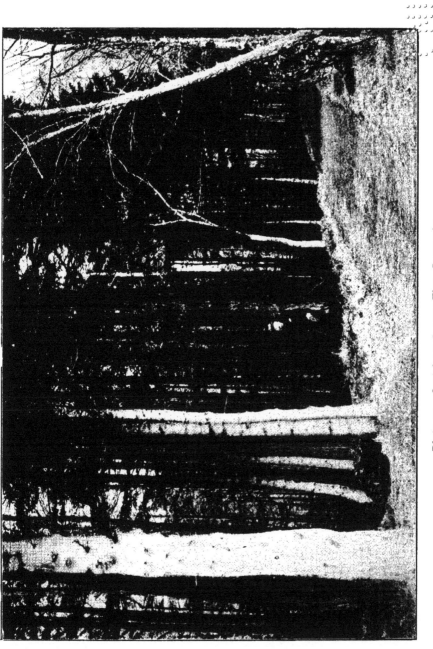

Plate 14.—Scotch or Spruce Firs, Cromarty

Taken for "The New Forestry" by Andrew McCritchie, Esq., Proprietor, Fairy Glen, Cromarty. Page 16.

PRESS AND OTHER NOTICES

OF THE FIRST EDITION.

" **The Scotsman**,"—*February* 23*rd*, 1900.

" An exposition of the Continental system of growing trees, according to which they are encouraged to grow into long straight poles, instead of being spoilt, as they often are in this country, by premature thinning. The chief merit of the book is that the author shows a practical knowledge of forestry, and has made a serious endeavour to propitiate game preservers, whose anxiety to have a thick undergrowth is one of the chief impediments to scientific forestry in this country."

" **The Field**,"—*February* 24*th*, 1900.

" The author of ' The New Forestry ' describes his book as an ' attempt to combine in a handy form all that is best in British Forestry of the past with what is now acknowledged to be the superior methods of continental forestry, and to adapt the latter to the conditions existing in this country, where the forests are owned by private individuals, instead of by the State.' . . . . . . ' The New Forestry ' is a good and useful book, and suggestive of much that is to be done in woodland planting if it is ever to be of any value either to the nation or to planters "

" The following has been received from **E. Floyer, Esq.**

" The Rayah Plantations, Manachi, Egypt, 6th March, 1900.

" Sir,—I do not know who sent me your book, ' The New Forestry,' but I am very glad to get it. I agree with nearly everything you bring forward. I plant between 5,000 and 6,000 (fir poles) to the acre. I trim all side branches when young, and leave only a crown for shade. Until the crowns join I cover the ground with arachis, which is useful in several ways. I think also that a chief function of a root is to fix the tree in its place.

" Yours faithfully,

" Ernest A. Ployer."

B

Sir Harald G. Hewett, Bart., refers as follows to " The New Forestry," in an article in **" The Field "** of December 21st., 1901.

" If you are going to grow Timber, let me entreat you at once to buy, beg, or borrow ' The New Forestry ', by Simpson. Simpson's book is dear, but it is worth any money to a beginner. I am advising you for your good, not for Simpson's. He needs no advertisement from me."

———

From the **"Agricultural Students' Gazette,"**—April, 1903.

Edited at The Royal Agricultural College, Cirencester.

" I should like to recommend most strongly ' The New Forestry,' by John Simpson, a practical forester, and published at Sheffield."

———

" Chambers' Journal "

In a prominent article in *Chambers' Journal*, of October, 1900, entitled " Forestry for beauty and use," the following reference is made to Mr. Simpson's book—" We have pleasure in mentioning the publication of an extremely practical book, ' The New Forestry,' by John Simpson. Mr. Simpson aims to set forth the continental or natural method of forestry, to reorganise the general management of woods on private estates, to encourage greater economy in their management, and the production of heavier crops of timber, of better quality, and better suited to the market. To proprietors, factors, estate agents and foresters, Mr. Simpson's volume is crammed with practical information of great value. We recommend the volume to all concerned,"

———

From **" The North British Agriculturist."**

" The chief interest of the book lies in the fact of its being the production of a practical forester, who has been brought up in the British school, who knows all the outs and ins of British practice, and who is thoroughly convinced that hitherto it has been conducted on wrong lines. As such it will appeal to practical foresters who have not had much in the way of a scientific sylvicultural training, and who might, perhaps, find some little difficulty to begin with in the more highly technical works of Schlich, Nisbet and others. The author himself has visited Germany, and has seen on the spot the methods which are practised there. He is therefore able to speak of the continental system from personal observation, and is thus in a position to put before his readers, in a way which he could not otherwise have done. The work is illustrated by several excellent photographs of typical bits .of dense forest in the Hartz Mountains and in the Thuringer Wald. These photographs were taken by the author's son, Mr. J. J. Simpson, Wharncliffe Estate Office, Newtyle, and are really splendid specimens of skilful selection and photographic art. The general get-up of the book is good.''

————

From **A. E. Wild, Esq.,** Darjeeling, India, February 23rd, 1902.

" I learnt the theory and practice of forestry over thirty years ago in' the very forest Mr. Simpson seems to have made his hunting ground, and have practised the profession in India for over thirty years. Mr. Simpson's book is a valuable addition to forest literature and should be welcomed by all interested in forestry. There are few books of its kind in the English language, and it should form a work of reference of considerable worth and utility to those named."

————

From the **" Yorkshire Post."**

" Mr. John Simpson's ' The New Forestry ' (Sheffield: Fawson and Brailsford) is a work we commend to the study of every estate owner and land steward in the country."

TO OWNERS OF WOODS.

The Author of "The New Forestry" begs to state that he has, as far as practicable, anticipated the wants of his readers in his book, but in consequence of the enquiries he constantly receives from owners of woods, he wishes to state that he advises on all subjects connected with woods and game preserves.

He inspects woods separately, takes stock of their contents, condition, and value; reports fully, sets out timber for sale, arranges planting operations, makes out lists and estimates, directs labour, and when engaged by the year over-looks the whole work of the woods. Terms moderate, according to distance.

He has for a considerable time been engaged in re-organising the woods on a number of estates throughout Great Britain, his acquaintance with woods and game preservation in nearly every county, and knowledge of Continental and British forestry, enabling him to advise under a great variety of conditions, so as to avoid the mistakes of the past and secure better crops of timber in the future.

When personal inspection is not desired, he advises by letter if particulars regarding soil climate and situation are furnished.

List of some of those Noblemen and Gentlemen by whom the Author has had the honour of being consulted, or whose woods he supervises.

His Grace The DUKE OF NORTHUMBERLAND.
The Most Honourable The MARQUIS OF NORMANBY, Mulgrave Castle.
The Most Honourable The MARQUIS OF AILSA. Cubzean Castle, Ayr.
The Right Honourable The EARL OF WHARNCLIFFE, Wortley Hall.
The Right Honourable The EARL OF LISBURNE, Crosswood, Aberystwith.
The Right Honourable LORD MONTAGU, Beaulieu Palace, Southampton.
The Right Honourable LORD CASTLETON, Ireland.
LADY CHERMSIDE, Newstead Abbey, Notts.
SIR EDWARD GREEN, Ken Hill, Norfolk.
SIR HENRY HOARE, Stourhead, Bath.
Colonel A. W HALL. C.B., Carlton Club.
Colonel J. GORDON MAITLAND, Esq., Cairn Edward, Galloway.
Captain P. LANGDALE. Houghton Hall, Yorks.
R. CHADWICK, Esq., Findhorn House Forres, N.B.
HENRY J. CAMPBELL, Esq., Lynford Hall, Norfolk.
W. J. H. MAXWELL, Munches, N.B.
ARTHUR J. DORMAN, Esq., Grey Towers, Yorkshire.
Mrs. BARNES, The Quinta, Wales.
Mrs. WYNDHAM A BEWIS, Tile House, Bucks.
DOUGLAS W. ESHELBY, Esq., Glen-Gorm Castle, Mull.
A. R. WARREN, Esq., Warren's Court. Ireland.
H. E. P. WELCH, Esq, Leck Hall, Northumberland.
EDWARD FIRTH, Esq., Hope, Derbyshire.
THOMAS BINGLEY, Esq., Ellerslie, Yorkshire.
FRED STRAW. Esq., Hykeham Hall, Lincoln.
H. N. B. GOOD, Esq., Shrewton Lodge, Wiltshire.
ANDREW J. MACRITCHIE, Esq., Faiey Glen, Cromarty, N.B.
C. SEBASTIAN SMITH, Esq., Estate Agent, Shipley, Derby.
Messrs. MACKENZIE & KERMACK, Land Agents, Edinburgh.
WELLWOOD MAXWELL, Esq., Kirkennan, N.B.
W. F. PEPPER, Esq., Shipton Court, Oxford.
HUGH MORRISON, Esq., Fonthill, Wilts.
PETRE HOARE, Esq., Luscombe Castle, Devon.
Honourable Company of Edinburgh Golfers, New Club, Edinburgh
        and many others.

PREFACE TO THE SECOND EDITION.

In offering the second edition of *The New Forestry* to the public the Author begs to thank those numerous Subscribers to the first edition who have expressed their appreciation of his work in such kind and flattering terms—not only to the publisher and himself, but also to their own friends and acquaintances—contributing in no small degree to the success of the first edition, and the publication of the second within a period of three years, and which the Author ventures to regard as a sign that the book has to some extent fulfilled its purpose.

Among other objects aimed at in the present edition one has been to show, more fully than has hitherto been attempted, the wide difference between the wasteful and unprofitable forestry system of the past, and the system proposed to replace it in the future, as nothing is more likely, the Author believes, to encourage planting as an investment than a clear understanding on that head. Another object has been to show owners of estates that they may begin the new system with the means and appliances at their disposal. Some owners are already moving in that way, and their woods will probably, ere long, serve as good examples of what may be accomplished by those who chose to try. It is suggestive that some who have invoked State aid and forestry education most earnestly have themselves undertaken the re-organization of woods on private estates with the ordinary staff and means usually provided, and so easily has the new system been put in operation that some have said "the only change effected has been to plant the right species thicker than formerly, and suspend thinning," which expresses part of the truth, but means more than such critics care to admit.

It is seldom anything of importance is said or written about forestry of which the text is not the millions of acres of waste land in Scotland and Ireland that might be planted ; but although that plea may appeal to the State, it does not interest many owners of private estates whose woods demand all their attention. The waste lands needing attention first are the blank spaces in existing woods, and which, in the majority of cases, are of greater extent than the ground occupied by trees. The fences are there but the crops are absent.

According to present agricultural returns there are, roughly speaking, nearly three million acres of woodlands in Great Britain and Ireland. Taking into account the thinly timbered woods of the south of England and the proportion of inferior species planted everywhere, the value of the three million acres may probably be about 70 or 80 million pounds. That is rating them at about their present market value, at any rate, as woods go in different parts of the kingdom, and it is a value that ought to be, at least, quadrupled under a better system. It represents the capital locked up in existing thin woodlands, and to restore these to the full crop condition would be an easier and a wiser thing to do than taking up fresh areas in out-of-the-way regions—so far at least as private owners are concerned.

In the present edition more illustrations have been introduced. Chapters I., III., IV., and V., have been considerably extended, and additions have been made where needful elsewhere.

Studfield House,
   Wadsley, Sheffield,
     January, 1903.

EXTRACTS

from the Report of the Departmental Committee appointed by the Board of Agriculture to enquire into and report upon British Forestry, 1903.

"The present condition of existing woodlands has been repeatedly and clearly reviewed by many eminent authorities. It is the common verdict that timber of the kind and quality imported in such large quantities from the Baltic and similar temperate regions can be grown as well here as anywhere. That foreign is so generally preferred to home-grown timber is in no way due to unsuitability of soil or climate, but is entirely due to our neglect of sylvicultural principles. It is hardly too much to say that until within the last ten years or so owners of woodlands, with few exceptions, failed to realize that the shape, size, and quality of trees could be influenced by anything that they could do. They seemed to imagine that the character of the final product was largely a matter of accident, whereas it is mainly determined by management. That the yield of our woodlands can be materially improved admits of no doubt, and the evidence before us unanimously favours immediate and effective provision for bringing systematised instruction within the reach of owners, agents, foresters, and woodmen. This has been on all sides emphasised as the first requisite in any project for the improve- of forestry, and consequently stands out as the cardinal point of our recommendations."

EVIDENCE OF THE EARL OF SELBORNE.

" I do not think there is any knowledge of the subject at all. I think that landowners, the agents, bailiffs, surveyors, and the whole heirarchy of people in England who have to do with land, are absolutely ignorant of the very elementary principles of forestry. They know how to grow a good tree for ornamental purposes, but of what forestry means as a commercial pursuit they have not the slightest idea."

CHAPTER I.

INTRODUCTORY.

THIS book does not profess to deal at length with every subject connected with the science and practice of forestry, as that would be impracticable in a handy book ; but it will be as practical and comprehensive as the author can make it, and the instructions given will be based on the best knowledge obtainable on the subject, and on the author's own experience and observation extending over a considerable period of time. It is an attempt to combine, in a handy form, all that is best in British forestry of the past with what is now acknowledged to be the superior methods of Continental forestry, and to adapt the latter to the conditions existing in this country, where the forests are split up, so to speak, into fragments, and owned by private individuals instead of by the State. The title of the book, " New Forestry," has a restricted significance which is explained in Chapter III. The time may come when some recognised system of forestry will be established throughout this country, but no such system exists at present, each owner disposing of his woods as may seem most expedient to him, often without any clear purpose or plan in his mind between the exigencies of game preservation and timber production, generally to the disadvantage of the one or the other or both. The main objects suggested in the following chapters are, first, re-organisation in the general management of woods on private estates ; second, greater economy of management ; third, the production of much heavier crops of timber of better quality than are produced now ; and, fourth, a more careful anticipation of the demand for timber for whatever purposes it may be wanted and can be profitably produced. The first of these objects concerns proprietors most, and depends upon their goodwill and assistance ; but the other three objects, we confidently believe, may be easily realised by ordinary care and good management.

The aim, therefore, of the present work is to enable the owner of woods or his forester to proceed to work on any estate where the system of forestry here advocated may be adopted and carry the foregoing suggestions into effect, it being hardly worth the while of either going through an elaborate schooling for what, on most estates, is but a comparatively small task—the care of a few plantations of no great extent. The author does not underrate the value of forestry schools and education begun at the fountain head, but that is a slow process when there is much work waiting to be done. Gardening in this country has reached a higher development than it has done anywhere else without any other school than a thoroughly good and widely diffused horticultural press, aided by horticultural societies, and handy practical books that enable gardeners to set to work with confidence and at once; and forestry might be advanced by similar means, but foresters and arboricultural societies have sadly failed to do for their craft what gardeners have done for theirs.

There is nothing, at any rate, to prevent any would-be planter of trees from beginning, with the aid of a few simple rules that can soon be mastered, to guide him. It is well known what kind of trees thrive best in almost every part of the three kingdoms, and there are few soils, however poor they may be, in which some species will not thrive more or less successfully if they are planted and tended on some definite and intelligent plan.

In our forestry of the past it is not the manner in which the work has been executed with which fault is found, but the system, which has been laid down at great length, and which has been just as difficult to learn, in all its bearings, as any other and better system. The work, with the aid of a few simple rules and instructions, has been well enough carried out by practical men who would be quite able to carry out another system equally well with similar assistance. Books and translations on the Continental system of forestry, recently issued, though good and suitable for students of forestry, are too elaborate and diffuse for immediate practical use, and present a syllabus to the working forester and his employer that neither think it needful to master. The author's experience is that neither owners of property nor their agents care to master volumes on every department of an estate, and shorter methods are preferred if something has to be left out. Nor do scientifically conducted Continental forests give one the impression, either, that the system of management is such a complicated business as books on the subject might lead one to suppose, although Continental forest officers are a much better trained class of men than British foresters are, and more thoroughly up to their business theoretically and practically. Continental forestry, as represented in Germany, is not the creation of any school, because the forests were there before the schools, and the science of forestry only proceeds on natural lines and principles systematically applied.

In the following chapters the author has not, except where needful, given the reason of every operation described or practice suggested, but nothing is advanced, he hopes, for which a good reason can not be given. This course has been adopted to avoid involved directions and save time. Some of the practices recommended have, in some form or other, appeared in the English and Scotch agricultural and horticultural papers within the last five-and-twenty years, during which period the author has been a contributor to these papers— especially in relation to the operations of planting, thinning, pruning of forest trees, etc., he never having subscribed to the opinions generally held on these subjects by foresters in this country. His convictions on these heads, though confirmed by what he has seen and read, are really founded on observations made long ago in the wood, in the saw mill, and in the timber market in a part of England where the consumption of timber, both home and foreign, is enormous. In the wood he saw the conditions under which the trees grew and shaped themselves in different ways; in the saw mill where the waste was; while in the market he quickly realised in which direction the forester must direct his attention if he wished to profitably compete with other countries in the timber trade. At this period there were practically no books on Continental forestry in the English language to read, and not much was known by foresters on the subject. The author has seen French forestry exhibitions and French forests, but a study of German forestry, as described in German works, induced him to personally inspect some of the most notable timber forests in the Hartz Mountain region and in Central Germany, where the climate and other conditions are similar to our own, and much that is advanced in this work has been suggested by what he saw there. Between German and French forestry there is not much difference, but Germany is the best school for an English forester, because a good deal might be attributed to climate in France, whereas the great German forests exist under climatic and geological conditions so similar to those of Great Britain and Ireland that the difference is not worth mentioning. The same trees can be grown in exactly the same way, and equally good in both countries, and even in more southern France it is not the climate that constitutes the difference but the system followed, both German and French practice being similar and equally unlike ours.

One great drawback to good forestry in this country is the great number of small estates on which the extent of woods is too small to employ a skilled forester, and which are neglected accordingly, though contributing largely to the supply of home-grown timber felled annually. Great mistakes are made and losses sustained on such small estates in the planting and tending, and in the selling of the timber periodically disposed of for the benefit of the proprietor. We have known many flagrant examples of this kind. A very little knowledge of forestry, or a little assistance from a qualified forester, would prevent such mistakes and failures, or, as in Germany (where many of the common and other woods not belonging to the State are supervised by a Government forest officer), a number of small estates containing timber might combine to secure the occasional services of a competent forester at a trifling cost to each owner and much to his advantage. County Councils now provide horticultural and agricultural teachers, and there is no reason why they should not take similar steps with regard to forestry. The writer is quite sure, from careful enquiry into the matter both in this country and abroad, that some such provision as this would result in an improved state of affairs and an enormous increase, before long, in the quantity of timber produced and improvement in its quality and value.

Another question of far-reaching consequence to the owners of woods is that of game preservation on well-wooded estates. Until a radical reformation is made in the present system of gamekeeping, in connection with the management of woods and plantations, there will be difficulty in carrying out any system of forestry to a successful issue. The subject has not been as fully dealt with in forestry books as it might be, and a chapter is devoted to it in this work in which the state of affairs is explained and suggestions offered for the future.

Some readers of the following chapters may probably think that too much has been said upon the errors and mistakes of past forestry practice and its advocates in this country. The reply to this is that it was felt to be necessary to explain old and utterly wrong methods, and dispose of them, before recommending new ones, because old methods have got a grip of the rank and file of foresters and their employers and have been followed too unquestioningly and too long. The author believes, and has been assured by competent judges, that our forestry system of the past, in its most important features, has been the main cause of failure and disappointment in the pro- duction of timber crops, and that a more intelligent system might alone turn the scale in the right direction.

The extent of the woods on the majority of estates in Great Britain are probably under 1,000 acres, while on many estates of from 2,000 to 5,000 acres, or thereabout, they are less than 500 acres in extent, but in all cases they represent a large portion of the value of the estate and have to be cared for.

On small estates the owners are obliged to take more interest in their woods than larger proprietors usually do, because they can seldom employ woodmen above the rank of labourers, who are generally ignorant of the rudiments of forestry, and such men prefer simple rules of work to general principles unless the latter are put in short and simple form. Owners, too, are often of the same way of thinking, and nothing is more likely to hinder an improved system from being adopted than making it appear difficult to carry out. Such are some of the conditions that have to be faced as ownership exists at present, and few, perhaps, have had better opportunities of knowing than the writer. We want a new system, but it must be made as easy as possible.

The mistake of some teachers, with a Continental training only, and unfamiliar with British woods and their wants, is that they can seldom conceive of anything less than a State forest, and State plans and re-organisation of woods on an English estate puzzles them, while their too comprehensive schemes frighten owners. Confronted with an average British wood, composed of a mixture of more species than a German forester, confined to spruce, beech, and Scotch fir, probably sees all the days of his life, and never contem- plated in his education, not to mention game, they might well despair and suggest, as some have done, that existing woods should go by the board and a fresh start be made on new areas—a scheme which would not work and which owners could not afford to entertain, not to mention the uncertainty of any system being continued from one generation to another. The German forester's education is thorough, but he is forced to acquire much knowledge which, like the short sword he wears under his tunic, he never uses, and which in this country would be of less use still. Keeping an accurate record of everything in the forest section under his charge and reporting to his superior officers probably makes a greater demand upon a German ober-forster's time and intelligence than anything else, and it strikes an English forester, after first impressions wear off, that when a German forester is appointed to a head charge with a system and a general routine of work, from which he cannot depart, laid down for him, and every inch of the ground mapped out in all its bearings, his duties cannot be difficult.

What has to some extent prompted these remarks is the impression existing among owners of woods, fostered by much that has been written about Continental forestry and forestry education, that the Continental system is difficult and expensive to put into operation, whereas in principle it is a far simpler and less expensive business than the kind of forestry hitherto practised in Britain, and only wants adopting culturally to suit private ownership. Continental forestry may be said to consist in sowing or planting very few of the most useful species, preservation of the overhead canopy with due regard to the shade-bearing power of the different species, and thinning but few times between the 25th, 35th, or 40th year and the end of the rotation period. Such a system costs less thought, less work, and less expense than our present home practice, and in most instances its adoption on estates would convert a losing investment into a paying one; but while in principle the system may be adopted on any private estate, working plans may have to be modified to suit restricted and special conditions.

The best advice one can offer owners of woods is to first inquire carefully into the state of these themselves, ascertain their actual extent and value, and then decide about their future management. Usually the woods are clearly enough marked on estate maps, copied from the Ordnance Survey, which, however, takes no account of the contents; and my experience is that owners seldom know what is in their woods themselves, hence the reason why such appalling miscalculations, sometimes amounting to thousands of pounds, are made by estate agents when estates are valued for sale. The woods are always the most difficult portion of an estate to appraise, and the professional estate agent's formula for such work is usually of the laxest description. Some estates are much more wealthy in the way of timber than their owners are aware, and instances have occurred in which the purchasers of well-wooded estates have sold timber, after taking possession, worth as much as the whole of the woods were valued at in the sale and still left a fair stock of timber on the ground. Nothing but a close inspection of the woods one after the other can be depended upon to give a correct account of their extent and value, and it is an amazing fact that on private estates owners and their agents have seldom more than a vague idea on that head.

In discussing this part of the subject in the following chapters, Brown, author of " The Forester," has been chosen as representing British opinion and practice up to the present time. Probably his " Forester " (original edition), which has seen five editions, has exerted more influence than any other work of the kind, and there is not much difference between his teachings and that of his contemporaries, and those who have followed him as writers on forestry. " The Book of Landed Estate," by Robert E. Brown, and well-known in private libraries, is, in the portion devoted to forestry, but a re-echo of James Brown's "Forester"; "Grigor's Arboriculture" is much the same; while as late as the year 1898, we have a Professor of Forestry in one of our most noted agricultural colleges publishing a work on forestry in which principles are laid down and practices advocated that are identical with those of the writers just named above, and who are now regarded as wrong by all competent authorities.

The new system advocated starts with the advantage that it is based upon rational and intelligible principles that the student can understand and appreciate, whereas the writings of exponents of the old system may be read through without finding any clear exposition of the principles on which that system is based. What the result of the latter system has been may be gathered from the opinion of Professor Schlich in the preface to the third volume of his Manual. He says :—
" In the first place, British timber cannot compete with the imported timber, because, as at present grown, it is of inferior quality, being generally shorter and less clean of branches and knots. Moreover, conifers generally grow much too quickly in Britain, because the woods are too heavily thinned while young ; hence the individual trees increase too rapidly, and produce timber inferior to that of the same species imported from the Baltic, and grown in crowded woods. Secondly, the home-grown timber is brought into the market in fluctuating quantities, so that neither a regular timber trade nor superior methods of working up the material, nor forest industries have a chance of developing and thriving ; in short, the whole business is far too haphazard."

The author has acknowledged the sources of any quotations he may have given from writers on forestry. For most of the extracts given on the subject of Continental forestry he is indebted to the "Manual of Forestry," by Professor Schlich, C.I.E., Ph.D., of Cooper's Hill College, and now so favourably known to foresters in this country. The plates at the beginning of the book, illustrative of German forestry, are from photographs taken by the author's son, Mr. J. J. Simpson, Agent to Captain Langdale, Houghton Hall, York, and represent typical bits of some of the most noted German forests. For the opportunity of securing these photographs and much useful information given on the spot, the author has to thank most cordially Dr. Kœnig, Prussian Forest Office, Lauterberg, Hartz, and Herr Kallenbach, Forest Office, Thuringer Wald, Eisenach, Saxe Wiemar—two gentlemen very favourably known in connection with their profession in Germany, and not unknown to owners of woods in this country.

CHAPTER II.

FORESTRY AND GAME DEPARTMENTS ON ESTATES; SUGGESTED REORGANISATION.

General Remarks.—Pheasant Coverts in Dense Woods.—Trees and Shrubs that produce fruits eaten by Pheasants.—Artificial System of Rearing Pheasants.—The Wild or Natural System.—Rabbits.

SECTION I.—GENERAL REMARKS.

THE object of introducing the subject of game preservation in a book on forestry, is to suggest, if possible, some plan by which the woods and game departments might be combined and managed under one intelligent and responsible head, instead of, as hitherto, being conducted separately to the disadvantage of both. Until something of this kind is attempted there is little or no chance of successful forestry in this country, and it is the duty of any forester to draw the attention of proprietors to the subject which is discussed here at some length, especially in regard to keepers' methods, simply with the view of making the proposed reorganisation easier. The results of the present system have been disastrous in the past to woods and plantations on estates, while the gamekeeping has not been up to the mark, although usually conducted on prodigal lines compared to other departments on estates. Every forester and every writer on forestry has lamented the hindrances to good forestry through perfectly preventable causes in connection with game preservation. Foresters in charge of woods are forced to concern themselves in the matter, and owners of woods only need to realise the actual state of affairs to see the need of reorganisation in some form or other. Gamekeepers—whose interest in their charge does not extend to the future, like those of the forester or farmer, and the results of whose work can be measured annually—rarely concern themselves about their masters' plantations, or anything else not connected with their own charge, and rarely assist the forester willingly to protect the woods and plantations. It was the gamekeeper, not his master, that was the cause of the Ground Game Act, that has lessened his employer's sport, exterminated hares on many estates, and embittered the relations between tenants and landlords. Now, it is a question of woods and game, and the question will not be solved satisfactorily while the irresponsible and often ignorant keeper has any authority in the matter. It cannot be supposed that owners plant extensively in the expectation of having their plantations destroyed, but they trust too much to their keepers, to whose carelessness much of the destruction of young plantations is due. The gamekeeper of the past is behind the times, and is usually in conflict with everyone else who has the general interests of his employer and his estate at heart.

The subject came before the Select Committee on Forestry, as it could not help doing in any enquiry of the kind. Professor Elliott, of Cirencester Agricultural College, in his evidence, dwelt on "the great drawback" to forestry in this country by the present association of woods with game, and Mr. McCorquodale, of Scone Palace, Perth, a forester factor of long experience, did the same, explaining to the Committee the extent of the ravages committed by rabbits to various species of trees up to one hundred years of age. There is, unfortunately, not the least doubt about the extent of the destruction to woods by rabbits. Young plantations especially are often quite destroyed, and always suffer more or less according to the number of rabbits on the ground. This itself amounts to serious loss, and when old trees are barked the loss is still greater. Smooth-barked plantation trees of ash, elm, sycamore, and beech suffer most. When the trees are in the pole stage they are often barked right round and die, and have to be removed. Others are partly barked, and while a strip of bark is left the tree lives, but the growth is checked, and the loss of increment thereby to the trunk represents a sensible loss in its value. The annual increment on a tree represents the interest on its standing value, and this may almost totally disappear in a tree crippled but not killed by being barked at the base of the trunk. Such losses often extend to thousands of cubic feet over large areas. Great numbers of trees in this condition are to be seen in nearly all woods, and the blank spaces usually represent trees that have been killed outright and removed. Keepers are in the habit of rubbing freshly barked trees over with soil and placing sods over the wounds to prevent the damage being discovered, but woodmen have been long acquainted with these tricks and are not deceived.

The expedients to which owners and their foresters are sometimes driven to protect plantations from destruction by rabbits are pitiable.   Wire-netting fences, as usually set up, are useless and expensive, and a substitute is provided by dealers in the shape of an offensive mixture with which plantations are expected to be smeared annually by men with brushes.   One of these vendors issues a long list of noblemen and gentlemen who patronise him, with testimonials from their foresters as to the excellence of his mixture, the price of which alone would be prohibitive.   One does not know which to deplore most, the mismanagement that suggests such futile measures or the forestry that has anything to do with them.   And all these evils arise from perfectly preventable causes, because, as has been proved, there are no kind of vermin more easily exterminated than rabbits, if followed up for a short period ; and had gamekeepers only been one tithe as anxious in regard to rabbits as they have been in their ghastly failures in pheasant rearing, they could have provided ample sport for the gun in rabbit warrens properly managed, and saved their employers enormous losses in their woods.   All that the proprietor needs to do is to decide what areas he will devote to the preservation of rabbits for sport or profit, and make it a condition with his keeper that they shall exist nowhere else.   Nothing else than a rule of this kind with a class of ignorant and careless servants, or legislation as on the Continent, will save our woods from damage at any time sufficient to turn the scale between profit and loss.   At present the woods and game are brought into frequent conflict, instead of working smoothly together as they should do, seeing how closely they are connected, and proprietors do not receive the benefit or satisfaction from either that they ought to have, and in many cases it would be better if, instead of working the two departments on a system of hopeless compromise, they were to stock their woods with game to their fullest capacity and abandon them to sport altogether.

Here is a description of what usually goes on wherever game, and particularly pheasants, are preserved to any considerable extent, and where the keeper's object is to show a good head of game regardless of the general interests of the estate.   From March till midsummer as little work as possible must be permitted in the woods, because the pheasants are either laying or hatching ; from midsummer till October the coverts must be kept quiet and free from intrusion in case the birds should be scared off the ground ; and from October till

February as little forestry work as possible must be permitted till the pheasants are shot. This comprises the whole year, during which the forester's work has to be done by fits and starts by the grace of the keeper. We are not here thinking of any single case but of many cases we have known, extending over a long period. There is above all the damage to young and old plantations by rabbits, which have probably destroyed a large proportion of trees planted in Great Britain over a long period, and contributed more than anything else to make ash and other kinds of timber scarce.* The keeper receives orders perhaps to clear the rabbits off certain tracts, and he promises to see to it; but the first fall of snow shows how he has executed his orders by the trees destroyed, all of which have to be made up, to be destroyed perhaps again and again, and so on. The loss sustained on numbers of estates in this way would appear incredible to some, and if only proprietors would take the trouble to enquire what they have spent in planting and replanting for a certain number of years, and then have a report of the extent and condition of their plantations sent to them, their eyes would be opened to a very disgraceful state of things indeed. When, as has been the case on a few estates, the keeper is made to understand that the woods are expected to be a source of income to his employer, and that he must conform to circumstances and produce game as well, it is wonderful how he can adapt himself to the situation; but the great mistake lies in the proprietor not insisting on the duties and responsibilities of his game department being clearly defined and accounted for, and in placing too much power in the hands of those who have no notion of conducting their work on rational or scientific principles of any kind, and who gauge their employer by his willingness and ability to spend in the way they suggest. No servant has such ready access to his employer as the game-keeper, who, unless he be a man of high principle, may easily abuse the privilege, and many keepers have done that without scruple.

The only way to obviate this state of things is to class the woods and game together, and place both under one responsible and capable head. It is immaterial whether the forester learns the keeper's duties or the keeper learns the forester's, but the former is by far the most likely man for both posts. As a rule he is a better educated man than keepers usually are; his duties as a forester furnish him with as many opportunities

* This estimate is based upon reliable information received from foresters on extensive estates in England and Scotland.

of acquiring a knowledge of game as those of the keeper do, and on most estates he already performs not a few of the keeper's duties. It is not proposed to abolish the office of head-keeper or upset generally existing arrangements, but it is proposed to class the game as a sub-department under the head of "woods" or "forests," and work the two conjointly. This is the German and French plan : the gamekeepers are foresters, and all sporting expeditions are conducted in Germany by the ober-forsters, who possess a knowledge of natural history, to which gamekeepers in this country are total strangers. By this plan the two departments would be worked without friction, and things would shape themselves accordingly and go on smoothly, with much advantage to the proprietor. The gamekeeper would have his daily working duties assigned to him as hitherto, but it is proposed to relieve him of the responsibility of keeping books and accounts, and to transfer these to the forester, who would assign them their proper place under the head of woods or forests, subject to the final audit of the estate office. As it is at present, this work is usually done by someone else than the keeper, whose books are generally kept by the agent or his assistants.

We do not wish to say a word more than can be helped against any class of servants on estates, but it is, we believe, universally admitted that the game department is the worst managed of any, chiefly because gamekeepers are, with here and there an exception, an ignorant class of men, who are recruited from all ranks, many taking up the business after they have failed in everything else. Why gentlemen should lay so much stress on securing skill and intelligence when engaging a forester, gardener or bailiff, and accept the services of a keeper, where both great skill and intelligence are required, on the strength of a certificate that he can keep moderately sober and kill vermin, is one of the puzzles of rural experience.

SECTION II.—PHEASANT COVERTS IN DENSE WOODS.

This subject is closely connected with the system of forestry adopted, the opinion of many owners being that the Continental system of dense cropping of the timbered area is inimical to the successful preservation of game, especially of pheasants, which is a mistake founded upon nothing better than supposition and the prejudices of keepers. The pheasant adapts itself readily to very different conditions as regards covert, although it prefers some kinds of plantations to others. On many estates, where the woods consist mainly of hard-woods, or deciduous species, there are plenty of pheasants, and the birds do well enough in summer; but such woods are usually over-thinned, and the trees being destitute of foliage from November till April they are the coldest in winter, being open to both winds and frost, and pheasants will forsake such woods in winter for more sheltered coverts, if such are to be found, or they will crowd into the warmest corners if they have no choice. They will forsake an open hard-wood plantation for a dense spruce or fir wood, if they have the chance, at almost any season, and the greatest number of truly wild pheasants we ever saw on any one estate was on one where the woods consisted of pure spruce or deciduous trees mixed with spruce. Keepers argue that in fir woods kept dense and close the tree trunks get bare under the branches, which is true, but even such woods pheasants prefer to naked hard-wood planta-tions. For years we have noted the partiality of pheasants for such woods because they were warm, the dense evergreen canopy overhead preventing radiation, and the crowded stems breaking the wind however hard it might blow. The wind blows through a thin, leafless hard-wood plantation like through a sieve, and even when dense, though then warmer, the hard-wood plantation is still the coldest. What we wish to make clear here more particularly, however, is that dense woods, cropped with an eye to timber, are not only just as suitable for game as thinly cropped, profitless woods, but that even if they were not so they can be laid out and planted so as to obviate any objections on that head, and can also be furnished with underwood of a suitable kind that will grow. Let it be borne in mind that the pheasant prefers the wood only for shelter and breeding purposes, and the quieter the woods are the better. It does not live in the woods continuously, but prefers the rides, margins of the wood, and the open fields as a feeding ground, where it also gets the sunshine. Sunny margins are invariably preferred, and if birds are flushed any-where in cold wintry weather it will be in such spots, or under or near to holly trees and other evergreens where there is shelter and warmth.

A point, the importance of which will be admitted by all sportsmen, is that nothing more promotes the successful raising of a good head of game than keeping woods and coverts quiet and free from intrusion. For this reason, on some estates, keepers are not allowed to carry a gun to kill vermin, trapping only being permitted. That being so, it follows that the system of forestry that necessitates the most frequent disturbance of the woods must be the worst for the game, and the system that answers to this description more than any other is our own system of forestry of the past, for nowhere, except in this country, are woods so needlessly disturbed under the pretence of thinning, pruning, inspection, or work of some kind or other. The quietness and repose of Continental forests, even of small extent, are a contrast to the bustle that goes on in English plantations. What disturbs game in coverts are sight and sound, and nothing prevents the one or deadens the other so much as a dense crop of timber. A gamekeeper's idea of a wood is one adapted to his own notions of game preservation, however crude these may be, and his own convenience. It must consist throughout of timber trees standing thinly on the ground, never to come down, sufficiently furnished with coppice or underwood for the shelter of his pheasants, but not so dense as to prevent himself or his beaters from facing the covert comfortably on a dewy or wet morning on a shooting day. Should it be a young plantation, so thick as likely to brush his coat tails, it is time, according to the keeper, that it was thinned, and many a plantation has been thinned for no better reason. Though the keeper's days of actual work, during the shooting season, often do not embrace a week or ten days throughout the whole year, and his shooting "day" does not begin before ten o'clock and ends soon after lunch, he would without scruple sacrifice his employer's crop of timber for the reasons described, if he had his way, when he ought to have men and dogs to do his bidding without trouble. Woodmen have to do the work of the woods in nearly all weathers, and are often drenched to the skin when felling, thinning, or draining, and no complaint is heard, but a keeper must not endure such hardships. It is, however, the southern keeper who is most fastidious. He knows least and wants most, and a training in the fir woods of Scotland for one winter would be a useful experience for him in his own line. These remarks are made in the knowledge that a prejudice exists against dense plantations in connection with game preservation, and that the prejudice has originated mainly through ignorant and incapable gamekeepers.

There are signs, however, that the gamekeepers will by and by have to conform to a different state of things. All that is needed to put an end to the present system is to show gentlemen that they may have both timber and game if they go the right way to work. The German system of dense cropping is being put into operation in the Crown forests and on private estates. According to Dr. Adam Schwappach, professor of forestry, Eberswald, Prussia, "the most extensive as well as the most scientific system of forestry," according to German notions, "is now being carried out in the large pine forests belonging to the Countess of Seafield, in Scotland, where game is also expected to abound; and also in the Raith forests, Fife, belonging to R. C. Munro Ferguson, Esq. With regard to the latter, it has been publicly stated that ' the woods are now to be worked with a view of profit, and that questions of sport and æsthetic considerations would have to take a back seat." In this chapter, however, we have suggested a plan of laying out young dense woods and planting up old ones that gets rid of the keeper's objections to density without sacrificing the timber crop, and it will be apparent, we hope, to sportsmen, that if a keeper cannot put up his game in such a covert it will be his own fault. A good rabbiter with two or three well-drilled fox terriers could certainly accomplish the last successfully.

A diagram of a combined timber forest and game preserve, showing how this covert may be formed, is given towards the end of this section.

All that is needed in this country to insure heavy timber crops and plenty of underwood or low bush cover is a slight modification of the German forestry methods by which clumps of coppice might be introduced here and there in small clearings in conjunction with the rides and paths, and so laid out as to admit sportsmen with the gun to every part of the wood. When traversing great tracts of dense forest in the Hartz Mountains and elsewhere in Germany, it occurred to the writer that clearings might be introduced frequently where a great variety of coppice bush (including a large number of species that produce fruit freely, almost anywhere in Britain, and that is greedily eaten by pheasants), might be grown in far greater abundance than has yet been attempted, in a systematic way in this country. Much expense is incurred on estates in providing artificial food, which is by no means so necessary as the artificial breeder imagines who slings his bag or bucket of food nearly every day in the year for birds that wait for his coming like domestic fowls, without trying to find their natural food; whereas it is perfectly well known that the wild pheasant can provide for itself all the year round, and has to do on some estates, where it thrives and affords good sport. The pheasant, indeed, displays a remarkable ability in catering for itself and discovering its natural food, even under ground, as gardeners have good reason to know. We have known almost whole collections of lily and other bulbs dug up and eaten during winter by a few pheasants, where there was nothing to indicate their whereabouts but the labels, while large seeds, like broad beans, dibbled in three inches deep and well covered, they unerringly find, unearthing each bean in succession almost as regularly as they are put in. The list of fruits and seeds, etc., which the pheasant eats is also an extensive one. According to Mr. Tegetmeir and other authorities, it eats with avidity nearly all kinds of seeds that the gardener and farmer sow— wild grasses, grass and weed seeds of various kinds, roots, numerous wild and garden fruits, herbs, insects, worms, grubs, acorns, beech mast, and hazel nuts; in fact, the pheasant will not starve while it can get grass to eat. We propose to augment this supply of food by furnishing coverts more plentifully, and in a different way than hitherto, with the various trees and plants that bear fruits and seeds and are known to grow anywhere in open spaces such as pheasants love to haunt, and the following descriptive list of these is here given, also the names of a few shade-bearing subjects suitable for dense woods. How we propose to establish masses of the subjects named in the following list will be shown further on.

SECTION III.—LIST OF TREES AND SHRUBS THAT PRODUCE SEEDS AND FRUITS EATEN BY PHEASANTS.

OAK.—Acorns shed on the ground in autumn and early winter, and greedily eaten by pheasants and rabbits.

BEECH.—The same as the oak. Good shade-bearer in dense woods.

COMMON CRAB.—Very abundant fruit-bearer. When the fruit begins to drop on to the ground it is readily eaten by pheasants; should be planted extensively in coverts.

HAWTHORN.—Bears heavy crops of haws regularly and abundantly, which are shed gradually during the winter, and much relished by birds.

MOUNTAIN ASH.—Rarely misses a crop of fruit. Berries much eaten by birds.

ELDERBERRY.—Bears heavy crops of fruit annually. Fruit devoured by game and other birds.

HOLLY.—Berries eaten to a moderate extent by birds. The tree is one of the best shade-bearers, and may be planted extensively as underwood.

2

COMMON BRAMBLE.—One of the very best covert and food-producing subjects. May be propagated by sowing the berries on the surface of the soil; endures shade well, but bears the most abundant crops of fruit in open spaces and at the margins of drives and woods. Fruit ripens in October and November, and is much sought after by pheasants and other birds; should be abundantly sown on the margins of woods. The common and parsley-leaved varieties are the best, and bear enormous crops.

WILD RASPBERRY.—This ranks next to the bramble as a berry-bearer and covert-plant. It grows in nearly all soils, propagating itself by seed and suckers, but prefers a moist soil and climate. Bears fruit in abundance, which is perhaps more sought after by birds than any other wild fruit.

ROSA RUGOSA.—A Japanese rose of recent introduction. A strong, rampant grower, not eaten by rabbits, owing to its branches being densely set with bristles. Grows about six feet high in a dense bush, and produces heavy crops of large crimson hips annually, of which both the skin and the seeds are eaten by pheasants and birds as soon as they are ripe. Thoroughly hardy everywhere—on the sea shore or inland.

BIRD CHERRY.—Hagberry in Scotland. A shrub or low tree with spreading branches drooping to the ground. Bears a profusion of small black fruit that birds are fond of.

HAZEL NUT.—As food for pheasants, only the common hazel nut need be grown, the nuts being small and easily swallowed. In the crops of pheasants that have been examined, large quantities of nuts have been found along with grasses and insects. Where crops of nuts are expected, however, the hazel must not be cut down as underwood too often— a portion should at least be left here and there.

SLOE.—In cool moist climates and rather cold soils the sloe fruits freely as a low shrub, and pheasants devour the fruit. The sloe is, however, a precarious fruiter on dry soils. On estates in Dumfriesshire, where such large numbers of wild pheasants are raised, sloes, nuts, wild raspberries and brambles are very abundant. The common damson plum succeeds well also in coverts along with the sloe.

PRIVET.—The common variety of this plant makes the best and most tangled covert, and bears fruit very freely, the fruit hanging on the plant all the winter and affording an abundant supply of bird food easily within the reach of pheasants.

According to our observations it does not, however, fruit so freely in some parts of England as it does in Scotland, where we have known it produce in great abundance. Is easily propagated by cuttings of the shoots simply stuck in the soil.

CRATAEGUS PYRACANTHA.—A member of the hawthorn family. A very abundant fruiter whenever the plant is allowed to spread and straggle in its own way. This shrub beats the hawthorn in productiveness, and the fruit hangs on the bush all the winter, but birds are very fond of it and will strip bushes growing close to dwelling houses as soon as the fruit begins to colour. Planted in the open, it is a low-spreading evergreen shrub and very hardy.

COTONEASTER.—Three varieties of this shrub produce berries in great abundance that last nearly through the winter, and are much relished by pheasants. These are *C. affinus*, *C. frigida*, and *C. microphylla*. The two first are deciduous, and much alike, and Mr. Harting, the accomplished naturalist and sportsman, in his book, " The Rabbit," says the first-named variety is every year laden with bunches of berries, and affords plenty of food for pheasants. All the three should be planted in abundance in the clumps and along drives.

COMMON BARBERRY.—In moist localities in Scotland this shrub sets the wood ablaze in autumn with its brilliant scarlet berries, which are produced in great abundance and fall on to the ground when quite ripe.

GOOSEBERRIES AND CURRANTS.—These are both natives of Britain, and although not commonly planted in coverts, succeed perfectly well and fruit freely, although, owing to the bushes not being pruned or cared for, the fruit becomes small. We have known bushes left in cottage gardens after the cottages were pulled down and the site planted, continue to live and bear for many years afterwards. The fruit ripens just at the season when the young pheasants begin to forage for themselves, and is greedily eaten. The free-bearing sorts and vigorous growers, like the Warrington gooseberry and common black and red currants, should be planted.

The above list does not exhaust the number, but it includes the best and such as are sure to succeed. It is not suggested that such subjects should be planted thinly here and there in the aimless way hitherto practised, but in open spaces left for the purpose in dense woods, as shown in the diagram, where they will get light and air and grow and fruit freely. Spots from half a rood to half an acre may be left, and if these are planted or sown thickly at the outset, keeping the taller species

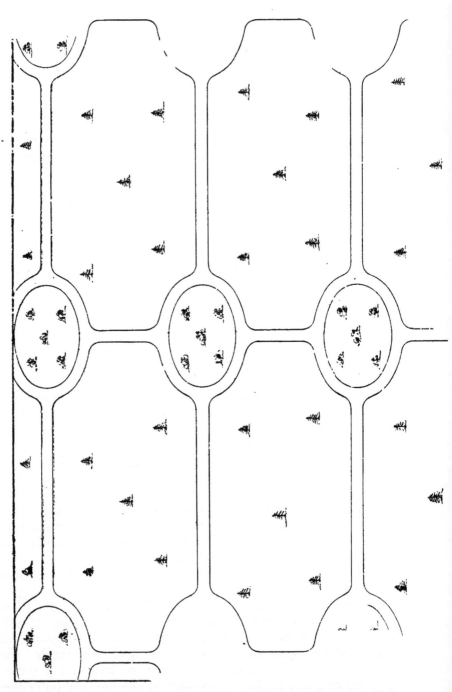

Combined Timber Forest and Game Preserve—Diagram.

in the centre and the dwarfed ones at the outsides, ideal nesting, feeding and flushing spots, in any number, might soon be established, surpassing anything practicable in our present over-thinned woods, which are for the most part a miserable compromise between a timber crop and a game preserve. Of course, drives and rides could also be planted in the above manner. The great point is to begin systematically and plant and sow freely so as to establish groups soon.

It will, we hope, be understood that we do not propose to plant any of the subjects named under the shade of the timber trees where, as is the case in many woods now, they struggle weakly on, without bearing fruit or affording good covert ; but to plant in the open where they will succeed. All our wild berry-bearing plants bear freely in open spaces.

The shade-bearers are the only species fit to plant as under-wood in dense woods, and they are few in number, consisting of the beech, spruce, horse chestnut and holly, and one or two others ; of these beech and spruce are the best, and the way they succeed in dense German forests, in deep shade, must be seen to be believed. Where such underwood is wanted, the spruce and beech should be planted thickly under the timber trees. This, however, is not a necessity, because if the groups suggested are regularly distributed over a wood, underwood is not really needed. What is aimed at by the plan suggested is really a dense forest of timber trees, alternating here and there with equally dense patches of open coppice consisting of trees and shrubs such as have been described.

The plan suggested in the foregoing diagram is based, as regards the distribution of the coppice clumps, upon the common experience of keepers that pheasants, and especially home-bred birds, run before the guns until they are driven into some "hot corner," with the guns behind them and the "stops" in front of them, and are forced to rise. Gamekeepers are constantly laying the woods under contribution for brush-wood to pack flushing spots here and there in the woods for the birds to run into and be put up from ; and what the keeper attempts in an imperfect way, with dead brushwood that soon decays, it is proposed to do in a more systematic way by means of living covert such as the pheasant loves to haunt. Naumann, in his "Birds of Germany," according to Tegetmeir, says the pheasant is certainly a forest bird, but loves "small pieces of grove where deep underbush and high grass grows between the trees, where thorn hedges, berry-growing bushes, etc., etc., are found ;" and such haunts it is

proposed to create.   The foregoing diagram looks formal on
paper, owing to the paths being straight, but the plan would
not look formal laid out in a wood.   The diagram, however,
only shows the principle on which such a wood might be laid
out, and any wood, of whatever shape or size, may be treated
in the same way.   The clumps may be large or small, few or
numerous, regular or irregular, but the fewer the better for the
timber crop.   There might be one clump of covert, of a rood or
more in extent, to every twenty acres of timber or thereabouts,
and the wood is supposed to be shot over lengthways.   In short
the wood is simply thrown into blocks of timber that beaters
and dogs can easily work, and the ovals are clearings with low
berry-bearing and other bushes, where the guns can be posted
as desired.   Although the paths are more numerous than are
needed in a wood, they will not seriously affect the density of
the crop, provided the margins of the blocks are kept close.
Since the first edition of this book was written, I have had
many conversations with gentlemen on this subject, who have
assured me that if the necessary density for the production of
timber could be secured in blocks of moderate size, the same as
in large areas, every objection would be removed to dense
woods so far as shooting was concerned, as better sport was
had with the gun in open glades and fields adjoining woods
than in narrow rides cut through them, such as are often seen.

In addition to the drives, narrow footpaths, about one yard
wide, and winding, may be made every ten or twelve yards
apart to admit beaters.   These paths we have made in very
dense plantations, not by removing any trees, but by nipping
off the lower branches, or a portion of them, up to a man's
height or a little higher.   In plantations arranged in this way
all objections to density are removed.

SECTION IV.—ARTIFICIAL SYSTEM OF REARING
PHEASANTS.

This is the only part of the keeper's business that the
forester is not quite familiar with, and which it is proposed to
abolish for reasons that will be given, and because it is, next to
the rabbit scourge, a branch of the keeper's business that
hinders the work in the woods more than anything else, conducted as at present.   It is, however, a business he may soon
learn to conduct with as much success as it is conducted at
present at least, and as will be shown; for if anything

approaching the same mortality prevailed among any other kind of live stock as commonly prevails among home-reared pheasants, there would be a panic on estates.

With regard to this particular branch of the keeper's business, and with a view to simplifying matters under the system of management now proposed for the sake of the woods, we venture here to discuss a subject that has, we believe, not yet been thoroughly ventilated, namely, the comparative merits of the two systems of rearing pheasants generally practised— the artificial system of raising birds under hens in coops, and the natural system of allowing the pheasants to breed wild in the coverts under due care. Assuming that the latter system may be carried out, at least as successfully as the former, there can be no doubt about its being by far the easiest and most economical, and the one which relieves the keeper of much care and anxiety which would be better bestowed elsewhere. We have seen both systems at work on an extensive scale on different estates, and we have taken great pains to get independent testimony on the subject.

The natural system we became quite familiar with on an extensive and most successful scale, many years ago, in one of the coldest and wettest districts in Scotland, where it has been always practised; and the artificial system we are also quite familiar with, as practised in England, and it is here proposed to discuss the two systems separately.

What takes place under the artificial system is suggestive, and is as follows :—The keeper first picks up all the earliest and best wild-laid eggs out of the coverts to set under hens, and he is often tempted to prolong this gathering until too late in the season, the wild birds continuing to lay as long as their nests are robbed, and hatching late and inferior birds from what eggs are left to them. Should the keeper not secure as many eggs as he requires in this way, he buys from other sources at an average price of about nine shillings per dozen, and sometimes more. The price is tempting, and egg poaching is common. Mr. Tegetmeir, in his excellent book on pheasants, last edition, p. 102, states that owners of estates have been known to buy eggs, from dealers, that had been stolen from their own coverts, and that, " in the great majority of cases," purchased pheasant eggs are stolen either from the rearer's own preserves or those of their neighbours. A leading article in the " Field," of April 20th, 1899, also deals with the subject of " illegal traffic in game eggs," and states that :—

" The chief sufferers from the nefarious trade are those

who preserve game extensively, and we do not hesitate to say that they themselves are in a great measure to blame for their own disasters in this respect. There are a legion of pseudo egg-dealers who parade a small egg "farm" as a cloak to their practices, and who are, as regards nine-tenths of their business, simply receivers of stolen eggs. Any customer who would take the trouble to inspect one of these bogus farms before committing himself to deal there would have small difficulty in seeing for himself that the supplies for which he is negotiating could not possibly be produced from the few small pens and coops which the establishment discloses."

"The result of this happy-go-lucky system is that a large proportion of the eggs bought by or for game preservers are proceeds of plunder from their own estates or from those of their neighbours. Out of every thousand eggs paid for by keepers or by short-sighted masters a large percentage, possibly as much as two-thirds, are not in any way additions to the resources of the district, but are simply passing through the hand of stealers and dealers to return to the several estates whence they were originally pilfered. The bona fide game farms of the kingdom will barely yield a fourth, if so much, of all the game eggs that are marketed in the May of any year. The rest of the supply come from illicit sources, and in no way swell the production of game in the country; they are at best transfers from Peter to Paul and vice versa, through the medium of thieves, who rob both in turn, and trade to their victims the proceeds of their own or their neighbours manors."

These are some of the serious objections to the system we propose to abolish, but not the worst. The question affecting owners of preserves most is the proportion which the number of birds brought to the gun bears to the number of eggs collected or bought, set and hatched, and the expense involved in their rearing. It is difficult to get at this problem from keepers. One gentleman in Norfolk devised a book that was to record everything from the setting of the eggs till the birds were finally distributed in the coverts; but he reckoned without the keeper, and it was a failure. By diligent enquiry from a number of estates where the artificial rearing is relied upon, we ascertained correctly the number of eggs put down and the number of birds shot over a series of years, from the same coverts, and we are within the mark when we state that the average proportion of birds brought to the gun amounted to from two hundred and fifty to three hundred for every thousand eggs, and no deduction was made for wild birds, which are included in the above figures. It will be admitted, we hope, that the number of birds brought to the gun ought to bear some reasonable proportion to the eggs set, bought, or picked up. In not a few instances we have heard of even a less proportion than the above being got. To be sure, however, we wrote to a well-known expert on this subject, a shooting estate agent, who is also a thoroughly practical gamekeeper and sportsman, and an advocate of artificial rearing, who is much consulted on the subject. He writes, June 29th, 1898 :—" Pheasant rearing is now skilfully reduced to a science in Scotland. I always think that a thousand birds brought up to the gun, out of two thousand eggs, a success." Now this is a loss of fifty per cent. by the most scientific and skilful process, and bears out our own calculations under ordinary conditions. We referred our correspondent to an estate where no artificial rearing was practised, and he admitted that " D—— was a celebrated place for pheasants, even without rearing," but added, " to me, whose business it is to study bags of large shoots, it is surprising how, generally speaking, they go down." It will be shown further on why the stock " goes down." Now, where is this discrepancy between the eggs and the birds accounted for? Undoubtedly, almost entirely, between the setting of the eggs under the hens and the turning of the birls into the coverts, or, in other words, during the time the birds are under the purely artificial care of the keeper. During this period the loss between eggs that never hatch and birds that die is always great and often frightful, far surpassing anything known in any other class of stock. The writer on the pheasant in the " Encyclopædia Britannica," last edition, who appears to have had access to excellent sources of information, speaking of hand-reared birds, states that the proportion that come to the gun may amount to three-fourths of those that are hatched (not of eggs set); but that, in many of the western counties, it would seem that more than half of the number that live to grow their feathers disappear inexplicably before the coverts are beaten. All that is here stated is corroborated annually by lamentable accounts of losses among artificially-reared birds.

Long experience has taught some keepers a few essential rules that must be observed ; but, as a rule, they proceed on no rational principle in what they do, despising scientific books relating to their duties, but readily adopting any ridiculous rule of thumb suggestions coming from others as ignorant as themselves. The system alluded to by Mr. Tegetmeir, of hatching the eggs in dry, insanitary pigeon holes, one above the other in tiers in dark sheds, is quite common among game-keepers who describe themselves as "experts" in the business. This applies more to England than Scotland, where, we are told, artificial rearing is practised more successfully and intelligently, the keepers often taking the work of rearing by contract, at so much per bird, till the birds are taken off their hands on the first of August by their employer. The expert whom we mentioned before, in writing to us on this subject, says the results of this system are very different from those he can remember, where a Sussex man, "who could neither read nor write," was employed on a Scotch estate to breed the pheasants—not an uncommon plan we believe yet.

One plea of keepers for picking so many wild-laid eggs out of the coverts to put under hens is, that the wild birds lay more eggs than they can hatch, and that it is better to at least remove some of them, although it is seldom the pickers-up discriminate very nicely. Now, as regards this point, we believe that where the coverts are stocked year after year with coop-reared birds, the birds become partially domesticated, or rather demoralised, in their habits, and run together like barn-door fowls, several hens often laying in the same nest; hence the large number of eggs sometimes found. We have often seen the hens running together in crowds at the beginning of the laying season, and under such circumstances over-full nests were often found; but nothing of the kind happens among really wild pheasants. We lived for years close to the extensive pheasant coverts belonging to the Duke of Buccleuch, in Scotland, all stocked with wild birds, the nests of which we often found, and the number of eggs rarely or never reached a dozen. It was, moreover, rare to find a nest in which all the eggs were not hatched off. The real wild pheasant, like other wild birds, does not, as a rule, lay more eggs than it can cover and hatch out, and that, we believe, is also the opinion of competent naturalists. Morris, in his "British Birds," gives the usual number laid, under natural conditions, at from six to ten, "sometimes" as many as fourteen; and Mr. Tegetmeir, p. 13, says the number is "usually about eight or nine." It is important to be accurate on this head in calculating the number of hens to be left in the wood where pheasants are bred wild.

In conclusion, the subject of the artificial rearing of pheasants may be summed up as follows:—First, that according to the testimony of the most intelligent advocates of the system, at least fifty per cent. of the eggs set never produce birds for the gun, and that, under the ordinary run of management, the loss is very much greater than that; second, that according to the testimony of those who have the best opportunities of knowing, pheasant eggs purchased from outside sources are, " in the great majority of cases, stolen from gentlemen's preserves by poachers; third, that eggs from penned-up birds are inferior, and a frequent source of disease in the young birds; fourth, that a very large proportion of good eggs picked up in the coverts fail when set under hens; and, fifth, that the practice of picking up the wild-laid eggs on estates is carried to excess, to the destruction of the wild stock.

Evidence of the above kind would be sufficient to condemn any system in any other department of an estate, and if it does not show the urgent need of reorganisation and a better class of gamekeepers, we do not know what would.

The foregoing remarks refer to rearing where the master pays all expenses and takes all risks; but it should be stated here, for the benefit of those who may still favour the artificial method, that the contract system is now coming into favour, especially in Scotland, and where this plan is adopted, the forester, with an assistant, could carry out the work as well as a regular keeper. One of the first authorities on game preservation writes us that in the North, keepers offer to rear the birds till the beginning of August (or when they can be fed on corn at from 1s. 7d. to 2s. per head), finding the field, the sitting hens and the food—the eggs to be picked up in the coverts. One keeper to a nobleman writes that he has carried out this plan on the same estate for seven years, at 2s. per head, and says that he did not make much by it, but that, on the average, he did not lose anything.

SECTION V.—THE NATURAL OR WILD SYSTEM OF REARING PHEASANTS.

The chances of raising a sufficient number of pheasants on an estate by allowing the birds to lay and hatch under purely natural conditions in the coverts, in conformity with the forestry working plans, must be calculated on the same principle as that on which the artificial breeder proceeds. For so many birds expected to come to maturity he sets so many

eggs, and the margin for losses, under the most favourable
circumstances, is always large.   This is a fundamental condition
with the artificial breeder, for it is one of the amusing features
of a system, ostensibly designed to multiply the stock on
economical lines, that the allowance for losses and failure must
be on the most ample scale.   In the natural system, allowance
must also be made for losses, but on a much less scale, while
the cost of the system is fractional compared to the other.
In wild-rearing, it is a question of the number of hens to be
left in the coverts after the shooting season is over ; but before
discussing this point, there are several other points to consider.
In the first place, it is admitted by keepers, and asserted by
competent and impartial observers, that if wild birds do not
always hatch out the whole of the eggs in the nest, they
at least hatch out a very much larger proportion than keepers
succeed in bringing out under hens.   Mr. Tegetmeir, giving
one gentleman's experience as an example, says, p. 105, that
in artificial rearing " The fault usually existing is that an over
careful pampering system is adopted, and miserable broods
are the result.   I have experimented in a manner which leaves
no doubt upon the subject.   Upon one occasion I was anxious
to test the fertility of certain pheasants' eggs, and continued to
remove the eggs from a nest in the woods until I found the
hen desirous of sitting.   I left twelve eggs in the nest, and set
thirteen under a hen at home ; the pheasant brought out
twelve birds, while at home I only had three miserable birds.
Similar results have many times occurred since."   Keepers
attempt to get over facts of this kind by arguing that although
the wild pheasant hatches out by far the largest proportion of
eggs, she loses the chicks afterwards, because she does not care
what becomes of them as long as she has one solitary chick
to follow her, which is a gross libel on the pheasant and on
nature.   The truly wild mother will hover about for days
within a few feet or yards of the nest, immediately after hatching, and, in addition to this, the young birds themselves are
surprisingly nimble on their feet from the very first.   In truly
wild coverts, a clutch of six, or even nine birds is much more
common than a clutch of one.   We have seen too many wild
clutches not to feel sure on this head.   The young chicks of
the common barn-door fowl are far more helpless than young
pheasants, yet we have known eggs of common hens hatched
out in the nests of wild pheasants, and the birds reared till
they could fly, with eight or nine pheasant companions.
    There is no doubt whatever about the practicability of

raising pheasants in the natural wild manner, and it is a mere question of breeding stock, as in the case of rabbits in warrens. It is an easy thing for a keeper to ascertain, near enough at any rate, how many hens are left in any covert under his charge after the shooting season is over. The question is, how many should be left? There is no doubt but that an average number of possible young birds from each hen could be struck, and we believe that that average might be put at half-a-dozen or thereabouts under ordinarily favourable circumstances, and the number expected would determine the number of hens to be left in the coverts. In Dumfriesshire, where the climate is unfavourable, and the rainfall about fifty inches, or just about double that of Norfolk, we used to consider the average higher. We have often there seen, long past the critical stage, clutches of nine or ten, and these birds, in most instances, received no artificial assistance whatever. But putting the average lower than the above, we still hardly get so low as the average reared on the artificial system; and look at the difference in the expense and trouble! There is no comparison. The question constantly asked by a gentleman in search of a keeper is, "Can he rear pheasants"? Here, by the simple wild system, the employer gets rid of the difficulty altogether, if only he can procure a man who will exercise some intelligent care in the maintenance of the wild stock. We commend this subject to the earnest attention of owners of woods and preserves, feeling perfectly sure that it can be dealt with in the way indicated by the forester.

In concluding this part of the subject, we may allude also to a modification of the wild system lately recommended by Mr. Te etmeir, in the "Field" for July, 1898, and described by himgas, "Pheasant Rearing Under Natural Conditions." He writes :—

"I have just returned from visiting Mr. Ward's shooting, where I find the pheasants are reared in accordance with natural principles, in a manner totally opposed to the general routine followed by keepers, and that the plan has been attended with the greatest possible success. In a covert two acres in extent, with close undergrowth and oak trees, which was wired round against foxes, which are numerous in the district, four hundred yards of two-inch wire netting being utilised, I found the result of his first hatch on May 22nd, when two hundred and sixty-five pheasants were obtained from three hundred and twenty-five eggs, gathered in the open from the wild birds.   Of these, as far as is known, not half-a-dozen have died from all causes put together.   These young pheasants are now loose in the covert, with the farm-yard and turkey hens that have hatched them.   There are no coops, but the hens roam where they like, and the young pheasants are all now roosting high up in the oak trees, flying from branch to branch with the greatest facility.   They are now too large to pass through the two-inch wire work which surrounds the covert, but they fly over into the neighbouring fields, and return in the same manner.

"Turkeys are not common in the neighbourhood, and Mr. Ward's manager was only able to obtain three hens.   One of these hatched out twenty-two young pheasants, all of which are now alive with their foster-mother loose in the covert, roosting with her, not on the ground, but safely out of the reach of all ground vermin, in the trees.   Some of the farmyard hens employed last year were left out during the winter. Their nests were searched for, and when found the eggs were taken away and pheasant eggs substituted.   The young pheasants that were hatched under the domestic hens were, in consequence of the absence of short grass and the prevalence of the wet weather in the early hatching period, kept in coops for a few days, but on the first opportunity removed to the wired-in covert, where the ground is heavy and not remarkably well adapted for pheasant rearing, which makes the success more remarkable.   Mr. Ward's manager, Mr. French, has entered warmly into the utilisation of the system.   As soon as the young birds are removed into the covert he bends down some of the branches of the trees towards the ground and places a wooden hurdle against them, so that the birds can readily ascend into the trees, and of this contrivance both hens and young birds quickly avail themselves.

"Now comes the account of the food which is employed. The first day or two some custard is given the chicks in addition to the general food which is prepared.   This consists of one boiled rabbit per day, the meat chopped up finely, the scalding broth used to scald the fresh barley meal with which the chopped meat is mixed ; to this is added a very considerable proportion of canary seed and dari.   No spiced condiments are employed, nor any dried stale animal food whatever.   As the birds advance their chief food is dari.   How well the birds have progressed, their flight to the higher branches of the oak trees testifies, and they have got on so well that they are now showing colour, and it is quite practicable to distinguish the cocks from the hens. Mr. French has fully entered into the merits of the plan of rearing. No keepers are employed, but his son—an intelligent lad of about fifteen or sixteen, who appreciates his work—is the feeder of the birds, which, reared in this way, require comparatively little attention.

"If this plan be compared with the usual method of shutting the hens up with their young charges for several weeks, shifting the coops daily, feeding entirely on artificial food, not allowing the old birds to scratch for ants' eggs, or obtain insects and other natural foods, the saving of trouble and labour is manifest; and as to the success, it would be difficult to find its parallel amongst those who pursue the old system. You wander about in this covert, and you find ants' nests scratched up, and doubtless other insects are obtained in large numbers, and the birds are now flying out over the four-feet boundary, seeking natural food for themselves in the fields of clover, wheat, and mangold which surround it."

SECTION VI.—RABBITS.

RABBITS.—In our little book on "The Wild Rabbit," which has had an extensive circulation, it is shown how hopeless it is to rear plantations wherever rabbits abound; and it is there suggested that the only plan of dealing with these vermin, on estates where rabbits are wanted for sport or profit, is to provide warrens of sufficient extent and keep the rabbits there, and exterminate them everywhere else. This can be done, is being done on many estates now, and where intelligently carried out is successful, at least as many rabbits being got as before, and usually more. Instead of shutting the rabbits OUT of the woods, as heretofore, by expensive fencing and protections of woods and single trees, it is proposed to shut them IN, and keep them in. We need hardly say that the worst opponents to this plan, that we have found, have been gamekeepers, whose stock arguments on the subject may, however, soon be disposed of. We never met a keeper yet who had any correct idea how many rabbits could be produced by good management in a warren, his idea of such an enclosure being a piece of poor waste, where the rabbits were expected to breed and thrive, year after year, under conditions that are known to exterminate every other kind of live stock in a short period. We have probably seen and known more rabbit warrens than any other single forester or keeper; and this, without exception, is our experience where the ordinary game-keeper was in charge. It need hardly be added that the plan here proposed meets with the approval of everybody else, and especially of farmers.

We trust the suggestions offered in this chapter will be received in the spirit in which they are made. They concern owners of woods principally, the suggestions offered are quite practicable, are worth weighing carefully, and can only be carried out with the sanction and encouragement of owners of woods and game preserves. We strongly advise gentlemen to, at any rate, organise working forestry plans, as described in Chapter IV., and to include in these plans the work of the game department, as far as it relates to the woods, at least. Well-matured working plans prevent vexatious changes, disputes and worry, permit work to be carried on without interruption, check irresponsible interference, and leave heads of departments in no doubt as to their duties and responsibilities There is abundant testimony to show that there is much room and urgent necessity for improvement in the direction indicated, and we are sanguine that the fact only needs to be fully realised by those concerned to induce them to take action.

CHAPTER III.

PRINCIPAL FEATURES OF THE OLD AND NEW FORESTRY DESCRIBED AND CONTRASTED.

British Forestry of the past.—The New Forestry.—Timber Trees of the older British Woods.

THE title, "New Forestry," is applied here, not because the system to be described is new, either in principle or practice, everywhere, but because it is practically new in Great Britain, as contrasted with the system generally recognised and practised in this country. It is important to understand the difference between these two systems; and to make the difference clear, and also to justify the title adopted, it will be necessary to describe both systems rather fully. There has been a tendency in some quarters to pooh-pooh the difference between the two, and where the difference has been admitted, it has been attributed to other causes than the right one— such as climate and soil, etc.; but the difference is real enough, and the causes assigned will not bear investigation, as will be shown. Besides, the old system, as it may be named, and as represented by long-acknowledged authorities, is now being condemned in its most important aspects by recognised and competent teachers of forestry, while books on the subject, that have long done duty as guides, have been withdrawn from circulation and others substituted in their place.

SECTION I.—BRITISH FORESTRY PRACTICE OF THE PAST.

In Great Britain, natural forests, such as exist abroad, have long ceased to be. On the Continent they are still of great extent, and have been the real schools of forestry there, particularly in Germany and France, and the absence of such schools in Britain has, probably, been the reason why the art of true forestry has been lost, and empirical practices set up, which, it is now seen, are wrong, and have been the cause of much loss. Primarily, the causes that have crippled forestry in Britain have been the want of a recognised system of general practice, neglect of working forestry plans, and the absence of anything in the shape of a methodical rotation system. The first has been the cause of much confusion of opinion and practice among foresters; the second has crippled the manage-

ment of woods on estates; and the third has prevented anything like a just balance being maintained between the
planting and felling of timber crops and a regular system of
successional cropping—planting and felling having generally
been carried on according to the whims and necessities of the
owner or the fads of the forester.   Hence the irregular aspect
which our woodlands generally present, the wide gaps in the
ages of the different plantations, and the absence of a regular
succession of crops such as one sees everywhere in German
forests.   Errors of practice in other ways relate to methods of
planting, thinning, mixtures of unsuitable species, roads, and
neglect in planting those species in most demand for timber.
On other points, British forestry does not differ widely from
that pursued on the Continent, but on the points named the
difference is marked.   A question that arises in proposing the
introduction of important changes is, "What is likely to be the
attitude of owners of private estates"?   Those who understand the subject reply that the gain to owners, from a
financial point of view, in a country where the demand for
timber is practically unlimited, cannot be doubted; that
opposition of a serious nature need not be expected from those
principally interested; and that there are no obstacles to the
proposed changes that may not be easily overcome.   Practically, the new system means making two trees grow where only
one grew before, and little doubt exists now in the minds of
those acquainted with forestry in this country that that can be
done.   It was the general conviction existing that forest
management in the three kingdoms was of the wrong kind, and
our woodlands unremunerative, that suggested the appointment
of a Select Committee on Forestry by the House of Commons
in 1885, and no one can read the evidence given before the
Committee without coming to the conclusion that that conviction was well founded, the evidence revealing not only a
deplorable state of things in the management of woods, but
irreconcilable differences of opinion among professed experts
in British forestry.   The report of the Select Committee contains a number of suggestions, but its general conclusions are
summed up in the following paragraph to the effect that,
"Apart from the question of actual profit derived from tree
planting, its importance as an accessory to agriculture is
shown by the effects which woods have in affording shelter
and improving the climate; and your Committee are of opinion
that, whilst on public and national grounds timber cultivation
on a more scientific system should be encouraged, landowners

might make their woods more remunerative were greater
attention paid to the selection of trees suitable to different soils
and to more skilful management after the trees are planted."
Some luke-warm supporters of the Continental system, while
admitting that our home forestry is more or less a commercial
failure, suggest that owners of estates will object because the
Continental system makes no provision for ornamental
features, has no respect for sentiment, and that hence, British
proprietors, rather than trust their woods to the new forester,
will prefer to go on in the old way, with all its imperfections.
This is a narrow and mistaken view that we feel sure not many
entertain. As regards ornamental planting, the Continental
system does not prohibit the laying out of woods or forests
in an ornamental manner, so far as their distribution is concerned. It does certainly advocate the planting of poor waste
lands in preference to lands that can be more profitably
devoted to other purposes ; but the system can be carried out
on good lands, in the ornamental style, just as easily as on
bad ones, by those who are so disposed. Better methods of
planting, rotation, and the production of trees of the right
shape and quality, are surely no hindrance to ornamental
planting, and can mean no disrespect to sentiment. German
forests, many of them, are scenes of sylvan beauty, established
on lands which, without the forests, would often resemble those
dreary wastes of moorland and bog so common in England.
If a slice of a German forest could be transferred to an English
park, it could not be distinguished from an ornamental English
plantation at a distance, but a close examination would show
that, unlike the other, it had been managed in a superior way,
and had a commercial as well as an ornamental value.

Apart from these considerations, the number and extent of
the timber sales on private estates all over the country show
that the commercial element does enter largely into the
wood management on estates. If there be any lack of interest
in this direction, it is due, as a rule, to the impression created
among proprietors, by past mismanagement, that things are
hopeless and cannot be altered. Reverse this impression and
a change will soon be noticeable. It is not long-deferred
returns from planting that influences proprietors so much as
the doubt of there ever being any returns at all. When the
larch was first introduced, and its value as a timber tree was
realised, almost all owners of estates planted it extensively,
even small freeholders, just as the Dutch are planting Scotch
fir now on their allotments, although it was seldom expected

that the crop would be realised by the planter. The same may happen again. Numbers of good examples of planting for the distant future might be cited—the Duke of Athol, for example, in Scotland, and the Earls of Yarborough, in Yorkshire—the latter having planted during the last hundred years some twenty millions of trees, according to an authorised statement in the "Field" of December 3rd, 1898. Such pleas will not, we think, interfere with good forestry, and those who are under the delusion that the introduction of the German forestry system into this country will banish beauty and sentiment from the land, must be woefully ignorant of German forests and that German forest lore and romance that has tinged so much of the literature of the world. There is one direction, however, in which German sentiment does not run, and that is in extravagant veneration for very old and useless dead trees such as encumber so many woods and parks in Britain. They believe in live trees and plenty of them. They do not excel in collections of relics like the Old Caledonian Forest for example, or like Sherwood, nor do they pride themselves on parks of stag-headed oaks or other species, except on a reasonable scale. Their rotation periods have long since put an end to all that, and they point with pride instead to the grand tracts of forest that clothe their mountains and waste lands almost everywhere, and which have become of so much importance to their country.

It may be remarked here that since the subject of forestry has been revived in this country it has often been asserted, and with truth, that if our present system be wrong, Scottish writers of forestry and Scottish foresters have been mainly to blame, and that, after all, the most profitable woods are to be found in England, where Scottish forestry practices have obtruded least. Scottish forestry practice, it is now admitted, has been a failure. So far as there has been what may be called any system of forestry in Britain, it has been of Scottish origin, been taught by Scottish foresters almost exclusively; and, in the belief that Scotch forestry was the best, foresters of Scotch training have been generally employed on estates in Great Britain and Ireland wherever the woods were important enough to require the services of a head forester. In that way forestry practice of a kind diametrically opposed to what is now recognised as true sylviculture, or the profitable culture of timber, has been spread throughout the country. Foresters are wedded to this wrong system, and it is difficult to get men at present who understand any other. The men are good, but their practice is wrong, and is based upon an entire misconception of tree growth as far as the production of timber is concerned.*

The following table of planting and thinning, etc., was published, as an example of good management, as late as the end of 1899, in a magazine devoted to the landed interest, by the head forester on a well-known ducal estate in England, and a member of the Royal Scottish Arboricultural Society, who claimed to have had a high-class Scotch training. The table affords a good example of the wasteful and destructive methods that have long been generally in operation and recommended. It does not even profess to be based on intelligent sylvicultural principles, takes no account of such important factors as density, overhead canopy, height growth, or protection of the soil; shows fewer trees per acre at the beginning than a German crop has at the end of 20 years—(see Chapter XII.)—a final crop 329 trees short of what is considered a fair Continental crop of the same age, and a loss of from 6,000 to 10,000 cubic feet per acre under conditions quite as favourable as those in Germany, and in many cases more favourable. Note the margin of difference in the number of trees and feet, reckoning the 120 trees, final crop, in the table, as equal to 3,000 feet, or a little over. The crop does not come within sight, so to speak, of what is regarded as an ordinary Continental crop, and such practice has often meant the loss of an income on estates, and should open the eyes of owners of woods in that direction. Look at the waste involved in the extravagantly severe thinnings during the first 25 years, the consequent loss of crop, and adverse influence on the trees left by destroying the overhead canopy and exposing the soil, not to speak of the cost of planting thousands of trees that were never to serve any useful purpose in themselves or benefit the trees left :—

* In his evidence before the Departmental Committee on British Forestry, 1903, the head forester to the Earl of Mansfield, at Scone, *Perthshire*, said that "plenty of foresters in Scotland still advocated the Scotch system," and that " It is undeniable that there has been and yet exists a general ignorance in the profitable growing of timber crops, even in such fundamental points as the following :—To what extent draining is necessary for the varieties proposed to be planted, what species to grow on various soils, etc. ; whether to plant pure or mixed—if pure, what variety and how close to plant ; if mixed, what varieties and what proportions of varieties, when and how often to thin, and when to realize the crop. It often occurs also that when the owner wishes to sell his mature timber he runs a risk of not getting its full value, as comparatively few foresters are reliable in the valuing of standing timber, and it not unfrequently happens that only half the value is offered for a lot by a timber merchant."

SCOTCH PLANTING TABLE, SHOWING DESTRUCTIVE THINNING.

PUBLISHED IN 1899.

	Per Acre.	Rate.
Number of trees planted ...	3546	
First thinning, at 10 years ...	1245	treated as of no value.
	2300	
Second „ at 15 „ ...	800	1s. per score.
	1500	
Third „ at 20 „ ...	500	3s. „ „
	1000	
Fourth „ at 25 „ ...	400	3d. each.
	600	
Fifth „ at 30 „ ...	250	9d. „
	350	
Sixth „ at 35 „ ...	90	= 360 cub. ft. at 6d.
	260	
Seventh „ at 40 „ ...	50	= 300 cub. ft. at 9d.
	210	
Eighth „ at 50 „ ...	45	= 405 cub. ft. at 10d.
	165	
Ninth „ at 60 „ ...	45	= 630 cub. ft. at 1s.
Number of trees forming final crop	120	

The history of forestry in Britain, especially in Scotland, shows that since anything like regular planting began there has not been time to develop a system of management, nor was there any proper foundation to begin on. British woods of importance have been chiefly confined to England.

The total area of Scotland is about 20,000,000 acres. Of that area in 1812 there were only 907,695 acres under woods, less than half of which consisted of planted woods, the rest

being natural.   The returns of 1872, as compared with those
of 1812, show a decrease of 200,000 acres in the forest area.
Whether it was the old or the new woods that had disappeared
during the sixty years interval is not known.   By 1881 the
forest area had increased again to 829,476 acres, the principle
increase having been confined to Aberdeen, Perth, Argyle, and
Inverness, which counties are, however, proportionately the
largest in Scotland.   Elgin, or Moray, is the best wooded
county in Scotland, nearly a sixth of its whole area being
under woods.

In England, Sussex is by far the best wooded county,
containing more than 124,000 acres of woods.   In Elgin,
however, the value of the woods is pulled down by the large
proportion of Scotch fir and spruce which the woods contain;
while in Sussex the woods consist to a large extent of unprofitable coppice, included under the head of woodlands.   These
statistics, relating to Scotland, taken from the last edition of
the "Encyclopædia Britannica," Agricultural Returns, and other
sources, show that with the exception of extensions of woods
in a few places Scotch forestry has really been going back
instead of forward.

Misconception exists also as to the relative extent, value,
composition, and general importance of English and Scotch
woods.   According to the Agricultural Returns of 1901, the
average acreage *per county*, of woods and plantations in the 41
English counties, was 40,627 acres; and in Scotland, 33 counties, 26,629 acres.   The waste land, and mountain and heath,
in England, was 2,305,823 acres; and in Scotland, 9,374,512
acres.   In the composition of the woods of the two countries
there is also a great difference.   English woods consist, mostly,
of the more valuable broad leaved species, and hardwoods;
and Scotch woods mainly of Scotch, spruce, and a small proportion of larch.   In the statistics of Scotland, in the last
edition of the " Encyclopædia Britannica," by T. F. Henderson,
modern plantations in Scotland are described as consisting
chiefly of Scotch fir, with a small sprinkling of larch, and it
might have been added, " much spruce."   We have little
information on this head, however, except in regard to Suther-
landshire, where, although the climate favours several kinds
of hardwoods, they have not been extensively planted, and
Sutherland may be taken as an example of other Scotch
counties.

According to the most recent Agricultural Returns, Sutherland contains 19,641 acres of woods.   Nearly the whole of the
county belongs to the Duke of Sutherland, and according to

the Duke's present head forester at Dunrobin, writing in the
" N.B. Agriculturist," of April 9th, 1902, there are less
than 3,000 acres of hardwoods in the whole county.   Whether
from ignorance, or because they have committed themselves
to the indiscriminate planting of spruce and Scotch fir, some
Scotch foresters, of professed experience, still write and speak
as if the production of hardwoods in the north of Scotland was
out of the question.   Quite recently, a well-known member
of the Royal Scottish Arboricultural Society and factor on an
estate, wrote in a Scotch paper that one might as well expect to
grow good grapes in our gooseberry quarters as expect the ash,
elm, sycamore and beech to grow equally well beside the Scotch
fir.   Comment on such ignorance is needless.* I have, in another
chapter, shown what might be done in growing pine timber
alone, to show what scope the timber grower has in this
country ; but trusting to one kind of crop is not suggested,
and the extent to which spruce and Scotch fir has been
planted in Scotland, almost to the exclusion of hardwoods,
has impressed me much during the past few years.   Owners
of woods cannot be too careful in the selection of the kinds
of trees to plant, and should never forget that density, a
hitherto neglected factor, has much to do with the production
of good timber trees in cold and exposed situations.   In
Scotland the oak does not reach the dimensions that it does in
England, but according to Grigor, second edition, page 270, it
produces a good crop ; and where the oak will grow, most other
broad-leaved species will do better.   Grigor writes :—" One
of the finest oak forests in Scotland is that at Darnaway, in
Morayshire.   Between the years 1830 and 1840 the sales of
timber and bark ranged from £4,000 to £5,000 yearly.   The
oak timber usually sold at from 2s. to 3s. per cubical foot, and
bark varied from £6 to £9 per ton.   The age of the timber
ranged from thirty to eighty years ; and, after paying every
expense during the growth of the timber, the revenue of the
forest per acre was double that of the finest arable land in the
country."

The same writer also furnishes remarkable examples of the
ash, beech and sycamore, and other hardwoods, in various
parts of the north of Scotland.

Col. F. Bailey, also writing on this subject in relation to the

---

* N.B. Agriculturist, April 2nd, 1902.—" On the Alps the ash, elm, beech,
sycamore, and Scots fir thrive respectively up to an elevation of from 4,000
to 6,000 feet, proving that these five species at least are likely to flourish
together at the two highest and most northern situations ever likely to be
planted in the British Islands."

Novar Estate, in Cromarty, in a booklet published in 1899, states that the prices per cubic foot now prevailing there for standing timber of oak and ash is 1s. to 1s. 6d., sycamore 1s. to 5s., elm 1s., beech 6d. to 1s., Scotch fir 3d. to 6d., spruce 3d., in fairly accessible places.

These prices are not much below the best English prices, denote timber of good size and quality, and speak for themselves as to the value of different kinds of crops.

There is now a tendency among Scotch proprietors to conform to the new order of things, both as regards the best kinds of trees to plant and methods of culture, and much will depend on the kind of men they employ in future; but the facts stated, and many more that could be given, show that Scotch woods have not hitherto provided either schools or teachers of forestry, as they are supposed to have done.

Scotch gardeners have always displayed a far more correct appreciation of the climatic conditions of the north of Scotland, arboriculturally and horticulturally, than Scotch foresters have done, if their writings and practice may be taken as an indication of their knowledge and observation.

The productions of gardens in the north of Scotland, in the shape of trees, shrubs, fruit and flowers, have often struck visitors from the south, but seem to have been passed unnoticed by foresters on the spot. Many years ago, the late Mr. Robert Thompson, of Chiswick, a native of Aberdeen, published in the " Gardener's Assistant" the following table:—

	Latitude.	Mean Temperature of March.
Paris	48° 50′	43·79
Rouen	49 26	41·12
Brussels	50 51	42·78
Chiswick (London) ...	51 29	42·23
Boston (Lincolnshire)	52 48	41·67
Dublin	53 21	42·46
Liverpool	53 25	44·44
Edinburgh	55 58	40·53
Dundee	56 27	42·20
Aberdeen	57 9	42·80
Elgin	57 38	40·53
Wick	58 29	41·94

showing how very little difference there was between the mean temperatures of the month of March from the north of France to Wick in Scotland, for cultural purposes; and since then (1884)

the Scottish Meteorological Society published a table of the
mean temperatures at Culloden, Inverness-shire, for every
month in the year, from 1841 to 1880, which quite corroborated
Mr. Thompson's figures.   This table is much too long to
give here, and it may suffice to state that the *mean* mid-summer
temperature every ten years, for forty years, was only a few
degrees below sixty—a temperature in excess of the growing
requirements of most forest trees, and almost as high as the
temperature in many parts of England, where the best timber
is produced.

In Wales there are 181,610 acres of woods, in Ireland about
340,000 acres.

Brown's "Forester," which, in its original form, has seen
several editions, the last issued in 1882, has been the generally
acknowledged exponent of British practice, and has been
followed unquestioningly, both in precept and practice, by
foresters, as our forest literature and our woods show conclusively.   Where Brown derived his ideas of practical forestry
from, such as they are, may be gathered from a perusal of the
works of the older and better-known English and Scotch
writers who preceded him.   His "glances" at the forests of
Europe, outside his own country, are vague, general and brief,
and show that he drew no inspiration from that quarter,
although he did profess to deal with the forestry of the
four quarters of the globe down to the issue of his last edition
in 1882.   His silence on the forestry methods of Germany
and France, carried on on well-established principles during
his time, seem to indicate an almost total unacquaintance with
the subject, and an entire ignorance of the fact that in these
countries timber culture was practised successfully on principles
diametrically opposed to his.   It can hardly be credited that,
had he known anything of the complete forestry system
already established in the countries named and elsewhere, he
would have ventured to suggest the necessity of an improved
system of forestry for the whole world, especially for European
States, which he does do (pp. 8—36).   Throughout Brown's
writings one sees evidence that he viewed forestry not so much
from an industrial and financial as from an artificial, cultural
point of view, and did not realise the possibilities of the home
timber trade, the nature of the demand, nor the extent of the
competition from abroad.

Forestry in this country, as a commercial industry, will
always be ruled by the timber trade and the nature of the
demand—a fact which planters must keep in mind in the

future much more than they have done in the past. As regards forest-tree culture, " The Forester" cannot be said to be a record of personal observation and experience, but it shows plainly enough that the author followed closely in the footsteps of his predecessors, old and obsolete as some of them were.

So far as we have been able to discover, there is hardly an opinion or practice of any importance, on the management of woods and plantations, in all Brown's work that is not dealt with by writers of the last and beginning of the present (19th) century, such as Nicol, Sang, Pontz, Marshall, Loudon, Sir Henry Stewart, and others, although Brown only incidentally acknowledges the existence of such writers. Brown's " Principles," his planting, notching, pitting, nursing, thinning, pruning, etc., etc., are practically identical with those of the older writers named. Indeed, the resemblance of portions of " The Forester" to the works of these older writers is suggestive, and does not harmonize with Brown's claim, p. 5, that the " vast advances " made in the principle features of forest tree culture were chiefly confined to a period of about thirty years previous to 1880—or the period covered by the several editions of his own book. This is particularly noticeable in reference to such subjects as thinning and pruning, - for example, which Brown dilates upon at great length and often, relating, p. 42, that pruning was the branch of forestry least understood some forty years before 1882, and how much had been learned since ; whereas he was anticipated nearly a hundred years before by Sang and others. Sang practically wrote Nicol's "Planters' Kalendar," 1812, a conscientiously written work, and a guide to both foresters and writers at the time.

The above references to Brown are not conceived in any hostile spirit. We know him only from his writings and his work on well-known estates which we are familiar with, and desire only to show here that a work which, up till now, has been regarded by some as a safe guide, and which professed to teach the latest and best methods of forestry practice, had little claim to be regarded in that light. We refer to the original editions, of course, not to the Germanised edition.

How or when Brown's system originated it is difficult to say. We once thought, and it is still held by some, that his system of growing timber-trees was simply the gardener's plan of growing trees for ornamental purposes, carried to the woods. It seems probable that it began with Evelyn, and filtered down through later writers till Brown's time, as there is a strong family resemblance running through the principal works on forestry since Evelyn's time.

Brown's system, in its most important aspects, was to plant the permanent crop thin, fill up with an extravagant number of profitless and often useless nurses, and thin early and often, until the final crop was reaped, if that ever happened; for rotation, which determines how long capital shall be locked up in standing timber and regulates successional planting, had no place in his system. Neither was density nor the shade-bearing capacity of different species regarded as factors in the production of good timber, nor, so far as we know, are they even mentioned in his book. Crowding, of course, he regarded as an unmitigated evil, and the protection of the soil in forests, according to the species, and over-head canopy, had no importance in his eyes, if we may judge by his practice.

From his frequent thinnings a regular and constantly augmenting revenue was expected and a profitable realisation anticipated at the end; but that did not happen, because the thinnings were unprofitable, the ultimate crop too light, and the timber of the worst quality.* Dr. Adam Schwappach, professor of forestry, Eberswalde, Prussia, in his report of a visit to the forests of Scotland, in 1896, comments adversely on Scottish forestry culture as practised in the past. Writing in the transactions of the Scottish Arboricultural Society, 1896, about what has hitherto been considered one of the finest examples of Scottish forestry, he says:—"The trees were showing vigorous growth, and one can only regret that the ground was not more fully stocked, as would have been the case under a different system of management, and which would have resulted in the production of finer and more valuable stems." Summarising the points having the most important bearing on the future of forestry in Scotland, he goes on, "the woods should be managed on sylvicultural principles, and not in the park-like manner at present so much in vogue;" and "the operation of thinning should be conducted in a more rational manner, and with more regard to the future of the wood."

In Chapter XIV. of "The Forester," fifth edition, at the beginning, Brown lays down his principles on the "nature and necessity of thinning plantations" in the following vague words, slightly abridged, which give the reader no idea what he actually means:—"Thinning is one of the most indispensable operations in arboriculture. The object which ought

* See Parliamentary Report. Mr. Dundas's evidence.

to be aimed at by the forester in the act of thinning, is the regulating of the trees in a plantation to such a distance, one from another, and that in such a manner as is known to be favourable to the health of each tree individually, as well as to the general welfare of the whole plantation. In order to grow any plant to that size which the species to which it belongs is known to attain under favourable circumstances, it is necessary that it have space of ground and air for the spread of its roots and branches in proportion to its size at any given stage of its growth. Upon this the whole nature and intention of thinning plantations rest." As a non-committal exposition of principles the foregoing would be hard to beat; but elsewhere, in the same chapter, these principles are overruled by quite another set of conditions, occupying about forty pages. Under eleven separate sections he distinguished between thinning plantations on all woodlands—and on properties; between thinning plantations on extensive properties —and on small properties; between oak plantations—and hard-wood plantations; between pine, larch and fir plantations —and pine plantations; and between fir plantations —and larch plantations; confusing and complicating in purely fanciful distinctions a practice in which the same general rule applies under all circumstances.

Trees, not timber, was what Brown was apparently thinking of. He assumed that the biggest tree, trunk and limbs, was the best, and that the tree that was allowed ample space in every way to develop to its fullest extent attained to the greatest size in the shortest time, and secured the desired end. This argument, applied in principle to plantation culture, necessarily leads to thin planting, wrong mixtures, early and frequent thinnings, and free lateral growth in the trees left; but, so far as the production of timber is concerned, either as regards quantity or quality, the reasoning is quite fallacious. It is true that trees grown as described do, individually, increase in bulk, including branches, more quickly than they do when crowded together; but it is equally certain, first, that fir trees, so grown, owing to excessive branch development, are too rough and tapering to yield good stems of useful dimensions; and that broad-leaved trees are spent in the production of far too great a proportion of small top wood of little or no value, instead of in trunk volume; and, second, that such trees produce the least quantity of timber to the acre because they take up more room, proportionately, than several trees of lesser size and better quality would occupy grown closely together.

The proofs of Brown's practice are scattered throughout
" The Forester." Whenever we have been consulted by
owners of woods we have been met by Brown's teachings on
the subject of thinning and nursing, both inimical to good
forestry. The opinion is almost universal among owners of
woods that as soon as a plantation gets crowded it is going to
ruin, whereas it is just in the condition it should be. Brown's
advice, as regards planting generally, is, that in high-lying
exposed situations, three-and-a-half feet should be allowed
between the plants, and in sheltered spots, four to five feet.
" On low-lying and naturally sheltered parts of the country,"
he recommends hard-woods to be planted five yards apart, the
space between to be made up with temporary nurses " to five
feet over all ;" and on exposed situations for pine and larch
from three-and-a-half to four feet. This is thinning to begin
with (p. 454). At page 43 he congratulates British proprietors
on having recently adopted a mode of thinning on what he
calls " a regular systematic principle, by which the crops are
kept at all stages of their growth in a regular state, one tree
from another, and from this at all times in an equally healthy
condition, and never allowed to become crowded before
thinning." Writing (p. 571) on the "nature and necessity
of thinning plantations," he again urges that in rearing up a
plantation " principally for the sake of the value of timber,
etc.," that " the object should be to keep the branches of each
individual tree from interfering with those of its surrounding
neighbours and no more." At p. 573, advising " how to proceed systematically in regard to the thinning of plantations
in all woodlands," he writes, " on all the properties respecting
woods of which we have reported, we have invariably recommended, as a means of improvement, that the several ages of
plantations should be divided into equal portions, and one
such portion should be periodically and systematically thinned
once in three, four, five or six years, according to the age
respectively." At p. 575, speaking of six hundred and thirty-
nine acres of trees of the respective ages of from forty-five to
sixty years, he writes, " the trees should have attained their
confirmed habit and should grow comparatively little in the
spread of their limbs." Clearly he is here thinking of trees
still retaining their earliest branches upon them.

Brown did not originate the system of planting "nurses "
in young plantations, but he elaborated it to an extravagant
extent, and probably few practices have caused more loss to
proprietors than that of planting so many nurses, or indeed

nurses at all.   We have been unable to find any clear explanation of the practice, but it seems to be taken for granted that
it means the filling up of the spaces between the trees, compos-
ing a thinly-planted permanent crop, with a hardier species, in
order to shelter the permanent crop until it becomes established, the nurses being gradually removed when no longer
needed.   The system is a practical admission of the soundness
of the principle on which density of culture at all stages is
based ; but owing to the way in which the nursing system has
been carried out it has defeated its purpose, and, next to over-
thinning, probably no practice has caused so much loss as
over-nursing.   In German forestry, a far greater number of
trees are brought on to the ground at planting than can be
found room for for any great length of time, the object being
to establish over-head canopy as soon as possible, and promote
shelter and height growth.   If in the British nursing system
the permanent crop had been planted thickly—say three or
four feet from tree to tree, and nurses put in between, reducing
the distance to from eighteen inches to two feet, the system
might have been defensible, but the mistake has been that
the nurses have taken the place of the permanent crop, and
while of little or no value in themselves, have not fulfilled the
purpose for which they were intended.   In other words, the
number of the trees to the acre of the permanent crop have
been far too few, and the number of nurses disproportionately
large, and both together planted so far apart that they could
afford no protection to each other when it was most needed,
viz., the first few years after planting.   In addition to this,
the nurses have often been of the wrong kind, and been left
too long, their removal then causing a severe check to the
permanent crop, as may be seen in the New Forest and elsewhere, where the oaks have become prematurely stunted.   So
far as we know, the nursing system adopted in this country
is unknown elsewhere, and one or two examples will suffice
to show to what absurd lengths the practice has been carried.
At page 584 of " The Forester," is a coloured diagram, made
out with much care, that has led many astray.   This diagram
shows the permanent or ultimate crop of timber trees, consisting of oak, ash, elm and sycamore, planted from twelve to
seventeen feet apart, or rather less than three hundred trees
to the imperial acre, where from four to five thousand ought to
be the number.   The spaces between the hard-wood species
named are filled up with larch and Scotch fir, from four feet
to six feet apart over all, or at a total average rate, hard-woods

and nurses together, of about seventeen hundred to the acre, of which number some *fourteen hundred are nurses to be removed before they can be of a remunerative size.* The worst feature of the business, however, is that all the four species to be nursed are as hardy or hardier than their nurses, the sycamore and beech particularly; the whole of the four species probably smothering their nurses early in the struggle.

This diagram of Brown's has been reproduced in many of the forest tree catalogues of the principal nurserymen in Great Britain, who supply trees and often conduct planting operations. The following is an example in which the spaces between the trees are even wider than they are in Brown's, and all the " L's " and " F's " represent nurses to be early removed, leaving a permanent crop of one hundred and eight trees to the acre! We do not blame nurserymen for following the lead of professed experts in such matters, but surely a little reflection might show the utter absurdity of a table like the following :—

PLANTER'S DIAGRAM,

SHOWING SYSTEM OF PLANTING TREES FOR A MIXED HARD-WOOD PLANTATION.

```
O   F   A   F   O   F   A   F   O   F
  L   L   L   L   L   L   L   L   L   L
F   F   F   F   F   F   F   F   F   F
  L   L   L   L   L   L   L   L   L   L
S   F   E   F   S   F   E   F   S   F
  L   L   L   L   L   L   L   L   L   L
F   F   F   F   F   F   F   F   F   F
  L   L   L   L   L   L   L   L   L   L
O   F   A   F   O   F   A   F   O   F
```

O. Oak, planted at 20 feet apart.
A. Ash, „ 20 „ „
E. Elm, „ 20 „ „
S. Sycamore, planted at 20 feet apart.
L. Larch, as nurses, and for early thinning.
F. Scotch Fir, Spruce, or Austrian Pine, as Nurses, etc.
O. A. E. S. Any of these or any other hard-wooded trees to remain permanently.

(From a Nurseryman's Catalogue.)

The next example relates to the Douglas fir—"The Forester," p. 355. This tree is to be planted "thirty feet apart as the permanent crop, and made up with larch as nurses to five feet over all"—the larch to be removed in about twenty years, so that "a complete plantation of this tree alone could be secured." Now here we have one of the most vigorous evergreen species known nursed by a deciduous species every way weaker than itself, and the permanent crop planted ten yards asunder for the production of timber. Plantations of Douglas fir raised on this principle are now to be seen, the worst examples of timber culture probably to be found anywhere—the trees tapering rapidly in shape and forming a mass of huge knots from top to bottom. In many cases the plan has defeated itself, and now plantations are to be seen in which the nurses have become the permanent and better crop, with here and there a hard-wood to denote the original purpose of the planter. We do not recommend nurses at all, but, instead, the planting, sufficiently thick, of the permanent crop, so as to establish overhead canopy as soon as possible.

Such are some of the cultural practices advocated by those who have hitherto been followed in this country, and the adoption of which has caused so much loss. More might be added, such as the absence of working plans, unprofitable methods of labour, methods of planting, the extent to which pruning, due to over-thinning, was carried, and extravagance in the general management of woods before the period of agricultural depression set in, that has paralysed forestry operations on many estates; but these will be dealt with in other chapters.

But although the majority of writers on forestry have apparently belonged to Brown's school, there were, previous to Brown's time, observers who had other and more correct notions of the subject of timber production, evidently, as now, derived from Continental sources, although the cultural process was not thoroughly understood. According to "Ree's Cyclopædia," 1819, Mr. Salmon, of Woburn, in Bedfordshire, writing in the "Transactions of the Society of Arts" on raising good timber, says, "it may be a fair question if our country be not capable of producing fir timber little or not at all inferior to foreign fir." Considering the purposes to which such timber is commonly applied, "it must occur," he writes, "that clearness of knots, straightness, length and equality of size of trunk, constitute its perfection, and that, if deficient

4

of all these, it is of no value but for firewood." His method
of producing trees of this kind was the wrong one—the
pruning knife; but his object was to secure the same ends
as the Continental forester aims at in crowding, viz., the
removal of the lower branches. Mr. Salmon began cutting the
lower branches off when the trees were five or six years old,
and kept on at it every few years till the stem of the tree was
clear up to a height of forty feet or thereabout, after which
such "side lopping" was left to nature.

SECTION II.—THE NEW FORESTRY.

This is really Nature's system, and is practically the system
reduced to method and adopted on the Continent. There is
nothing novel about it, nor, as far as we are aware, has it ever
been claimed that the system originated in those countries
where it is practised so successfully. All that has been done
has been to maintain and extend the forests on principles
derived from a close study of nature, and that is all. Were
it not that the trees in the later German forests are seen to
have been planted in rows, or in some kind of formal order,
the visitor could not tell the artificially planted sections from
those that had grown up naturally. Much of the timber
imported to this country from Germany and Northern Europe
is from purely natural forests—from Russia, Sweden, and
Norway, almost wholly so; while from the natural forests of
America, Asia, Africa, and the Colonies, come vast quantities
of timber of all descriptions, rivalling, if not surpassing, the
productions of the scientifically-managed forests of Europe,
and produced under exactly the same conditions unaided by
the cultural hand of man.

Reduced to practice then, this system consists in the
division of the forest into areas and compartments in which
the timber crops are regulated on a strict rotation system
according to the species; in the reproduction of crops by seed,
or by plants raised in the forest nurseries from seed and
planted out small; in planting thickly, so as to cover the
ground speedily; in crowding the trees judiciously at all stages,
so as to secure height growth and clean cylindrical trunks;
and in thinning sparingly at long intervals. The rotation
period determines the length of time that any crop of timber
shall occupy the ground, and is regulated more by the size of
the trees than their maturity. It is found that the Scotch fir

and spruce reach their most useful maximum dimensions at one hundred years of age or thereabout, and the final crop, or what remains of it, is then swept away and the ground re-sown or re-planted. On the same principle, the beech, mixed with a few other hard-woods, is allowed one hundred and twenty-five years, and the oak one hundred and fifty years. Practically all the species grown come within these three groups. There is no irregularity and no blanks. When all the main divisions of the wooded area have reached the productive stage, each yielding its annual quota of timber, the "working circle" is said to be complete—reproduction, of course, going on in proportion to the fellings. Supposing this method was applied to a well-wooded estate in England, the wooded area would have to be arranged in divisions of workable size, which, when fully stocked, would each yield a certain and regular quantity of timber. The average annual income expected from the woods, and the nature of the demand would probably, in any case, determine the number of divisions, their size, and the period of rotation. The woods on any estate in this country might be laid out and conducted on the foregoing principles, and once the divisions were set out, an estimate of their value and the cost of stocking fully could easily be made out.* In German forests the ultimate or final cutting is the best, but is not the only crop, as large quantities are cut before the end of the rotation period. Where the forests are on a large scale, the above rotation periods are found to answer, but in order that capital may not be too long locked up in standing timber, and to meet the most profitable demand, they may be shortened. By way of illustration, supposing that on an English estate it was found that the crop of larch could be grown and disposed of most profitably within the space of forty years, that period ought to be the end of the rotation, and so on with other species, according to the age at which it was found most profitable to reap the crop.

First, the general theory of the system is that thick planting at the outset and dense culture throughout are the first essentials in the production of good timber; second, that thick planting leads to the early establishment of the overhead canopy, promotes height growth, and protects the soil, preserving its fertility and keeping it at a more uniform degree of

* On the Raith estate, belonging to Mr. Munro Ferguson, M.P., in Fife, 800 acres of woods have been recently re-arranged on the above principle, and are expected to render a sustained annual yield of at least 60,000 cubic feet on a forty years' rotation.

temperature and moisture than is found in open woods or where the ground is exposed; third, that density, or crowding, causes the struggle for existence to set in early, in which struggle the trees begin to shed their lower branches while they are still young, grow in the desired cylindrical shape in their stems, are free from knots, and produce timber of the best quality for all purposes; lastly, that the quantity of timber produced to the acre is greater than can be produced by any other system, and the value of the crop proportionately greater. (See Chapter XII.)

In practice, the Germans often plant several young trees in one hole, the holes being from two to four feet apart, according to the situation and soil—poor and exposed situations receiving the most plants, and vice versa. Frequent and severe thinnings are avoided as unmitigated evils, and so is the admission of light and currents of air below the overhead canopy; shelter to the stems of the trees from both being of the utmost consequence. The trunk of a tree in a dense forest is regarded as but the channel between the soil and living branches high up at the top of the tree, where growth and elaboration is carried on. In the tended forests of Germany, thinning is seldom attempted before the trees are from twenty to thirty years of age, in the case of firs, while hard woods, like the beech, coming up naturally in dense masses, are often left unthinned for thirty-five or forty years. When thinning is done, the greatest care is taken to preserve the overhead canopy, and exclude air currents and winds, even dead trees being often left standing if their removal is going to create a gap. Crowding at all stages is the rule, the live top of branches decreasing in proportion as the trees grow older, until, at the end of the rotation period, in the case of the spruce, only about one-sixth, or even less, of the entire length of the tree will be furnished with branches, forming just a tuft at the top, the trunk by this time having long shed its lower branches, and formed a clean straight pole with very little taper from end to end. In the case of hard wood the proportion of top is much the same, a mere wisp, comparatively, carrying on all the functions of growth successfully to the end. However small the top of live branches may be, within reasonable limits, it is sufficient to add a layer of timber to the trunk annually, and given the required number of years, a tree of the required dimensions is produced. Big trees of mature timber are not so much sought after in Germany as trees of moderate girth and of good useful quality. A crop of pit-props, for example, averaging from five to six inches quarter girth in the middle, can be produced in from twenty-five to forty-five years without any thinning at all, but trunks larger and thicker are also produced from forests which have been sparingly thinned a few times in the course of the whole rotation period. Increment of bole depends upon the amount of living top of branches and foliage the tree is allowed to carry, and between youth and middle age, or even later, these may be permitted to increase, when thick trunks in the mature crop is an object, consistently with the preservation of the overhead canopy. From the British forester's point of view, what appeared objectionable to us in those German forests was the large proportion of under-sized trees existing in the middle-aged and even older crops. We do not mean short trees, for all were tall and clean, but under-girthed, slender-stemmed trees, such as could not be disposed of profitably in this country. In Germany, of course, firewood has to be produced as well as timber—something like thirty per cent. going for that purpose, and the small trees and cordwood supply this demand, which in Britain is unimportant.* If the forests were a little more evenly regulated, much of the small stuff would be got rid of, and the trees left would be larger and more useful. This German foresters understand, and before the end of the rotation period they do sometimes thin to promote girth, but in this country that would have to be the rule, while still acting on the German principle of first securing height-growth, clean trunks and an unbroken leaf canopy.

It will be seen by the foregoing that in the dense system of forest-tree culture, underwood, of the kind allowed for covert and other purposes in the over-thinned woods of the past, is not contemplated. In dense woods it cannot be grown as a crop, its place being taken by timber trees. As far as game covert is concerned, it will, however, be seen, by a reference to Chapter II., that an equivalent for underwood is provided in the shape of open glades or spaces filled with trees and bushes of the usual underwood kind, and where they are sure to thrive far more successfully than under trees. Underwood or covert, in dense woods, is, however, not an impossibility if the right species are selected, and the subject is dealt with in a short chapter towards the end of the book.

---

* Since the above was written I find that more firewood is consumed on many estates than has been supposed, wood being almost exclusively burnt in both mansion and cottage for economical reasons—usually loppings and unsaleable butts—some mansions using nearly 100 tons per annum.

SECTION III.—TIMBER-TREES OF THE OLDER BRITISH WOODS.

It must not be supposed from what has been said that the timber produced in Britain has always been of the description produced by the cultural methods of Brown and his predecessors.   There are good reasons for supposing that before the empirical system of forestry in vogue during the last century began, our forests were, to a large extent, of natural growth, and that much of the best timber which was supplied for the navy and other purposes came from such forests. A reference to the navy estimates in " Haydn's Dictionary of Dates," from the beginning of the eighteenth to well on in the nineteenth century, will show that the demand for timber for ships must have gone up by leaps and bounds, and during that period the woods of England must have been ransacked for timber of large size.   That this was the case is proved also by the records of private estates a long way from the sea, and which show that the timber was simply felled and squared by the axe in the wood and hauled by horses to its destination. It was this demand which has led writers on forestry to dwell so much on the wants of the navy when timber was the material used in ship-building, and the demand for which only fell off with the advent of iron and the use of foreign timber. According to Marshall, 1785, a gentleman of leisure who travelled much in England in search of information on the subject of planting, great inroads had been made in the forests of this country in his time, but much was still left.   With the decline of the demand for ship timber, however, arose the demand for oak and fir for railway carriages, waggons, and sleepers, and we believe that the demand for railway material of that description has, during the last fifty years, exceeded the demand for the navy at the time referred to above, with the result that our stock of home-grown big timber is now approaching the vanishing point.   The main timbers of railway carriages are still, by preference, made of English oak of good size, and, as only the very straightest and soundest trees are used, and only the best portions of these, the consumption of oak, in the shape of railway material alone, may be imagined when it is added that some of our great companies will now own from one to nearly two hundred thousand carriages and waggons.   Railways, of course, use a great variety of other kinds of timber ; but oak for carriages and Scotch fir for sleepers for the permanent way represent the two kinds of timber for which the demand is by far the greatest, and it is constantly increasing.

That the oak and fir of these older British woods were produced in dense forests, quite unlike those existing now, and that the trees were tall and straight, is evident from the fragments of our older woods still left, and other examples. This applies to oak and Scotch fir principally, the first in England and the latter in Scotland. The beams, joists and fittings in many old houses and cottages attest this. These beams are long, straight, and of good girth from end to end. In many cases the logs have not been sawn, but simply squared by the axe in the forest and used in that way. In England bridges over streams were constructed of home-grown oak logs of great length and stoutness. Some years ago the timber of an old bridge of this description, in Norfolk, was still so good that it was advertised for sale and was bought by a Yorkshire timber merchant. The logs were from sixty to seventy feet long, and squared only a little less at the small end than they did at the other. The purchaser had to send his own team to Norfolk to have them removed. That accurate and conscientious observer, Gilbert White, in his "Natural History of Selborne," records similar examples, apparently scarce in his time. "On the Blackmore estate," he writes, "there is a small wood that was lately furnished with a set of oak of a peculiar growth and of great value. They were tall and taper, like firs, but, standing near together, had very small heads, only a little brush without any large limbs. Some trees were wanted that were fifty feet long without bough, and would measure twelve inches diameter at the little end. Twenty such trees did a purveyor find in this little wood, with this advantage, that many of them answered the description at sixty feet. These trees were sold for £20 a piece."

The remains of many old woods in Yorkshire, and records connected with them, seem to show that that county must have been famous for its oak in times past. We have never seen the Yorkshire oak surpassed for size and quality, and it has struck us several times that the oak trees of Hampshire, Surrey, and other parts south of London, were short and inferior to those produced in Yorkshire of the same age, particularly the plantation oak in the New Forest and neighbourhood. In "Hunter's Hallamshire" (Yorkshire) it is stated that a Mr. John Harrison made a "minute survey," in 1637, of the Manor of Sheffield, for the Earl of Arundel, in which he thus describes the "stately timber" growing in Sheffield Park and Rivelin Chase:—"The Haugh Park is full of excellent timber of very great length and very straight, and many of them of great bigness, being about sixty feet in length before you came to a knott, insomuch that it hath been said by travellers that they have not seen such timber in Christendom." Evelyn, we also learn from the same source, "accounts for the noble timber with which the hills about Sheffield were once graced." Mr. John Halton, the Duke of Norfolk's auditor, told Evelyn that "in the Park alone there were not fewer than a thousand trees worth at least six thousand pounds, another thousand worth four thousand pounds, and so on in proportion." We are acquainted with the extent of the locality here mentioned, and judging from that, and the number of trees given, they must have grown up in dense masses, as their shape and length seem to testify. Not very far from Sheffield we once valued, and saw sold by auction, a number of lots of old and sound oak equal to those described by Evelyn, the remains of an old and dense wood. The sale was put into the hands of a well-known London auctioneer, who brought purchasers from far and near. All the trees were large and old, some of the lots averaging eighty cubic feet per tree throughout, and the others not much less. They readily realised from 2s. 6d. to 3s. per foot standing in the wood, although nearly four miles from a station. Such examples are yet to be found in old and once dense woods near mansions, but they are not common and are seldom for sale. Some of the finest timber trees, probably in England at the present time, are to be seen at Shipton Court, Oxford, the seat of W. F. Pepper, Esq. These trees are growing in a small wood near the mansion, and consist of a mixture of hardwoods, larch, and Scotch fir, remarkable for their length of trunk, freedom from branches, and clean, cylindrical shape, qualities due to the wood having been left unthinned—accidentally it is surmised—until the trees had passed middle age. The oaks in Sherwood Forest are large, but they are not good sylvicultural examples, and the noted Major Oak, the biggest tree in the forest, is an excellent example of what a timber-tree should NOT be, covering, as it does, a large portion of an acre with its numerous boughs, which spread out from a rough, short trunk. A nice little crop of trees, of the dimensions and value described by Gilbert White, could be reared on the space occupied by the Major Oak. Sherwood has long been an open, thin forest, hence the park-like form of the trees there.

In Yorkshire and elsewhere, before iron was substituted for timber to the extent it is now, and before foreign timber became common, good home-grown timber fetched a much higher price than it does at present, and labour and cultural expenses were less, as many estate records could show. The demand in those days was good, and no doubt led to the undue thinning of woods on many estates, and the production of rough timber in that which was left to grow. In fact the decay now noticeable in many old woods is due to nothing else but exposure by over-thinning after the trees had reached mature age. If a strict rotation system of clearing off and re-planting had been followed, instead of a timid system of repeated thinnings and mismanagement, in all probability our woods would have been in a very different condition now. It is plain to the most casual observer that in many old oak woods the lower branches (which in park trees would be the oldest and the largest) are much smaller than the branches which form the tops of the trees, and the explanation is that the lower branches have been produced at a much later period than the tops, their production being due to the broken over-head canopy encouraging the late growth. These branches often clothe the trunks of old oaks from top to bottom, and have a pleasing effect to the eye, but they are in the wrong place, and in aged trees are produced at the expense of the proper top, as they absorb the sap as it ascends, and which should flow to the top of the tree. French foresters, according to Bagneris, call such growths " epicormic branches," and prune them off, believing them to be one cause of old oaks becoming stag-headed prematurely.

The past system of thinning oak woods until the trees left were too few, too far apart, and consequently exposed at a period when they were least able to bear exposure, has, no doubt, led to premature decay in the trees left in many woods. Trees now going off fast at their tops, and becoming hollow in their trunks, might still have been in good health and adding to their size and value if thinning had been arrested as soon as it was seen that it was going to open the wood out too much. Clear cutting in sections should then have been begun, followed by re-planting, so as to keep the area fully stocked.

CHAPTER IV.

WORKING FORESTRY PLANS.

Allotment of the Wooded Area.—-Period of Rotation.–Choice of Species.—Cultural Methods.—General Routine of Management.—Forestry Book-keeping.

By working plans is meant the general scheme of management throughout all the woods on an estate. Wherever a forester and a working staff are employed, working plans are a necessity, although they are rarely found on estates, the work being usually carried on in an irregular fashion from year to year, the forester being left too much to his own resources. Good working plans provide a safe guide to both the proprietor and his agents, make the work of management easier and cheaper, and promote order in every department. The work may not go on with the same regularity in the woods every year, but it can be taken up, according to the plan, where it was left off, and should even a change of foresters occur, the management can still go on the same lines as before. Well-considered forestry plans should not contemplate nor permit any material change of management or practice with a change of foresters or whims of an untried man, a thing which has often happened on estates to the disadvantage of the woods where no plan of work existed. It should be clearly understood that in the new forestry here advocated there is little that the usual practical training of the Scotch or English forester, combined with a little knowledge of vegetable physiology, should not fit him to carry out perfectly well. He should soon master the general principles on which any system of culture is based, and need only conform to the working plans. On the Continent, and particularly in Germany, the first duty of the forest officer in any section is to master the system that controls all important operations connected with his charge. Writers on the German forestry devote much attention to the working plans, going into the subject on a far more comprehensive scale and minute way than it is proposed to do in this work, where woods of very limited extent, compared to Continental forests, are dealt with, and the working plans modified accordingly. Woodlands in Britain have almost everywhere been so injudiciously planted, and so severely and irregularly thinned, that on almost all private estates there is sufficient scope for planting and regeneration, without taking up any fresh land ; and in many cases the restoration of existing woods to the full-crop condition would provide owners with quantities of timber for sale in simply clearing away what ought to come down to make room for successional crops.

As given in this chapter, little else than the titles of the working plans and the general duties included under each head are stated ; the reader being referred to the other chapters in the book for details of practice and operations that come under one or other of the different heads given in the following working plan that has been thought sufficient to meet the wants of the British forester : —

    1.—Allotment of the wooded area.
    2.—Period of rotation.
    3.—Choice of species suitable for the locality.
    4.—Cultural methods to be adopted.
    5.—Control and general management.

SECTION I.—ALLOTMENT OF THE WOODED AREA.

Under this head should be included existing woods, and any areas proposed to be planted at any future time. In dealing with this part of the work, the forester should first provide himself with a good map of the estate on which the woods are clearly set out. This map will be found in the Ordnance Survey ; if on the new and larger scale of twenty-five inches to the mile, all the better. Having ascertained the extent of the existing woods and plantations, and decided on the areas yet to be planted, the first should be coloured a dark-green shade on the map, and the last a light-green, to be deepened after planting. Both should be numbered distinctly on the map, and consecutively from one side of the estate to the other side, and the numbers should correspond with the numbers in the wood register book here described. The words "wood," "forest," or "plantation," should be applied only to such planted tracts as are not separated by fields or fences, and the different divisions of such woods, whether distinguished by age or species, should be indicated in the register by letters of the alphabet, but popular local names need not be omitted. This register should begin with a descriptive reference table or index, setting forth the number and name of the wood, its extent, elevation, aspect, number of divisions, soil and formation, and record in the register ; and to each wood should be allotted a sufficient number of pages in the register book for the entry of further particulars, in a concise form, showing the age and extent of each division, what it consists of, when thinned or cut down, how the produce was disposed of, and the value received, etc., as shown in accompanying examples.

REGISTER OF WOODS AND PLANTATIONS ON THE W—— ESTATE.

DESCRIPTIVE LIST.

No.	Name of Wood.	Extent.	Elevation.	Aspect.	No. of Divisions.	Soil and Formation.	Record in Register.	REMARKS.
1	High Wood.	60 acres.	385 to 450 feet.	South-west.	Three—A. B. C.	Poor Loam on Millstone Grit.	Pages 1 to 9.	
2	Black Plantation.	200 acres.	750 to 910 feet.	North-east.	One.	Thin Peat on Rag.	Pages 10 to 19.	

REGISTER OF WOODS AND PLANTATIONS.

SUB-DIVISION.

No. 1.—High Wood—continued. Division A.—Mixed. Planted in 1836. Consisting of oak, ash, elm, birch, alder, and larch.

When thinned or clear cut.	How disposed of.	Value.	REMARKS.
Thinned first time 1860.	Sold to Mr. L—, of Leeds, for ... ... Small Poles and Cordwood	£100.	Growing fast. Disease appearing on Larch.

REGISTER OF WOODS AND PLANTATIONS.

SUB-DIVISION.

No. 1.—High Wood—continued. Division B.—Pure. Planted 1859. 20 acres. Common spruce.

When thinned or clear cut.	How disposed of.	Value.	REMARKS.
Thinned first time sparingly, 1875.	Used on the Estate.	Valued at £30.	

E O WOODS AND PLANTAT ONS.

SUB-D v s on.

o. High Wood—con nued. Division C. M xed.
    Sco ch fir, Cors can fir, and ar

Planted 1880. 20 acres

When thinned or clear cut.	Disposed	Value.	Remarks.
C eaned in 1880.	For firewood to house.	£40	

A register like the foregoing may be modified to suit circumstances, but such a record may be kept with little trouble, and will provide a useful ready reference to the proprietor and his forester.

SECTION II.—PERIOD OF ROTATION.

Rotation in forestry does not necessarily mean the same thing as the rotation of crops practised and enforced in agriculture, viz., a change of crop. In forestry, rotation means the period that any crop shall occupy the ground from the time it is sown or planted till the ultimate crop is swept away and the ground re-stocked by natural regeneration or planting. Over great tracts of forests on the Continent of Europe, the same species appear to have succeeded each other from time immemorial, but under later and more particular management in Germany, it has been found necessary to regulate the crops and limit the period according to the species. It is significant that in British works on forestry of the past, rotation is hardly alluded to. Yet there is no part of working forestry plans of more importance than the adoption of some scheme of rotation wherever the woods are moderately extensive. Rotation, properly carried out, regulates the amount of forest produce to be disposed of annually or periodically, and necessarily determines what the equivalent is to be in the shape of regeneration by planting or sowing. These in turn regulate the income from the woods, the expenditure upon them, and the work generally. At present, in British woods, there is no attempt at periodical rotation, hence the confusion in many cases. Let, however, a period of rotation be decided upon on an estate, and the age and condition of every plantation be ascertained, and things at once assume a definite shape, and the owner can look ahead and forecast his plans accordingly. The rotation period need not be fixed on hard and fast lines, but might be regulated by climate, the rate of growth expected, and the purposes for which the timber is grown. On the Continent, oak is allowed about one hundred and fifty years, beech and other hard-woods about one hundred and twenty-five years, and spruce and Scotch fir one hundred years. On private properties, according to Bagneris, short rotations are preferable, in order to guard against the accumulation of a large capital in the shape of standing timber. The want of a rotation system in Britain has frequently led to loss in this way, and great irregularities in management. Rotation, in the agricultural sense, has hitherto been deemed necessary by British foresters, the idea being probably derived from agricultural practice; but in natural forests, and also in Continental forests, rotation in that sense can hardly be said to exist, the same species following each other on the same ground. In Germany hard-woods have followed hard-woods, and firs firs, from time immemorial. In the great American forests it is the same, and according to the recent Government reports of the forests of Australia, by Mr. J. Ednie Brown, the same species appear to have followed each other from a prehistoric period. In the Jarrah forests of West Australia, at the present time, vigorous natural regeneration at all stages is found going on, from the seed of the previous generation of trees, wherever a clearing has been effected by natural or artificial means. It may be occasionally wise to change the crop, but it is not always necessary.

SECTION III.—CHOICE OF SPECIES OF TIMBER-TREES FOR THE LOCALITY.

Under this head should be set down a list of any species that are known to thrive and grow quickly in the district, and such as are likely in the future to find a good market. Careful ·enquiry over estates in the neighbourhood will soon reveal what species succeed best; but soil and aspect should also be considered in drawing conclusions on the subject. As to the probable comparative value of the different kinds of timber that may be produced, the consumption within a radius of about twenty-five miles will pretty well determine that question, if the timber has to be sold in the rough, in the wood, as distance from the consumer is a main factor in determining the price in the wood. Having determined the species most suitable and the right proportion of each, a list should be made out for future use. Of course this arrangement does not prohibit the planting, for experimental purposes, of new or likely species, but extensive plantations of these should not be made until their adaptability to the climate and usefulness as timber-trees have been proved. The Continental forest authorities are careful on this head. They may be said to have scarcely as yet added to the species indigenous to the country, and they select but few of these for the main crop. This important aspect of the subject will, however, be more fully dealt with in the chapter on " Species most suitable for planting."

SECTION IV.—CULTURAL METHODS TO BE ADOPTED FOR
THE WOODS AND PLANTATIONS.

What the owner has to decide here is the method of
cropping and culture to which his woods shall be subjected,
with the object of producing profitable crops of timber, if
necessary in conjunction with game and sport. By culture
and cropping is meant everything pertaining to the actual
management of the trees in the plantations, from the time they
are sown or planted until the crop is reaped, and includes the
raising and preparation of the trees in the nursery, the age
and size at which the trees shall be finally planted out, as far
as that is practicable, the season of the year at which the
different species shall be planted, the method of planting, and
the times and conditions under which any thinning shall be
begun and conducted until the crop has reached maturity—all
of which shall be specially dealt with in the chapter devoted to
these topics. The principles on which all these conditions and
operations are based are of almost universal application, and
are easily mastered by the forester, whose instructions as to
the general system to be pursued should be definite and
clear. Without adherence to guiding principles of culture,
neither methodical practice nor continuity of plan is possible,
and the want of both has been the great drawback in the past.

SECTION V.—CONTROL AND GENERAL ROUTINE OF
MANAGEMENT.

By control is meant the general superintendence of the
woods and game preserves on an estate subject to the general
estate supervision ; and by routine of management is meant
the ordering of the work throughout the year. The full
control should be vested in the head forester, whose duty
should be to keep all books, collect accounts, arrange the work
of the staff, prepare plans of work proposed to be executed
annually in the woods, and estimates of expenditure and
income, etc., etc. Keeping a correct debtor and creditor
account is one of the forester's most important duties, because
without that his employer cannot possibly know how his
woods stand. This applies as much to estate accounts and
charges as to outside transactions in forest produce. It is easy
to do this, but in too many cases correct accounts are not kept.

It is popularly supposed that woods in this country do not pay—and, as a rule, we believe they do not as at present conducted; but the receipts would often be much greater if the other departments on the estate always discharged their liabilities to the woods. If all departments on estates were to render a faithful account of their mutual transactions, the woods would often appear to better advantage; and there is nothing so likely to impress heads of departments with a sense of their responsibility as keeping a full and faithful record of all transactions connected with the expenditure under their control. The woods are usually laid under contribution to the other departments of the estate to far the greatest extent, and because no cash passes between them the accounts are often but loosely kept. The wages and labour are probably charged in the usual way in the forester's pay-sheet for thousands of faggots and tons of firewood supplied to the mansion, for thousands of feet of timber supplied to the estate for many purposes, and for constant assistance and material given to the gamekeeper; but, in all probability, none of the three are ever charged with the debt which goes to swell the woods accounts at the end of the year.

Among the other important duties of the forester is the preparation, at the beginning of every year, of a statement showing the extent of the planting, thinning, draining, fencing proposed, quantity of timber to be felled and sold, and a general estimate of the expenditure anticipated, and returns expected from all sources. The latter can seldom be given exactly, but on a methodically-conducted estate they may be approximately estimated, while the work proposed to be executed may be very closely gauged. Such statements and estimates should be submitted to the proprietor, who, with the general working plans and wood register before him, may soon decide to what extent the forester's plans for the year are to be carried out. That settled, and all working plans thoroughly understood, the work should go on smoothly.

One point of much importance in forestry labour is to decide what work shall be done by the day and what shall be done by contract. By contract, under superintendence, is by far the best plan, as by it the workman earns better wages and the proprietor gains largely. All such work as planting, felling, draining, road making, mowing of rides, cleaning of walks, hedging and fencing, can be done by piece-work easily, provided the forester understands his business. Much superintendence is obviated by the contract method, provided the specifications are clear, and they are usually simple enough. We believe that in most cases at least thirty per cent. is saved by letting the work by contract, and the workmen prefer piece to day-work.

In setting out the planting to be carried out during the year, the extent should correspond with the quantity of timber to be felled and disposed of.   In all fairly well-wooded estates the quantity of produce disposed of should defray the cost of management and planting, and leave a balance to the good. Where this system is carried out methodically, it will be found that a comparatively small extent of planting is required to provide an equivalent for the number of trees felled and disposed of.   The extent of ground cleared should be approximately reckoned, and the ground to be planted set out accordingly.   By these means a regular succession is kept up, the expenditure is moderate and more regular, and no gaps should occur in the plantations.   These suggestions apply to existing conditions where a complete working rotation " circle " cannot be soon established.   That means systematic stocking throughout to begin with, and many owners are not prepared to launch out on that scale at once.

SECTION VI.—FORESTRY BOOK-KEEPING.

In certain well-known books on forestry the book-keeping for the forester is a great feature—nearly sufficient to employ one clerk, at least, on a moderate-sized estate.   For example, there should be entered in the time-book, we are told, the days of the week, the days of the month, the daily state of the weather, the thermometer, each man's name, where he works, what he is doing, and the amount of his wage for whatever fraction of time he may be employed at any spot.   The pay-sheet has twenty-five columns, and the items of each man's time and wage are entered in every column opposite his name, the total number of entries for twelve men being exactly three hundred.   Everything relating to the woods accounts is on the same scale, and the labour involved thereby to the forester and the estate office may be imagined.   Although this remarkable " System of Book-keeping adapted to Forest Operations " has been recommended by the same authority up till quite a recent date, we believe very few estates indeed are to be found where it is adopted, and there are still fewer proprietors who take the trouble to master such records when they are presented. Every practical man knows that such red-tape systems of book-keeping in every department of an estate are a farce and a waste of time. Men's time and work have often to be kept by subordinates, and it has too often been found that, when a man is expected to give account of every hour that he may have spent doing one job here and another there, he usually does his book-keeping quietly at the end of the week, distributing his time over the separate heads by guess, as judiciously as he can, the forester seldom being able to find out whether he is right or wrong. Complete accounts should be kept at the estate office, and the books that the forester requires are a labour and sundries book, in which the day labour, contract work, accounts against the woods, and all incidental expenses should be entered under their separate headings in due course. Other books are a day book for all credit transactions connected with the woods, and a cash book in which all receipts and payments are balanced up periodically.

On some estates the attempt is made to keep a separate debtor and creditor account of every separate plantation, but that is not practicable when there are numerous small and large woods. The different woods may be divided into groups or divisions, corresponding with the woods register, and a separate account kept of each group; but more need not be attempted, and the men's time and labour account should be as simple as it can be made, and not be encumbered with useless entries.

CHAPTER V.

WHERE TO PLANT TIMBER-TREES.

Elevation and Aspect.—Rainfall.—Value of the Land.—Soil.—Accessibility.

IN planting for timber the rule, generally speaking, should be to plant where no other crop is likely to be as valuable. This is practically the rule in Germany, the difference in that respect between that country and our own being marked. In the cultivated regions of Germany lying near the mountain ranges, where the climatic conditions are similar to our own, the best land is devoted to agricultural crops, no room being found even for fences, shelter-belts, or hedge-row trees, and the farmer pushes his corn and other crops up the mountain side as far as he can do with advantage, and no further. Where his crops end the forest begins, the two looking at a distance as if dove-tailed into each other. There is no ornamental planting, as that is understood in this country. What strikes German foresters who visit this country is the way in which poor waste lands, suitable for timber-production, have been neglected, and the extent to which good land, often of the highest agricultural value, has been planted. It has to be explained to him that one of the worst features of our forestry has been that the landscape gardener has had more to do with the laying-out of our woods and plantations than anybody else, and has indulged his "æsthetic" tastes at the expense of true forestry, of which he is usually ignorant, dotting the landscape with his belts and patches of woodland in much the same way that he lays out borders and beds in a flower garden, regardless of soil, species, or utility, and this not unfrequently when he has scope for much better things.

The conditions affecting the choice of situations for timber-crops are, first, elevation and aspect; second, rainfall; third, rental value of the land proposed to be planted; fourth, soil; fifth, accessibility and proximity to a market. Any one of these conditions may materially affect the prospects of success, and are here dealt with separately and in order.

SECTION I.—ELEVATION AND ASPECT.

The altitude to which timber culture may be carried no doubt varies between the southern and northern limits of the three Kingdoms, but no exact data exists on the subject. The broad-leaved species like the oak, elm, chestnut, lime, ash, sycamore, and beech, etc., attain their greatest development the further south we go in Britain, or low down in valleys; while the best examples of Scotch fir, larch and spruce, and other firs are found north of the Tweed. But the Scotch and other firs also succeed well in the south, on poor land, in high and low situations. But although the beech, ash, and sycamore succeed best in the south, they yet grow to a large size in many parts of Scotland, both north and south, and are well worth planting there on a large scale as timber trees. Good examples of the oak are also found in Scotland, in favourable localities, but the oak timber trade is, and has always been chiefly confined to England, where the trees are generally larger and of superior quality. In ancient buildings in Scotland, the beams of buildings, etc., are commonly of Scotch fir, and in England of oak. The comparatively diminutive oak trees still existing in fragments of the old Caledonian forest show that the oak never did thrive in Scotland as it does in England; and Professor Lindley has shown, in his " Theory and Practice of Horticulture," by the Admiralty tests, that by far the best quality of oak is produced in the south, and that the trees grow much faster there. Latitude should therefore enter first into the calculations of the planter in determining what species are likely to produce the most profitable crops on his estate; and, next to that, in hilly districts, the elevation and aspect, which are more under his control. Quality of soil or severe frosts hardly enter into comparison with these two factors so far as growth is concerned. Late frosts may occasionally injure the extremities of the young shoots of forest trees, but new shoots are immediately produced again from the older wood, below the injured parts, and all signs of injury have usually disappeared by the end of the season, or at latest by the following year. Serious injury is rarely done to any of our forest trees by frost after the leaves have fallen, in the case of deciduous trees, and as seldom to any of the conifera, commonly grown, that ripen their annual growth perfectly. We are here speaking of frost as distinguished from a low mean temperature, which, whether due to elevation or latitude, must always exert a sensible effect on vegetation in the aggregate, even though the difference may not exceed one or two degrees. But high or low, north or south, exposure to cold winds, or even persistent winds not necessarily keen, always exert an injurious effect upon forest trees, inasmuch as they check or repress growth to a greater extent than all other causes put together. This is seen in any wood on the side exposed to prevailing winds, where, by repressed growth alone, the trees are often not half as large as the trees in the middle of the wood or on the sheltered side. It is seen in a marked manner in young plantations before the trees meet and cover the ground and shelter each other, when a sensible increase in the rate of height-growth is always observable; and also in over-thinned plantations where the wind reaches every tree individually. German foresters are well aware of the ill effects of cold winds, and take every precaution against them. These precautions consist in selecting the most sheltered situations for the tenderest species, and on exposed situations in planting the margins thickly—in planting thickly generally and thinning sparingly.

The following table, contributed by the writer to the "Transactions of the Royal Horticultural Society," in 1895, bears on this point, and shows to what an extent the weight and value of a crop of timber may be affected by exposure to winds alone. All the trees grow under the same conditions, except that on one side the plantation is exposed to severe west and north-west gales about seven hundred feet above sea-level.

TABLE showing the effects of Exposure and Shelter on the growth of Forest Trees in Mill-Moor Plantation Belt on the Wortley Estate.

Kind.	Average Height of trees on most exposed side of belt.	Average Height of trees in the middle of belt where less exposed.	Average Height of trees in the inner and most sheltered side of belt.
Beech ...	31 feet	37 feet	43 feet
Sycamore	28 ,,	36 ,,	45 ,,
Ash	26 ,,	35 ,,	44 ,
Oak	21 ,,	36 ,,	40 ,
	106	144	172

The bulk of timber in each tree is, of course, in proportion to the height. With these general remarks, we shall now deal with the question of elevation more particularly.

Our mountain ranges and hills represent by far the greatest extent of our waste-lands which it is desirable to afforest, and present almost every variety of soil and aspect up to between two and three thousand feet, above which it is perhaps not desirable to go, generally speaking. It is not so much a question of soil as tempertaure and aspect, and probably all our mountain ranges in England would grow timber-trees to their summits, or nearly so, if the species were judiciously selected; while in Scotland, even in the north, some species might be expected to succeed up to two thousand feet. In glens and ravines, which are always more or less sheltered, success need not be doubted; but it is not desirable to encroach on alluvial bottoms of good land anywhere.

The accompanying diagram on page 74, kindly sent me by F. W. Burbidge, Esq., Trinity College, Dublin, author of "Cultivated Plants," and other works, shows the conditions which favour height-growth in trees, whether these are created by dense culture or the configuration of the ground.

For the purpose of comparison, let us glance at the forests on some of the Continental mountain ranges. Beginning with the Hartz Mountains, in about the same parallel as Norfolk, and travelling north to a point in Norway considerably beyond the most northern point of Scotland, we find the mountain ranges to a great extent covered to high elevations with spruce, Scotch fir, beech, birch, alder, and other species. The Hartz Mountains are almost entirely covered with forests to their summits, over three thousand feet high in many instances; even the Brocken, about four thousand feet high, being clothed to its top or nearly so. In Norway, a country much resembling Scotland in climate, only colder, spruce, Scotch fir, and birch grow up to the snow-line, and in the upper valleys of the high ranges, too high for any other form of cultivation, the best spruce and Scotch fir is produced that is exported from Norway. What, therefore, might not be attempted in the same direction in this country, where the conditions are more favourable? In fact, numbers of small plantations are to be found, scattered here and there at high elevations all over Britain, that show well enough what is practicable on a large scale. The following list of well-known species, brought together from Professor Schlich's "Sylvi-

Effects of Shelter.

RAVINE PLANTING.—Shelter and Exposure.

Sketch of Scots Fir growing in a gully, Newry, Co. Down. Arrow showing prevailing wind.

cultural Notes," in his "Manual of Forestry," vol. ii., gives the elevations at which they grow more or less successfully : —

SPECIES.			ELEVATION.		
Beech	1,200 feet,	Derbyshire.	4,500 feet,	Alps.	
Hornbeam	1,200 „	Hartz.	3,000 „	Alps.	
Oak	1,500 „	England.	1,350 „	Highlands.	
Ash	1,350 „	Yorkshire.	4,000 „	Alps.	
Elm	1,500 „	Derbyshire.	4,000 „	Alps.	
Sweet Chestnut	2,800 „	Alps.			
Sycamore	5,000 „	Alps.			
Alder	1,600 „	Highlands.	4,000 „	Alps.	
Birch	2,500 „	Scotland.	5,000 „	Alps.	
Poplar	1,600 „	Yorkshire.			
Lime	2,800 „	Tyrol.			
Hazel	1,900 „	Highlands.			
Silver Fir	2,500 „	Central Germany.			
Norway Spruce	6,000 „	Alps.	3,000 „	Norway.	
Scotch Fir	2,200 „	Britain.	6,000 „	Alps.	
Austrian Fir	4,500 „	Alps.			
Weymouth Pine	4,000 „	Alps.			
Larch	2,000 „	Scotland.	3,000 to 6,000 ft.,	Alps.	

We know a good portion of the high-lying portions of Yorkshire, Lancashire and Derbyshire, and Scotland, where there are woods, and do not regard the above figures as extremes, if one may judge by the behaviour of such species as the oak, ash, beech, chestnut, sycamore, birch, Scotch fir, spruce, and others. If any of these species be found attaining to the size of timber-trees at elevations approaching those given in the foregoing table, they may be expected to succeed higher up still in plantations. Take the oak, for example, which in the past has not been regarded as a tree likely to succeed either at a great elevation or in a poor soil. Yet, fifteen hundred feet in England and thirteen hundred and fifty feet in Scotland are the limits of its distribution, as regards elevation, which may surprise some foresters; but we ourselves know of oak plantations at elevations over one thousand feet in Yorkshire on the thinnest and poorest soils. In 1887 we sold one hundred and seventeen trees, the last of an old wood standing at this elevation, and the trees averaged about sixty cubic feet each—the largest reaching one hundred and seventy feet. At the same elevation, or a little higher, are younger plantations from forty to eighty years of age, of oak, birch, larch, chestnut, beech, and sycamore, growing at a fairly rapid rate, though the situation is north-east, or east, and extremely exposed.

Of course, in speaking of trees at high elevations plantations are meant, because these will succeed on the dense principle, where single trees would never be much better than scrub. The sycamore, although Brown recommends it to be nursed with Scotch firs, is a very hardy tree, isolated specimens on the most exposed sites attaining to large size. The sweet chestnut also grows freely at high elevations and so does the beech.

The late Mr. John Macgregor, forester to the Duke of Athole, in his evidence before the Parliamentary Committee, stated that from one thousand to twelve hundred feet should be the limit for the larch, and averred that the difference in the value of a crop of larch per acre, at one thousand feet elevation and lower down, would probably amount to £80— that is to say, the crop highest up was worth £20, and that lower down worth £100. We know the larch woods from which these valuations were taken, and our opinion is that the crops might have been worth more if they had been less severely thinned. We have known larch crops, not valued, but sold, at £50 per acre, at an elevation of twelve hundred feet, and from soil of the poorest description. This wood was near the summit of the Pennine Range.

As regards aspect in planting, that, of course, may make much difference. The warmest and most sheltered spots should, as a rule, be chosen for the most tender species—mostly hard-woods—and the coldest spots for the firs, beech, birch, and alder, etc., which, in the south, seems to prefer northern exposures where the soil is suitable. This is found to be the case in the mountain ranges of the Black Forest, in about the same parallel as Central France, at an elevation of from two thousand feet to three thousand five hundred feet, where the common silver firs and Scotch fir attain a height of one hundred and forty feet. Here reproduction is generally good, but "a marked difference is found between northern and southern slopes, the growth and reproduction being far more vigorous on the former than on the latter."—Schlich, vol. iii., p. 366.

Gales are another subject to be noticed under this head. Both owners and their foresters in Scotland are under the impression that nowhere in Europe are gales so destructive to woods as in Scotland, and it is asserted that dense woods suffer worst; whereas, if the case was stated fairly, it is a fact that nowhere in Europe are the woods so severely thinned as in Scotland, and if they do suffer more severely from gales it is a fair conclusion that over-thinning is the main cause of it. We have visited frequently the worst gale-devastated districts in the south and north of Scotland, and our impression was that the most destruction occurred in middle-aged and older woods in which the trees were thin on the ground, the over-head canopy nil, and the margins open. The worst windfalls seemed to occur in woods with unprotected margins, near to highways and railways, where the wind found an entrance. In other instances the gale seemed to have behaved in the most erratic manner, sometimes making a clear gap in one part of a plantation and missing higher and more exposed parts of it altogether.

Another erroneous impression is that German forests exist in a comparatively windless region, otherwise the dense system of timber-culture could not be practised. The answer to this is that Germany is not the only country where the dense system of culture is pursued. Norway and Sweden are worse situated than Scotland as regards gales and climate generally, and yet owners there do not thin their forests at all, and send us the best samples of timber that comes to this country from north Europe. Moreover, Central Germany is not windless, nor are forest windfalls unknown there, but, on the contrary, they make serious inroads in the forests as with us, not to speak of destructive snowbreaks of which we know practically nothing in this country. According to Schlich, vol. iii., p. 366, in certain sections of the Black Forest, from which example results are given, the percentage of total fellings include twelve per cent. from snowbreaks, and sixteen per cent. from windfalls, which per centage is described as " fairly moderate." At pages 383-4, a sample page of a working plan and detailed control book is given, in which such entries as " excess due to windfalls" and heavy windfalls occur frequently. Professor Schlich, who was one of the most reliable witnesses that appeared before the Select Committee on Forestry, was asked by the examiners to give an instance of destruction by gales in Germany equal to that recorded as occurring on the Duke of Buccleuch's estates in Scotland, where, in two successive gales, 1,250,000 trees went down; and the answer to the question was that in the Bavarian Forest, in 1870, a gale " threw down so much timber that, in spite of the efforts of the officers in charge, all the available labour had not removed all the timber in 1885, fifteen years afterwards, when he was there."—(Question and answer No. 307, "Report of the Forestry Committee," 1886.)

In fact, the windfall plea against a better system of forestry in this country will not bear investigation, and there can hardly be any doubt that the "notch" system of planting and planting trees too old and too large has greatly contributed to the losses caused by gales in Scotland and elsewhere.

SECTION II.—RAINFALL.

The rainfall is another factor that has to be taken into account. Continental experts who have visited this country have remarked that the Scotch fir they saw cut up at saw-mills in the north of Scotland was inferior in quality to the German timber, and attributed the difference to the moister climate and less constant summer temperature. No doubt these conditions do affect the quality of timber in Britain, but they are not the same everywhere, in either Scotland or England, and the rainfall varies greatly in different parts of Britain, and consequently the amount of sunshine, which in turn influences the quality of the timber. A glance at the little-known but excellent coloured rainfall map of the British Islands, published by the Scottish Meteorological Society and here given, by permission, will show that over nearly the whole of the western part of Scotland the mean annual rainfall is excessive—ranging from sixty to eighty inches and upwards; that over a broad irregular belt running through the centre of the country from Sutherland to the Clyde, and extending over the greater portion of the lowlands, the rainfall is from forty to sixty inches; and that over a broad belt, stretching inland, and following the contour of the east coast from Berwick-on-Tweed to the Pentland Firth, the rainfall varies from forty inches inland to less than twenty-five inches nearer the coast. In England (with the exception of a few portions of it confined chiefly to Cumberland, Westmoreland, West Yorkshire, Wales, and Cornwall, where the rainfall varies from forty to eighty inches), the mean annual fall over all the counties is from twenty-five inches, or less, to forty inches, the Eastern Counties and Midlands being the driest portions. In Ireland, over the western half of it, forty to sixty inches is the rule, falling to from thirty to forty inches on the eastern half. There are a few local exceptions on both sides, but of small extent.

MEAN ANNUAL RAINFALL
OF THE
BRITISH ISLES.

FOR THE 24 YEARS FROM
1860 TO 1883.

EXPLANATION.

25 inches or under	
25 „ to 30 inches	
30 „ to 40 „	
40 „ to 60 „	
60 „ to 80 „	
80 „ and upwards	

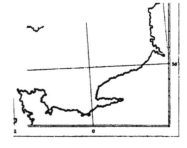

That a difference in the rainfall in different parts of these Islands, amounting to about sixty inches annually, or six thousand tons to the acre, implies a corresponding difference in the amount of sunshine, exerting, in its turn, a corresponding effect upon vegetation, goes without saying ; while the quantity of rain should also to a large extent determine the extent of the drainage of woodlands if any, the species to be planted, and the season of planting. Soils which in a dry climate might not need draining, might, under a heavy rainfall, be water-logged during a good portion of the year. Some species of trees, like the spruce, might be quite unsuitable for planting where the rainfall was light or the soil dry, and vice versa, while nearly all the pinus family and broad-leaved species, except the birch, alder, and mountain ash, would probably succeed best where the rainfall was lightest and the sunshine more constant. As regards planting, where the rainfall is regular and sufficient, operations might be carried on in either autumn or spring, but in those parts of England where the rainfall is light, we are assured, by those able to judge, that spring-planting is most unsafe because of the risk of drought in April, May, or June, in which case the trees perish. According to Mr. Buchan, of the Scottish Meteorological Society, a rainfall exceeding 40 inches might be considered a wet climate, and the heaviest rainfall follows the mountain ridges.

SECTION III.—VALUE OF THE LAND : PLANTING AS AN INVESTMENT.

On this point it may be stated that on private estates in this country it is risky planting, for profit, land that already yields a fair rent for any other purpose ; but it is difficult to set any precise limit to the value that might not be exceeded by the production of timber, so much depends on culture and management which may involve a difference of thousands of cubic feet to the acre. There is scarcely any data on the subject in British forestry records that is thoroughly reliable, but it is pretty generally agreed amongst experienced men that it would pay to grow timber on land, other conditions being favourable, the rental value per acre of which did not exceed ten shillings. An agricultural rent above this figure, paid annually, and the accumulated interest on the same calculated for the period that a crop of timber would occupy the ground, would be likely to exceed the value of the latter in the end considerably. It is from poor lands of little value that the most profitable results may be expected. The quality of the soil makes so little difference to a crop of timber that we can easily conceive of the latter ultimately reaching a value that would greatly exceed an agricultural one for the same period.

As regards planting, considered as an investment, pure and simple, no reliable conclusions can be drawn from past experience, as forestry has been conducted in this country, because there has been no system, and crops have been poor both in quality and quantity. A mistake too frequently made, also, in estimating profits from woods consists in comparing these profits with that from capital otherwise and safely invested at four or five per cent. compound interest for the same period. No agricultural investments should be measured by that test, because it is not a fair one, and few owners of estates do sink their money, for long periods, in the way suggested. What does not go for planting is usually spent some other way on the estate, and probably not so profitably as it might have been in planting. The view taken by the Forestry Committee was the practicability of raising the value of poor and second-rate lands on estates by planting, and most sensible landowners look at the subject in that light. What the owner of land has to consider is the value of his land before planting and its probable future value under timber crops. If he can substantially and permanently raise the value of his estate, by planting the worst parts of it, that ought to be a sufficient inducement, and under ordinarily good management that can be done.

The time that must elapse before a crop of timber can be reaped depends on the length of the rotation period and the nature of the demand. Much timber, both home-grown and foreign, is disposed of under forty years of age, especially larch and other fir, birch, ash, and sycamore; and still larger quantities between forty and a hundred years of age. Much depends on the species planted, and intelligent management. There must be a certain number of trees to the acre at all stages, and the greatest number of trees, of measurable dimensions, in the shortest possible time, should be the aim of the forester, who should dispose of his crops at any age at which he can do so most profitably. The income from woods ought to be as sure and as regular as that from other sources on an estate.

Good useful timber has always fetched a higher price in this country than it has done anywhere else in Europe; we grow a greater number of species than are grown on the Continent, and it is admitted that the climate and soil of Great Britain and Ireland produce all the most useful timber trees in perfection. We have a good market for timber, we can grow it; and the only question is, can we produce crops heavy enough to pay? We have not the least doubt on that head. If we can produce a certain number of cubic feet to the acre the question is solved. German authorities give the final clear cut, alone, of Scotch fir, at nearly ten thousand cubic feet to the acre; spruce and silver fir at from fourteen thousand to seventeen thousand cubic feet; and other species in proportion. We ought to be able to do the same in this country, and at the very least we should be able to produce from eight thousand to ten thousand feet to the acre under dense culture. Less than that quantity ought to pay, and pay well, and at the average prices long given for timber in our woods, owners of estates ought to be able to satisfy themselves whether planting is likely to prove a safe investment or not.

SECTION IV.—THE SOIL.

The question of soil in relation to the production of timber is one of much importance in connection with the planting of poor soils and waste lands. Much ignorance has existed on the subject in this country up till now, and has caused great loss owing to good land having been planted that might have been more profitably devoted to other purposes, and waste land to be neglected that was quite suitable for timber trees. Brown's teaching, and those of others of the same school down to the present day, have contributed greatly to mistakes in this direction. Nothing could be cruder or more misleading than Brown's definition of a tree in the last original edition of "The Forester," 1882, page 61, where he states that "the body of a tree is formed out of a few earthy substances, together with water and air, and is fixed to the earth by its roots." Fostered by teaching of this kind it has become a fixed idea among foresters that the quality of the soil is of first importance in the production of timber, whereas it is realy of secondary consequence. Correct ideas on the subject have only recently been derived from France and Germany, although the subject has been understood there long enough. The true theory of the growth of timber or wood in trees, as far as relates to soil, is simple. Trees derive by far the greatest portion of their

6

food from the atmosphere, and, comparatively, only a fractional·
portion from the soil in the shape of mineral substances,
and there are hardly any soils, however poor, that do not contain the latter in sufficient quantity for the growth of timber
trees, provided the moisture is sufficient. That much has been
proved by practical observation and scientific investigation.

Paul Charpentier, one of the best European authorities on
this subject, in his book on "Timber," translated by Kennell
(Scott, Greenwood & Co.), advises "the planting of every kind
of soil which it is found cannot give any other remunerative
product;" but one condition he considers essential on sloping
lands apt to become dry, and that is, the "retention of water
which favours in a high degree the growth of trees of all ages."
In other words, do not drain without good reasons.

The following table, by the same author, shows the properties of the wood of the beech, oak, aspen, birch and willow,
and represent pretty fairly the properties of all our forest trees.
The three first columns show the percentage of carbon, or
charcoal, and gases derived mainly from the atmosphere; and
the right-hand column—"ashes"—the mineral substances
derived from the soil:—

Nature of the Combustible.	Carbon	Hydrogen.	Oxygen and Nitrogen.	Ashes.
Leaves	45·015	6·971	40·910	7·118
Small branches, bark	52·496	7·312	36·737	3·454
„ wood	48·359	6·605	44·730	0·304
Medium-sized branches, bark ...	48·855	6·342	41·121	3·682
„ wood	49·902	6·607	43·356	0·134
Large branches, bark	46·871	5·570	44·656	2·903
„ wood	48·003	6·472	45·170	0·354
Trunks, bark	46·267	5·930	44·755	2·657
„ wood	48·925	6·460	44·319	0·296
Large roots, bark	48·085	6·624	48·761	0·129
„ wood	49·324	6·280	44·108	0·231

The author drew particular attention to this subject in a paper
of his, read before the Royal Horticultural Society and published in its Transactions in 1895, and an extract from that
paper may perhaps be usefully given here:—

"Given a root-hold in a healthy soil, however poor, a tree
will grow and produce a timber trunk of surprising dimensions.
Innumerable examples widely apart could be furnished to

prove this, a few of which may be given.   At Wharncliffe
Chase, the scene of the opening chapter of 'Ivanhoe' and
the reputed haunt of 'The Dragon of Wantley' of nursery
lore, there still stand a number of the 'broad-headed, short-
stemmed, wide-branched oaks' referred to by Sir Walter
Scott, and, considering the soil and situation in which' they
grow, their bulk is surprising.   Wharncliffe Chase is described in the Doomsday Book as a natural 'waste,' and in that
condition it remains for the most part to this day—the soil
being so thin and scant, where there is any, and rocks projecting so above the surface in all directions, as to make it
unfit for cultivation.   Yet this poor tract, lying about 1,000
feet above the sea-level, was to a large extent once covered
by forest, and, if it were not now tenanted by deer and rabbits,
it would produce timber again, as its young plantations abundantly testify.   The geological formation is the millstone grit
lying above the coal measures, and, according to Professor
McConnell,* usually the basis of one of the poorest and
hungriest soils.   Where the bulky oaks referred to grow, the
surface soil consists of a poor, thin sod, lying on the rock,
which forms a deep bed, fissured in all directions, and so per-
mitting the roots to descend deeply into it.   One of the trees
has apparently sprung from an acorn dropped into one of
these fissures on the edge of the crags on an extremely lofty
and exposed spot, and fulfils in every particular the description
in Scott's 'Lady of the Lake' :—

> Moored in the rifted rock,
> Proof to the tempest's shock,
> Firmer he roots him, the ruder it blow.

" This gnarled and starved specimen is twelve feet in circumference a little way above the rock, and once contained about
sixty cubic feet.   Not far from it is another ancient example,
where the soil consists of a thin sod through which the rocks
project on all sides, which girths twenty-two feet five feet up.
Another close by girths twelve feet, and contained, before it
lost some of its limbs, about two hundred and seventy cubic
feet of good timber.   Another tree on the same poor ground
contained one hundred and seventy cubic feet in the trunk,
and about fifty feet in the boughs.   Growing under the same
conditions are many birch, ash, hollies, beech, yews, etc., and
throughout Wharncliffe Wood there are numbers of oaks of
various sizes growing on the rock ; and these trees, as can be

* McConnell's "Agricultural Note Book."

seen, have produced a second and third crop of timber from the same stools. These examples are mentioned to show under what poor conditions, as regards soil, timber-trees will thrive, for, unless the Wharncliffe trees were there to speak for themselves, I have no doubt that even some practical foresters would hardly believe that they could grow under such conditions. On the same rocks, about one thousand feet above the sea, on a peaty sod two or three inches deep, we have the Corsican Pine *(Pinus Laricio)* growing beautifully and beating the larch and Scotch fir.

"Not less remarkable than the size of the trees produced in poor soils is the variety of poor soils in which the same species will thrive. At Lord Salisbury's, at Hatfield, I was much struck by the great size of the oaks, limes, yews, and the usual forest-trees, when noticing at the same time in the kitchen-garden close by that the pure chalk was turned up everywhere at a spade's depth. Equally striking are both the young and old plantations on the deep, poor sandstone in some parts of Nottinghamshire. In Thoresby Park the sandstone is of great depth, and the surface soil is so poor that only high culture keeps it up to the mark. Yet the size and health of both young and old trees there are remarkable, though, according to Professor McConnell, Sherwood Forest, with its great oak trees, lies on a member of the Upper New Red Sandstone, where the surface soil is 'a barren gravel.' So at Bournemouth, again, there are extensive and thriving tracts of Scotch and other firs growing, for the most part, on pure sand-banks. In the Highlands of Scotland, again, in many parts, the size of the larch and Scotch fir trees, growing in very poor soils, has often excited the surprise of travellers, for in many places the soil consists of poor peat or gravel only. In the part of Yorkshire where I live, I daresay travellers have often noticed considerable tracts near collieries covered by deep mounds locally called 'pit-hills.' These hills, which consist wholly of a poor blue shale, brought out of the coal pits in getting the coal, do not contain a particle of what one would call 'soil,' and would probably be regarded as the worst rooting medium that could be found. Yet it grows timber trees. About thirty years ago some of these pit-hills on the Wortley estate were planted with a general mixture of forest trees, which now form a dense and thriving plantation. In short, the indifference of forest trees to their rooting medium, so long as the moisture is sufficient, is surprising, and I lay stress on the point to show that however unfit for farming purposes, and however poor land may be, it will almost certainly grow good timber.

" I do not know of any theory that is better sustained by facts than that timber trees can be grown to good size on soils chemically poor from an agricultural point of view, because they need a much smaller quantity of the usual plant-food derived from the soil than farm and garden crops do. When I first studied analysts' tables on this subject, I confess it was a kind of revelation to me, for it explained much that had before puzzled me, viz., why great trees should grow out of soils in which, according to our gardening and farming ideas of plant culture, they ought to starve. Schlich's conclusions on this subject, from Ebermayer's tables, briefly summarised, are that the substances required by forest trees are qualitatively the same as those required by field crops, but quantitatively so much less that almost any soil can furnish a sufficient quantity of mineral substances for the production of trees, provided the leaf-mould accumulating from the fallen leaves is not removed. And, further, that conifers require the least amount of such substances of any known plants."

SECTION V.—ACCESSIBILITY AND PROXIMITY TO A MARKET.

Generally speaking, every mile further the wood is from the consumer the less the timber is worth to the owner, till a limit may be reached where the margin of profit may disappear altogether. This applies more particularly to estates where the woods are not very extensive, nor the supply sufficient to make it worth the consumers' while to put down plant to convert the timber on the spot. It might be different in the case of large areas maintained by the State, and that would probably create permanent work and industries in the woods, as in Continental forests which have a population of their own. Good roads and forest paths and proximity to railways are of course an immense advantage in all cases, and any facilities that reduce the cost of haulage increase the value of the crop to the owner. We have often known these conditions to affect the price of timber at a sale to the extent of from five to twenty per cent. one way or the other; and they must always affect the prospects of planting on private estates. Much has been said about planting waste lands in the Highlands of Scotland; but instances are on record there in which the very best timber has been worthless to the owner because it could not be delivered to the consumer at a price that left a margin of profit.　　In the " Highland Society's Transactions," vol. vi., p. 271, we are told that, " in 1841 the wood cut down in Glentanar brought little or nothing more than the cost of cartage to Aberdeen, owing to the almost inapproachable position of the best trees in the forest, most of them being too heavy to be floated by the river except in the time of flood." Many such examples might be recorded.

CHAPTER VI.

PURE AND MIXED WOODS.

Pure Woods.—Mixed Woods.—Conifera Mixtures.—Mixtures of Broad-leaved Species.—General Mixtures.—Grouped Woods.

SECTION I.—PURE WOODS.

WOODS are said to be pure when they consist of only one species, and mixed when they consist of several. Great tracts of pure natural forests exist in different parts of the world. Mixed forests are not so common, and where they do occur they usually consist of but few species of similar habits of growth, as when the disparity is great in that respect the weaker species disappear in the struggle for existence. It is held by some that certain species succeed best when mixed with others, as, for example, the larch and oak ; but we believe all the species usually grown for timber in this country can be grown successfully by themselves. Pure woods are more easily managed than mixed woods, because there is less inequality in the rate of growth among the trees than exists in the latter, unless the species are very carefully selected. From a landscape point of view pure woods are most effective, particularly when composed of any of the pine or fir family, which may be planted so as to give a rather tame landscape a beautiful sub-alpine aspect, very different from that produced by round-headed, broad-leaved species. Pure woods are also considered most profitable, and in the planted forests of European States they are the rule, or the mixture consists of few species. One disadvantage of pure woods, on private estates, is that they do not permit of as many species being grown as might be desired, but that might be got over to some extent by adopting the " grouping system " described elsewhere in this chapter.

SECTION II.—MIXED WOODS.

There are various kinds of these, some bad and some good. Unfortunately the excessive number of species included in British tree lists, and recommended for planting has been the cause of a great deal of indiscriminate mixing, resulting in little else than trouble and loss in the end.   Generally speaking, mixed woods in this country may be divided into four classes, viz., mixtures of different varieties of the conifera only ; mixtures of broad-leaved species only ; mixtures consisting of both the conifera and broad-leaved species ; and grouped woods.   The three first are common, and it may be asserted that probably nothing has tended more to make the forester's task difficult in this country than the indiscriminate mixing of species of greatly dissimilar habit.   It has caused endless trouble in thinning, and much pruning that should never have been needed   Our very mixed woods would puzzle a Continental forester who does not contemplate such mixtures as ours ; hence a good deal of the confusion that has arisen when home and foreign forestry has been compared.   If a German forester had to deal with an English wood consisting of a general mixture of numerous species, and had to proceed on his own principle, he would not dally by pruning and hacking the biggest and best trees in the wood to give the weaker species an equal chance, but would remove what he calls the dominated and suppressed trees ; and as these would be the weaker species, the result, in no long period, would be that the wood would consist of the species that should have been planted exclusively at the beginning.   The English forester, on the other hand, wants to preserve his mixture as he began ; and to give weak and strong a chance, he has to fight the battle with the pruning knife, without regard to overhead canopy. The fast-growing poplar will be many feet above the tallest of its neighbours and extending its branches over their heads at an early stage ; the beech, while asserting itself in height-growth, will, from its shade-enduring power, extend its lateral branches to the ground and smother all the weaker species within its reach ; and so on with other species in mixtures in which much disparity of habit exists.   The same remarks apply to conifera mixtures when planted in nearly equal proportions.   Such species as the Douglas fir, for example, will oust most of its neighbours, and the common and silver spruces will soon dominate such weak species as the white spruce, *Abies alba, Pinus cembra,* and others.   Plantation mixtures in this country are planted on the principle that if one species fails another may succeed and be useful ; whereas such a practice is not defensible, because the species that succeed together and the conditions that suit them are now pretty well known, and judicious mixtures may be easily selected.

SECTION III.—CONIFERA MIXTURES.

The best guide to go by with conifers is the rate of growth in height, which in all the species is indicated from the first, making due allowance for transplanting. Thus it will be as easily seen, in a nursery quarter as in a plantation, that the Corsican fir and the Siberian fir, for example, are unsuitable companions, because the one soon overtops the other and becomes the dominant tree. Rapid growers and slow growers should not be planted together, and, of course, what are called the "dwarf" conifera are unsuitable for mixed plantations altogether. Our object in restricting the species according to their height is economy where timber production is an object. It must be plain to anyone that, quality and other conditions being equal, the tree that grows soonest to profitable dimensions must be the best to plant, and that the species that associate best together in this respect must make the best mixture, and the difference in this respect among different species is very great indeed. If the above rule is adhered to, the planter cannot go far wrong, and for further information on the habits of different species he may consult Veitches' "Manual of the Conifera" and other works, and any respectable nurseryman will give him information on the subject.

Another question in connection with the conifera is that of mixing the *Abies* with the *Pinus* family. They are commonly mixed, but they do best separate. The Scotch, Corsican, Austrian firs, and other members of the pine family grow equally well in a moist or dry climate, provided the ground is well drained; but the *Abies* family do not like either a dry soil or a dry climate, and the common spruce, for example, often perishes outright under such conditions, or falls a prey to disease,—cold, dry, cutting winds especially causing much damage to the tree. Inside of mixed woods it succeeds better, but it is not a tree for the margin of a wood on a dry soil or an exposed easterly aspect. In selecting the species for a mixed wood, it should in any case be remembered that the common Norway spruce, silver spruce, Scotch fir, Corsican fir, and larch are proved timber-trees—the three first supplying most of the pine timber used everywhere—and in any mixture of the conifera they should predominate.

SECTION IV.—MIXTURES OF BROAD-LEAVED SPECIES.

The different species of this family that grow almost as evenly together as by themselves, and therefore suitable for mixed plantations, are the oak, ash, elm, sycamore, cherry, and lime. They do not all increase equally in bulk of trunk, but when judiciously mixed they do not smother each other, and the same soil and conditions suit them all. The species unsuitable for a mixed plantation are the poplar, willow, beech, Spanish chestnut, birch and alder. The two first prefer a wet soil, and the poplar overtops all other species in a destructive fashion. The two should therefore go together, the poplar being planted thickly and under-planted with the willow. The beech is a bad tree in a mixed wood owing to its great shade-bearing power, which enables it to retain its lower branches, which push out and usurp the surrounding space, smothering everything near it. This is the reason why beech trees in mixed woods are usually found full of limbs and occupying so much space. Grown by itself, or with its equals, like the Spanish chestnut, for example, it behaves differently, producingpa tall, cylindrical trunk of fine timber. The birch may be planted in mixed woods, where it will keep pace in height-growth with the other species till well past middle-age, but the trunks are usually small. Planted with the oak alone it is seen at its best, and the oak does well with it, and both may be planted thickly. The French also recommend the birch as a companion to the oak. Referring to the beech again, it may be used for under-planting in mixed woods with every prospect of it growing well and of the right shape, always provided that it is planted after the general crop has got well-established and grown up to a good height. The beech has not hitherto been nearly so much used as an underwood as it might have been. We have seen it sixty feet high under the deep shade of a spruce forest in the Hartz Mountains, and in numerous cases in this country found it growing well under the shade of other trees where no other broadleaved species would have long survived, except the hornbeam and horse chestnut.

SECTION V.—GENERAL MIXTURES OF BROAD-LEAVED
SPECIES AND CONIFERA.

Where it is desired to plant some of the conifera among broad-leaved species, the larch, Scotch and Corsican firs, *Pinus excelsa*, *Pinus strobus*, common and silver spruces and others may be planted. These will give effect to the plantation from a landscape point of view, and afford shelter to game, but the extent to which second-rate species may be used should be carefully considered. The rule should be not to mix all the species in equal proportions, but to give preference to the most valuable species, and keep the strongest-growing and perhaps least valuable species within bounds. The oak, ash, and sycamore, for example, might be the most profitable crop, and should be planted in largest proportion; fewest of the elm, lime, and pines, and fewest of all of the spruce. The larch does as well in a mixed wood as anywhere, and it is always safe to plant a good proportion of it.

SECTION VI.—GROUPED WOODS.

These may be regarded as a kind of compromise between pure and mixed woods, and are composed of groups of distinct species running from one rood to an acre or thereabout in extent. As yet, systematically grouped woods are not common. Their advantages are that when the land to be planted varies in quality and depth, etc., portions perhaps good, others poor, or wet, the species may be selected accordingly. Oak, ash, elm, sycamore, and the like could occupy the good spots; poplar, willow and spruce the lower and moister situations; and the beech and pines the driest and poorer soils, as they make the least demand on the soil for food. Grouped woods also afford scope for planting a greater number of species than the general mixture system does, because if a patch of any species fails, it can be cleared and re-planted without encroaching on the rest of the wood. Many species of our exotic firs might be tested as timber-trees on the grouping system and in a practical manner, quite out of the question in the garden or park. Where game preservation is carried on, the grouped wood would also be found to possess greater attractions for the feathered tribe than any other, if groups of suitable species like the spruce, yew, low cover, and coppice were also introduced in some proportion.

CHAPTER VII.

SPECIES MOST SUITABLE FOR PLANTING AS TIMBER TREES IN GREAT BRITAIN AND IRELAND.

Number of Useful Species.—Kinds of Timber in most demand.—List of Species.

SECTION I.—NUMBER OF USEFUL SPECIES.

ACCORDING to some writers, the principal timber-trees (hard-woods) recognised by botanists as being of spontaneous growth in the British Islands, exclusive of their varieties, number twenty-seven.   The number of species actually in demand, however, as timber-trees, does not amount to more than half the botanists' list or thereabout, and in the list given in this chapter only the well-known kinds will be described, and a few others that promise to be good timber-trees.   Lists of coni-ferous species given by writers as usually planted in this country, together with such newer kinds as are sufficiently hardy and said to be worth cultivation in Great Britain and Ireland, include seventy-seven species, and this number will also be much reduced.

The most judiciously compiled nurseryman's lists of trans-planted forest trees contain between thirty and forty species altogether, including the thorn and hazel, and this number, Schlich, in his " Manual," vol. ii., reduces to twenty, but thinks a few less important species might possibly be added.   In Germany less than a dozen would probably comprise all the species grown, while in Britain, as is well-known, a few species really supply the chief demand.

SECTION II.—KINDS OF TIMBER IN MOST DEMAND.

At the present time we have no means of knowing what the total timber consumption in Great Britain amounts to, because although we know what quantity is imported into this country from abroad annually, there is no record of the quantity of home-grown timber disposed of from estates wherever there are plantations; but that the quantity is large there can be no doubt, and when added to the nearly £18,000,000 worth annually imported, shows what scope there is for the British planter. The home-grown timber generally offered for sale is oak, ash, beech, sycamore, elm, birch, rough Scotch fir, spruce and larch, but this list only represents the kinds we have most of, and does not indicate the kinds of timber in most demand. In fact, the question of demand has never been sufficiently considered in this country. The demand for Scotch fir for railway sleepers would of itself absorb a very large portion of all that could be grown in this country, north or south, the creosoting process having made consumers less fastidious as to quality. Many of the sleepers laid down now represent the full diameter of the tree, squared, including the sap wood or a portion of it. There are nearly twenty thousand miles of railways in the British Islands, or about forty thousand miles of single lines furnished with sleepers laid from two feet six inches to two feet nine inches apart, each sleeper being nine feet long, ten inches wide, and five inches thick. These are being constantly replaced, and, for reasons known to engineers, wooden sleepers are not likely to be replaced by steel except in tropical countries. The number of telegraph and telephone poles, of considerably less girth than sleepers, amounts to some seven millions or more—Scotch fir also—and will increase. Scaffold poles and pit-props are generally of spruce, and the demand is enormous.

Hitherto we have been accustomed to associate the Scotch fir chiefly with the Highlands, but the extent to which it has already established itself in the south of England and elsewhere and spread naturally, and the opportunities which poor lands afford for planting fir tree forests, seem to indicate that England may yet become the chief fir region of Great Britain.

With examples of Scotch fir from the north we are all familiar, but of its value as grown in the south we have heard but little, although the question has presented itself to the minds of planters at different times. Rees, quoting from the "Transactions of the Society of Arts," 1819, states that the steward to the Marquis of Bath had proved conclusively on poor lands he had to deal with that neither oak nor beech was as valuable at sixty years of age, on the best spots of land, as Scotch fir would be on the very worst land at thirty years,

adding that poor land will produce Scotch fir to perfection
that will produce nothing else.   Batty Langley also (an
ancestor of one of the present Members for Sheffield), in his
quaintly written "Sure Method of Improving Estates," 1728
had advanced ideas about the value of the Scotch fir planting
in England.   He considered it the most likely fir for the purpose, stating that, "in his time there were many Scotch firs
in Devonshire, planted by gentlemen then living, and fit to be
felled for the use of builders, adding that "he was in hopes
that our English gentlemen would speedily make large plantations thereof, since they thrive with great celerity where few
of or any other kind of trees will grow."

The consumption of foreign pine timber in the building
trades alone is enormous   There is hardly a mansion, cottage,
or building of any kind in which the wood-work from the
floor to the roof does not consist almost wholly of pine timber,
nearly all foreign.   Except in the case of large oak of fine
quality, and a small quantity of other kinds of timber, almost
the whole of our home-grown timber is used for rough purposes, much of it going to the railways, collieries, waggon
builders, boat builders and the like.   Of the nearly £18,000,000
worth of timber imported from abroad, over £14,000,000,
according to Government returns, represent pine timber, consisting of Scotch fir, spruce, and, to a less extent, Weymouth
and pitch pine.   The three first succeed well enough in this
country, but the Scotch fir is the most valuable of the three
and the most extensively used.   And the consumption of pine
timber is increasing at an almost incredible rate, especially
since the wood-pulp trade assumed such dimensions.   This
consumption takes no account of the larch and fir timber of
home growth also consumed, which is large, only it does not
enter into competition with the foreign timber of the same kind
in the uses to which it is put.   Here, then, we have three
species—the Scotch fir, spruce, Weymouth pine, to which
should be added the larch, making four species which supply
by far the greater portion of the enormous quantity of timber
used in this country, which could be grown more quickly and
probably as successfully and profitably as any other species in
almost every part of the British Islands—of a varying quality,
perhaps, but of good dimensions and of a quality sufficiently
good for a great multitude of purposes.   The rotation period
—that is, the period that the crops may most profitably occupy
the ground until the final clear cutting—is a factor here.   In
Germany the Scotch fir and spruce yields the earliest returns

in the shape of poles, and the mature crop is reaped at the end of one hundred years, or about twenty-five years sooner than the hard-woods, such as beech, and fifty years earlier than the oak. These are a few of the species then that the forester should plant largely wherever they will grow, because while the demand for the other kinds of timber is local or limited, the demand for pine timber is great and universal. The four species named should succeed well in almost every county in Britain and Ireland, under dense plantation culture. The spruce may be a little capricious, preferring a rather cool and moist climate and sheltered gullies, but the larch, when it escapes the disease, grows well and fast, north or south As to the Scotch fir, it seems equally at home in the Highlands of Scotland, on the shores of the English Channel, or the sandy flats of Holland. Schlich says "it is eminently" a lowland tree and prefers southern aspects in mountains. We have had opportunities of examining the principal Scotch fir tracts in the New Forest and elsewhere in the south, and wherever the ground was naturally well-drained the timber appeared to be equal, age for age, to much of the Scotch fir grown in the north. Fine red-hearted stuff that we saw cut up in the saw mills in the forest, the consumers told us, was superior to much of the foreign red deal imported, and much of it is used for indoor joinery. On the Beaulieu estate, not far from Lynd-hurst, there are mature plantations of Scotch fir, fairly crowded, where the trees run from one hundred to one hundred and thirty feet in height, and the timber of which, the clerk of works there and others assured us, was of the best quality. The groins or break-waters which protect the beach on the Solent, opposite the Isle of Wight, are all constructed of Scotch fir from the New Forest, and both strength and endurance are required. To us, this New Forest Scotch fir appeared to be superior to much that is produced on the level lands of no great elevation in Central Germany and in Holland, and superior to much of the north of Europe " red deal " imported from abroad. There need be little or no fear, indeed, of clean Scotch fir timber finding a ready market, no matter where it is grown in Great Britain. A well-drained soil and dry climate has pro-bably more to do with the quality of the timber than anything else. In those parts of England where the Scotch fir thrives so well, as in Hampshire, Norfolk, Surrey, and elsewhere, the rainfall is the lightest in England, and the soil sandy, or dry and poor ; and although the Scotch fir is not indigenous to the south of England, it is said to have long been spreading spontaneously there on heaths and other poor tracts from which large quantities of timber are disposed of successfully. There can hardly be any doubt that a dry climate, with its greater amount of sunshine, must have a consolidating effect upon the tissues, and that the difference in quality observable in samples of Scotch fir from different parts of the country may be explained in that way. It is worth noting that the remains of natural and other Scotch fir forests in the north of Scotland are mostly, if not all, situated within the drier and sunnier belt on the eastern side, where also the cereal crops come to the greatest perfection. The whole of Forfar, Kincardine, Banff, Nairn, Elgin, the greater part of Aberdeen, and part of Perth and Inverness, lie within the dry belt, and in some of these localities the best Scotch fir in Scotland is produced. Mr. Alexander Smith, C.E., and surveyor, Aberdeen, writing in the "Highland Society's Transactions," vol. vi., p. 277, states that, on the well-wooded estate of Moneymusk, in east Aberdeen, the Scotch fir is the best produced on Don side, and always commands a ready sale. Moneymusk is within the drier belt, and we can endorse the above statement from enquiries made by ourselves on the spot.

After the fir and pine timber comes that of the oak and ash. The demand for English oak exceeds that of all other sorts of hard-woods put together, and a good deal of the finest goes to America. Trade reports of 1898 mention the export of oak to the States as steadily increasing. Railway companies consume enormous quantities of oak, sometimes quite clearing the market of certain sizes, according to timber-trade reports, which state that, "it is not an uncommon occurrence for a railway company to take the whole of what is obtainable in a season."

Ash is more profitable to grow than oak, as it soon reaches a saleable size and fetches a good price. Of course, although forest trees thrive in a great variety of soils, it is a good plan in deciding what to plant on an estate to look round the locality and see which species succeed best, especially under plantation culture, because although almost any species which will succeed as an isolated park tree or garden specimen will also succeed under plantation culture, there are some species that will grow well in a sheltered plantation that may not succeed in the open. Of the latter may be mentioned as examples, the common and other spruces, the Douglas fir, and the Wellingtonia, which in keen, cold localities on the east coast and far inland refuse to thrive when planted as isolated

trees, but grow fast in plantations where they are not likely
to overtop their neighbours and expose their tops to winds.

SECTION III.—DESCRIPTIVE LIST OF SPECIES.

The following list is intended principally for the use of
planters and those who have timber-trees to dispose of. The
descriptions are taken chiefly from numerous carefully recorded
observations of our own, made in woods where the trees have
grown up in dense masses or groups, wherever these could be
found, in different parts of England and Scotland, and may be
relied upon as being near the mark. The behaviour of trees
under dense plantation culture is, we conceive, what the timber-
grower needs to understand first of all. In almost every work
on forestry in the past, the descriptions of our forest trees are
taken from park, garden and hedge-row examples alone, and are
consequently quite misleading. Probably for every tree grown
under the last-named conditions there are thousands grown in
plantations, to which a quite different description would apply.
Take the oak, for example, as described by a well-known
writer on forest trees. It is, we are told, a massive-stemmed,
spreading, flat-topped tree; whereas under true plantation
culture it would be more correctly described as a tall, branchless, stemmed tree, with a small, round top.* Again, the
common alder is described as an almost worthless timber-tree,
seldom attaining a height of more than forty feet except where
attention is paid to it. This is a good enough description of
the rough and worthless riverside specimen, but we have seen
alder, and sold it out of a thick wood where no attention had
been bestowed upon it, nearly seventy feet high, the result
simply of plantation culture; and we have examples in the
woods here now of that height, branchless and shapely for fifty
feet up, squaring about ten inches at that height and over
sixteen inches at the bottom. These examples are growing
among oak and ash of the same shape. Indeed the difference
that plantation culture and density produces on a tree in
increasing its length of trunk and altering its shape and
general habit of growth is not sufficiently understood except
by those who are familiar with our forest trees.

The prices given in the following list are the average
prices ruling now, 1898, or thereabout, and are for plantation
timber, standing in the wood, after allowing for the cost of

* See Plates No. 8 and 9.

7

felling and delivery within a radius of twenty-five miles, the timber to be removed at the purchasers' risk. When felled and sorted by the owner, the expense should be added to the prices given. Much depends on quality—clean, straight trees invariably fetching much the highest, and hedgerow trees the lowest price. The species are given in each class in the order of their importance as timber-trees, beginning with the broad-leaved species.

LIST OF SPECIES DESCRIBED.

BROAD-LEAVED SPECIES.

1.	Oak	*Quercus pedunculata or sessiliflora.*
2.	Oak (Turkey Quercus) ...	... *Quercus cerres.*
3.	Ash	... *Fraxinus excelsior.*
4.	Elm	*Ulmus compestris.*
5.	... ... •	... ,, *Montana.*
6.	Beech	*Fagus sylvatica.*
7.	Sycamore	*Acer pseudo platanus.*
8.	Maple	,, *Platanoides.*
9.	Birch	... *Betula alba.*
10.	Alder	... *Alnus glutinosa.*
11.	Mountain Ash	*Pyrus aucaparia.*
12.	Poplar (Black)	.. *Populus nigra.*
13.	Willow (White)	... *Salix alba.*
14.	Lime	... *Tilia Europea.*
15.	Chestnut (Sweet)...	*Castanea vesca.*
16.	Chestnut (Horse) ...	... *Æsculus hippocastanum.*
17.	Hornbeam	*Carpinus betulus.*
18.	Cherry	... *Prunus avium.*
19.	Walnut	*Juglans regia.*

CONIFERÆ SPECIES.

1.	Scotch Fir...	*Pinus sylvestris.*
2.	Corsican Fir	*Pinus laricio.*
3.	Cluster Fir	*Pinus pinaster.*
4.	Austrian Fir	...*Pinus Austriaca.*
5.	Weymouth Fir	*Pinus strobus.*
6.	Common Spruce Fir	*Abies excelsa.*
7.	Silver Fir...	*Abies pectinata.*
8.	Douglas Fir	... *Abies Douglasii.*
9.	Noble Fir	... *Abies noblis.*
10.	Nordmans Fir	*Abies Nordmaniana.*
11.	Great Fir	*Abies grandis.*
12.	Larch...	... *Larix Europea.*
13.	Larch. Japanese	*Larix leptolepis.*
14.	Deodar	*Cedrus deadora.*
15.	Wellingtonia	*Wellingtonia gigantea.*

OAK. *Quercus pedunculata* and *Quercus sessiliflora.*—
These are said to be distinct by botanists, but intermediate
varieties are common. The oak is a comparatively slow-
growing tree, but its timber is used for a great variety of purposes, from young poles squaring three inches in the middle
up to trees of mature age, poles fetching from one shilling to
eighteenpence per foot, and trees squaring ten inches and
upwards, from one shilling and threepence to two shillings and
sixpence per foot, fine butts often considerably more. The
heart-wood of the oak varies in quality and colour, even in the
same wood, but its strength and toughness begins to give way
when decay sets in and the tree becomes " stag-headed." At
that stage the timber is described as " tender," but it is still
valuable for many purposes—for furniture, and for cutting up
into thin veneers. The usual colour of the heart-wood of the
oak is well-known, but old trees are sometimes as dark-
coloured as walnut, and are known as " brown oaks," while
others are of a pleasing red shade, and others again are
figured. Such trees always sell at a considerably higher price
per foot than ordinary oak, and purchasers of old trees
generally hope to find a few red or brown ones amongst them.
We have known a red oak tree containing a little over four
hundred cubic feet sold by auction in Yorkshire for over one
hundred pounds, and it is not at all an uncommon thing for
timber merchants to give a high price for coloured oak,
although the tree may be hollow inside and little else than a
shell. Batty Langley, Esq., M.P., Sheffield, had a pollard oak
of this description sent from Stowemarket, in Suffolk, to his
yard in Sheffield, in 1898, for which he paid a high price on
the spot, the cost of haulage being also great. Mr. Langley
told us that had this tree not been hollow it would have
measured close upon seven hundred and forty feet, although
a pollard oak only fifteen feet in length. Great art is shown
in sawing up such oaks into veneers, almost as thin as paper,
to show the figuring ; one cubic foot producing some hundreds
of superficial feet, each foot worth from sixpence to one
shilling, according to quality. There is a steady and increasing
demand for this kind of oak for the American market, and
good trees are shipped from Liverpool to New York uncut.
Red and brown oaks are usually old and tender, and the
colour is always deepest at the junction of the trunk with the
root. The cause of the deeper colour has never been explained,
and red and brown oaks are usually found growing within a
few feet or yards of other oaks of the ordinary colour. The

oak prefers a good deep soil, but will succeed and, in time, become a very large tree in the poorest soils up to one thousand feet elevation in Yorkshire.

TURKEY OAK. *Quercus cerris.*—Since the first edition of this book was published, I have seen many fine examples of this oak, and that, together with the favourable account from other countries, has induced me to give it a place here. The tree is as hardy as the common oak, grows twice as fast, and the wood is hardly inferior to an English oak for many purposes. It is used in our dock-yards for ship-building, and is the chief timber employed for that purpose in those European countries where it abounds. The tree is, besides, almost an ever-green, and may often be seen green in this country in December—a quality which should recommend it for cover planting. I am of opinion that there would be no risk in planting it with the common oak, in equal proportions, where, owing to its fast growth, it would yield an early supernumerary crop. In some parts of England it is said to produce a tree one hundred feet high, with a trunk four feet in diameter in 80 years. It is a tree of robust growth wherever the common oak will succeed, and its rapid growth to plank dimensions is a strong recommendation in its favour. For a crop of small poles of saleable dimensions, in a short rotation, it would probably be a profitable tree.

ASH, COMMON. *Fraxinus excelsior.*—A tall, quick-growing tree, succeeding best in mixed woods, but becoming stunted and bark-bound on poor, dry ground. It likes a fairly moist soil and shelter. Ash timber is always in good demand, and is saleable from a small size at from ninepence to one shilling per cubic foot; large butts fetching from one shilling and sixpence to two shillings per foot. It comes very late into leaf, casts little shade, and is a good plantation tree, producing a trunk of exceptional length, free from breaks, sometimes overtopping the oak. It may be under-planted with beech and the common spruce, the two best shade-bearers, and should be planted out the first or second year from seed, as older plants get bark-bound and are long in moving.

Ash timber is becoming scarce in this country. More than a hundred years ago Marshall lamented the want of foresight among planters in not planting more ash in " close plantations," considering the multitude of purposes for which the wood was used and its value. One certain cause of the scarcity is the destruction of the tree by rabbits, trees of all ages being barked and killed. There is no tree so liable to be attacked by these vermin as the ash, and they fatten upon the bark. The quality of ash timber is much affected by situation. In warm, sheltered situations it grows fast and is tough, while on cold northern aspects it is " tender." We know woods on northern aspects in which the quality of the ash is so well known to local consumers that they will not buy it, while accepting readily that growing on the south side of the hill under the same conditions, excepting aspect. The texture of the wood can at once be told on applying the woodman's scribe to the end of the tree, and woodmen know the quality of ash timber as soon as they apply the axe.

ELM. *Ulmus montana* and *Ulmus campestris.*—Some confusion exists among foresters and timber dealers concerning these two elms, the first-named being supposed to be common to Scotland and the latter to England; whereas the Scotch elm is, if anything, more extensively grown in mixed woods in England than is the English elm, and some of the oldest elm avenues in England are a mixture of the Scotch and English varieties. The timber of the Scotch elm is preferred to the other, is in greater demand, and fetches a higher price, being tougher and often substituted for ash. The two kinds are easily distinguished. The Scotch elm is a tall, free growing tree with sweeping limbs, strong twigs, broad rough leaves, and deeply-furrowed bark in old trees. The English elm, compared to the Scotch, is upright and stiff-looking in habit, denser in its foliage, smaller in leaf, rugged and corky-looking in the bark, and sheds its leaves later than the other. In Yorkshire, timber merchants know the two kinds well, and name the Scotch elm " English " and the English elm " Dutch." The Scotch elm is in good demand at from tenpence to one shilling and twopence per foot. English elm fetches less.

BEECH. *Fagus sylvatica.*—This is a tall-growing tree of vigorous habit, laying on timber fast after middle-age, a good shade-bearer, but bad neighbour in mixed woods, and is best grown by itself, or with spruce and larch, thrives in poor soils, if dry, and at high elevations. The beech is one of the best trees for planting as underwood in thin woods, either as shelter for other trees or covert for game, owing to its shade-bearing power. Timber in fair demand if of good girth; price from tenpence to one shilling and fourpence per foot.

SYCAMORE. *Acer pseudo platanus.*—It is a rather remarkable fact with regard to this first-class timber-tree that, although it propagates itself more freely than any of our forest trees except the birch, makes a big bole quickly, and fetches a high price as timber, good butts are scarce and not often offered in any quantity. One explanation probably is that in the past the tree has not been valued by foresters for its timber, and that the demand for sycamore has greatly increased within the last forty years or so for various purposes connected with the Lancashire mills and other branches of industry. From eleven inches upwards it is sought for at from one shilling to three shillings and sixpence per cubic foot. The articles made from it, many of them, are cut out, not longitudinally, but across the grain, hence the usual stipulations about girth by purchasers who buy sycamore for special purposes, such as rollers for machinery, as in the case of the beech. The sycamore grows quickly, and in a mixed or pure wood produces a fine, clean, cylindrical trunk, is extremely hardy, withstands gales, and is not particular as to soil. The tree sows itself freely, and in some parts it has extended itself naturally from older trees. When planted, one year or two-year-old plants should be used.

NORWAY MAPLE. *Acer platanoides.*—A hardy tree, less vigorous than the sycamore, which it resembles. Timber not in demand, but may be sold with that of the sycamore.

BIRCH. *Betula alba.*—This species and the alder and mountain ash are here grouped in succession, because the timber of all the three is used for similar purposes, and they thrive well together at high elevations and under similar conditions. The birch is a very useful timber-tree, reaching saleable dimensions on dry or moist soils of almost every description, thriving at a higher elevation than most other trees, also in valleys, and reaching a height of sixty feet. The timber is light and is extensively used for clog soles in England, the cloggers felling the trees at any season of the year, cutting out the soles and leaving them to season stacked in piles in the wood. Trees of from one to five cubic feet dimensions are preferred for soles, but lots of all sizes are readily sold at from fivepence to sixpence per foot. The birch sows itself readily, and may be sown artificially without any preparation of the soil. When planted by itself, about six thousand small plants may be put out to the acre, and they need not be thinned until the best reach three-and-a-half inches quarter girth in the middle. Birch is a good companion for the oak, and both may be planted very thickly together without fear, as they do not incommode each other and grow at about the same rate till past middle-age in the case of the birch. Birch timber is now imported in the rough from the north of Europe in the shape of clean, straight butts of small size, but of a quality inferior to English birch. Large quantities of the timber are used for making bobbins and other purposes in Lancashire, Yorkshire, and elsewhere.

COMMON ALDER. *Alnus glutinosa.*—(See birch.)—The timber of the alder is not in such demand by itself as the birch is, but good clean stems are readily disposed of. The tree prefers a moist soil, but thrives in any well-drained soil that is deep. Water-logged soils do not suit it. It may be planted or sown with the birch in the more moist situations.

MOUNTAIN ASH OR ROWAN. *Pyrus aucuparia.*—This tree succeeds well with the birch, and although not specially in demand, cloggers accept it for the same purposes. It grows, when young, as fast as the birch, propagating itself freely, but soon shows a tendency to become branchy and round-headed. When in flower or in berry it is one of the most beautiful trees we have, particularly in those districts where the rainfall is heavy and the air moist. In some parts of the Highlands, especially in Argyleshire, the size and brilliancy of its fruit are remarkable. In the chapter on game this tree is referred to as a food producer.

BLACK POPLAR. *Populus nigra.*—There are several species of poplar all producing timber of much the same quality, but the black poplar is perhaps the most rapid grower of the family, the hardiest, and the most profitable to grow. It exceeds all other broad-leaved species in the rapidity of its growth, towering above its neighbours at an early age, and hence it is an undesirable tree in a mixed wood. Moist or wet soils suit it best, and in such situations it should be planted thickly alone, or mixed or under-planted with willow. As the timber is not durable, and is used mainly for indoor purposes, the demand is not great, but it can always be disposed of in moderate quantities at from tenpence to one shilling per foot.

WILLOW, COMMON. *Salix alba.*—Like the poplar, this species thrives in swampy soils, where it attains to a large size. The timber is in moderate demand for special purposes in which lightness and toughness are required—as in cricket bats, oars, etc., but recently there has been an increasing demand for this wood for brakes for railway trains and waggons, it being found that willow timber, owing probably to its peculiar fibre, wears rough and takes a better grip than harder and heavier woods that wear smooth by friction. The only other wood that is used for the same purpose is poplar, which is sometimes substituted for the willow, both fetching the same price.

LIME TREE. *Tilia Europœa.*—The lime is well-known as
an ornamental tree that attains to a great height in parks and
avenues, but as a timber tree it is not much grown.   London
and some of the larger towns are the best markets for this class
of timber, which is used in turning and for cutting-blocks, as
the wood does not blunt the knives.   Nice butts fetch from
one shilling to one shilling and threepence per foot.   The tree
is liable to be broken and disfigured by gales when grown in
the open.

SPANISH CHESTNUT. *Castanea vesca.*—This would be one
of our most valuable forest trees but for its liability to ring-
shake after middle age, and which, as purchasers and foresters
know, renders any kind of tree almost worthless.   In a ring-
shaken tree the annual rings shrink and part, and when the
tree is sawn up it falls to pieces.   On this account consumers
do not care to buy Spanish chestnut standing, and felling
always reveals a large proportion of shaken trees.   Ring-shake
may be worse in some localities and soils than in others, but
timber merchants who buy over wide districts say that it is
common everywhere in this tree.   Up till forty or fifty years
of age the Spanish chestnut ranks in value with the oak, which
it much resembles in the outward appearance of its trunk,
but is a quicker grower.   Although in a park or hedgerow it
has a very wide-spreading straggly habit, often throwing out
limbs of a distorted shape, it is an accommodating plantation
tree, producing a trunk of model shape and good bulk with
other species of the same rate of growth as itself—like the
beech, for example, and the same conditions suit both.   The
poplar, as stated elsewhere, overtops most other species, but
the Spanish chestnut beats most species in laying on timber,
and that, too, in very poor soils at high elevations.   Where
it bears heavy crops of fruit regularly it may perhaps not grow
so fast, but in cold localities, where the fruit comes to nothing,
the growth is rapid.   One fine park tree that we have had
under observation for many years is about ninety years of age
and contains over four hundred and forty cubic feet of timber,
which is at the average rate of close upon five solid cubic
feet per year for the ninety years.   But as in all trees the
annual increment increases with age, the increase in this particular tree must have much exceeded five feet after middle-
age.   The timber of the Spanish chestnut resembles the oak,
and when sound is valued at about the same price.   It is a
good tree for producing a crop of small poles in a short time,
coppice wood and hop-poles, etc.

HORSE CHESTNUT. *Aesculus hippocastanum.*—An ornamental park tree, but worthless as a timber-tree, and an obnoxious tree in a plantation, as it bears shade well and is a persistent side-brancher like the beech, smothering its less vigorous neighbours.

HORNBEAM. *Carpinus betulus.*—Although the timber of this species is useful for several purposes and can be sold in mixed lots at a low price, it is rarely asked for, and is not a profitable tree to grow in this country. It is a good shade-bearer and is useful for under-planting.

WILD CHERRY. *Prunus avium.*—The wild cherry, or gean, is seldom planted as a timber-tree, but is common in woods where little colonies of self-sown trees spring up round older trees, and also single trees here and there sown probably by birds. The timber is used by cabinet makers, but is not much sought after, although nice butts are readily disposed of when offered, at about the same price as ash. The tree grows fast and attains to a large size.

WALNUT. *Juglans regia.*—The timber of the walnut is not often offered for sale in this country, but the tree attains to a good size, and no doubt the wood would find a ready market, judging by the quantity used up of foreign origin. The walnut prefers a good soil and favourable climate, but large trees are frequently found at considerable elevations in England and Scotland.

SCOTCH FIR. *Pinus sylvestris.*—The value of the Scotch fir as a timber-tree has been adverted to already. Here it may be added that probably none of the fir tribe have such a wide geographical distribution in Europe as this species, extending as it does, as a useful timber-tree, almost from the Arctic Circle southwards to the Middle Rhine, where it joins the vine ; and eastward to Asia, covering hills and plains alike and thriving on the poorest soils. The quality of the timber varies greatly, even within the British Islands, being best on dry and worst on moist soils, and in a cool, moist climate ; but seldom so inferior anywhere as to be unfit for many useful purposes. No ordinarily healthy soil that is well-drained or naturally dry comes amiss to it, and, if anything, it is more at home, once fairly established, in poor sands than anywhere else. This is particularly noticeable on the sand dunes near Bournemouth and in many parts of Germany and Holland. It makes a useful pole of pit-prop dimensions in from thirty to forty years, if planted thickly and sparingly thinned or not thinned at all during that period. We have seen Scotch fir like this grown in Yorkshire and elsewhere, but, as a rule, poles of the above age, owing to their having too much room, are usually so rough as to be unsaleable. It is best grown as pure forest, and it should be planted on a large scale. The price of Scotch fir varies from sixpence to ninepence per foot.

CORSICAN FIR. *Pinus laricio.*—If the Scotch fir is ever superseded we venture to think that it will be by this species, which appears to have all the good qualities of the Scotch fir, with the advantage that it beats the latter in bulk of timber from the first. This is due, no doubt, to the fact that the leaf surface of the Corsican fir is considerably greater, than that of the Scotch fir, and timber is consequently laid on more quickly. It has been planted extensively on the Wortley estate in a variety of soils and situations and at different elevations, and this description holds good in every instance. It is also very favourably reported on by foresters, generally, in these respects. It does not·transplant well in winter, but if planted early in August, September and October, or in April and May, the failures are quite as few as in the Scotch fir. When the Corsican fir began to be planted it was often confounded with the Austrian fir, which was often substituted for it; but however nearly related botanically the two may be, they are perfectly distinct as forest trees, and both kinds are now easily distinguished by their foliage and habit anywhere and at all ages. The Corsican fir is of a rather cylindrical, thin habit, and the leaves have a twist and colour by which it is easily distinguished from the rigid-spined, bushy Austrian. The latter also varies considerably in habit, while the Corsican is generally true to its character. It thrives in almost any soil, and were it desired to plant fir extensively anywhere we should certainly plant Scotch and Corsican firs, and expect the latter to take the lead from the beginning.

CLUSTER FIR. *Pinus pinaster.*—This is another very useful fir for planting near the sea-side. It has been extensively 'and successfully planted on the west coast of France within the last hundred years, and now yields a variety of useful forest products there, including pit-props, quantities of which are exported to Wales for the coal pits there. It also grows well close to the sea near Bournemouth and elsewhere.

AUSTRIAN FIR. *Pinus Austriaca.*—This is an exceedingly hardy species anywhere and in any soil. It varies in habit, but generally it is of bushy, dense habit, and of a slower height-growth than the Scotch or Corsican firs. It is one of the very best species to plant for shelter purposes, but is an

inferior timber-tree, owing to its rigid and thick horizontal side
branches, which are not soon shed unless the tree is planted
thickly by itself, hence its timber is very knotty and rough,
but otherwise it is equal to the Scotch.   Owing to the bushy
habit of the tree it is apt to be blown to one side and consequently grows up with a bent trunk.

WEYMOUTH PINE. *Pinus strobus.*—This tree has never
been really tested as a timber-tree in this country, and descriptions of it given hitherto, of British-grown specimens, are
clearly taken from park and lawn examples where neither the
height-growth of the tree nor its suitableness for plantation
culture could be tested.   It is the Scotch fir of America, its
timber being more extensively used than that of any other.
In Germany it is one of the few exotic species that has been
favourably reported on.   We saw fine examples, taller and
bulkier than the Scotch fir among which it grew, at over two
thousand feet elevation, not far from Eisenach.   It is said to
be more fastidious as regards soil than the Corsican fir, doing
best in cool, moist situations and deep soils, in which respect
it forms a suitable companion to the spruce.

COMMON NORWAY SPRUCE. *Abies excelsa.*—As at present
grown in our over-thinned woods, where it is more or less
branched too near the ground, this tree is one of the most
worthless to the producer.   Thinnings and small poles are
practically unsaleable, and large trees only fetch from one
penny to threepence per foot if within a reasonable distance
from the consumer.   Trees of large size, free from knots, are
in fair demand for waggon bottoms and other purposes, but
only a portion of our home-grown trees can be used, the upper
portion of their trunks being usually a mass of large bulging
knots which are sawn off as useless, except perhaps for firing
the engines of the saw mill.   Good, clean trees of cylindrical
shape, like our telegraph poles, would find a ready market, as
they make good deals and are also likely to be by-and-by used
as railway sleepers, as they are now used in the spruce regions
of Germany.   Spruce is now also used to such an enormous
extent for making paper that an early scarcity is feared both
in Europe and America.   It likes a cool, damp soil and situation, and is a good subject for under-planting, as it bears shade
well.   Dry, exposed situations and dry soils do not suit it, but
it will grow in a dense plantation where it will scarcely live
standing by itself.   It is one of the best subjects to plant as
covert for pheasants.

SILVER FIR. *Abies pectinata.*—This tree lays on wood

faster than the common spruce, which it resembles in its habits
and wants, and its timber is used for similar purposes. The
two are commonly planted together in Scotland. Probably no
forest tree involves so much work in felling and cleaning as
this fir when grown in thin woods, where it is always heavily
branched. In Continental spruce forests we have seen trees
one hundred and thirty feet high, felled, that needed scarcely
any cleaning save the cutting off of the short top, whereas in
Scotland, trees of less size we have known to occupy two men
nearly a day in cutting off the branches alone.

DOUGLAS FIR. *Abies Douglasii.*—Within the last few
years a new variety of this species, called "Colorada Douglas
Fir," has been introduced, and recommended as superior to
the original variety. Planters should, however, be cautious in
substituting the new for the old. The Colorada variety is still
dear, and wherever we have seen it side by side with the original
form, its slower height growth was very marked; and as the
rapid growth of the original Douglas fir is its best recommendation, as a timber-tree, the superior value of the new kind
may be doubted. The latter is of a more squat habit, and
varies in the colour of its foliage from light to glaucus green.
The old variety comes true and is the safest to plant for
timber. The vitality of this tree exceeds that of all other
firs in suitable situations. Like the spruce, it fails on dry
soils and exposures. We have known it tried repeatedly and
carefully in such positions far inland on the eastern slopes of
the Pennine Range in Yorkshire and fail completely, but have
seen it growing freely near the sea on the Norfolk coast along
with other spruces. In the New Forest it is as much at home
as in Perthshire, where it is seen at its best—the fine lawn
specimen at Dunkeld, planted about 1845, and containing
about one hundred cubic feet, being one of the finest examples
in Scotland. The tree should be grown in crowded plantations by itself in order to cause the lower branches to be shed
early. Under such conditions, probably no other forest tree
would reach large and useful pole size so soon, but, unfortunately, it has not been grown in that way as yet, and
examples we have seen have been of the worst description as
timber trees, being clothed to their base with branches that
produced huge knots at their junction with the trunk, which
was also too tapering. In one well-known plantation the
forester had sawn the lower branches off, a practice that would
have been unnecessary had the trees been sufficiently crowded.
The timber of the Douglas fir has been sold at one shilling

per cubic foot, it is said; but as that price probably included the cost of delivery to the consumer, the net price might be much less. We have seen the best plantations, and our idea was that the timber was not worth the above figure in the wood. We believe that by planting the tree from 4 to 5 feet apart, and letting it alone for fifteen or twenty years, a crop of pit-props of excellent quality could be produced that would pay the grower, and probably no other fir tree would produce good deals so soon. Sections of trees about nineteen years old, that we have seen, had a diameter of eighteen inches, indicating an extraordinary rate of growth. Sections from trees ten years old, or more, showed heart-wood colouring to within two-and-a-half to three inches from the bark, the sap wood being white and the heart-wood of a fine reddish shade, both taking on a finely polished surface. We should say that this tree would produce a good useful deal at an early age of a quality between that of the spruce and Scotch fir. Such rapid formation of the heart-wood is remarkable, and is certainly not found in any other fir that we know of. In all the plantations of this tree that we have seen the trees have been rough and extremely tapering—of bad shape for commercial purposes, that is to say; but reckoning from such data as we have, there is little doubt but that in a plantation sufficiently crowded to cause the trees to begin shedding their lower branches early, trees squaring from ten to twelve inches in the middle, cylindrical in shape, and clean, could be produced in from thirty to forty years—a rate of growth exceeding that of all our other forest trees, and representing a rate of production per acre far exceeding anything yet recorded. The capabilities of the tree as a timber producer have really not been tested yet, owing to the severe thinnings it has been subjected to, but it is well worth experimenting with under dense culture on a large scale.* The Douglas fir flag-staff at Kew is one hundred and fifty-nine feet in length, twenty-two inches in diameter at the base, and eight inches at the top—a run off in the taper of fourteen inches only in fifty-three yards. This pole shows every sign of having grown up in an excessively crowded forest where it probably never had more than a few feet of branches at its top. It is free from large knots for its whole length, and in general shape and appearance it is so unlike British-grown

---

* Since the above was written the author has secured photographs of promising plantations of this fir. See plates 10 and 11.

samples that the two would hardly be recognised as belonging to the same species. The largest examples of Scotch-grown trees are in shape like an elongated candle-extinguisher, with a lumpy exterior, while the Kew pole is almost cylindrical, and smooth from end to end.

THE NOBLE FIR. *Abies noblis.*—This is not only a beautiful tree, but promises also to be a useful timber-tree. It is perfectly hardy, a quick grower, is not a very wide brancher, and forms a fine, clean pole of cylindrical shape. We have noticed in many places that it is not so fastidious as to soil and climate as the other spruces, and that it thrives, if it does not grow so fast, in dry, thin soils, and stands exposure fairly well. We have seen it in mixed plantations in Argyleshire doing remarkably well, and would advise its use as a timber-tree. Taking up little room laterally, it may be planted from two-and-a-half to three feet apart.

NORDMAN'S FIR. *Abies Nordmaniana.*—This promises to be another useful tree, being a good grower and hardy. Its rigid, horizontal branches are, however, wide-spreading, and, like the Douglas fir, it should be planted by itself and but sparingly thinned.

GRAND FIR. *Abies grandis.*—This species has the fault of the more tender spruces—a dislike to dry soils and keen windy exposures. In the sheltered dens about Murthly Castle in Scotland, it makes a grand tree, and in a plantation would no doubt soon provide a trunk of large size.

LARCH. *Larix Europœ.*—This tree needs no description. But for the disease to which it is extremely liable everywhere and which renders it useless, it would be the most valuable species among all the firs. Under ordinarily favourable conditions a crop of larch is sure to pay. Its timber is useful and enduring at an early age, and large trees fetch from one shilling to one shilling and sixpence per foot in the wood. As pure forest, a large number can be grown to the acre, and although it has been said to succeed best mixed with other species, it is well-known that many of the pure crops of larch of mature age in this country have been very fine. Mixed with the beech it holds its own in height-growth, but the beech is of poor quality owing to its liability to branch under the thin shade of the larch. The larch succeeds in a great variety of soils, on lowlands and on hills, where they are well drained, and grows rapidly. The leading shoot in young trees frequently exceeds three feet in a year, and we have known plantations on gravelly lands in Leicestershire where the annual growth on many of the trees exceeded four feet. We strongly recommend the larch still to be planted in mixed woods of hard-woods, where it holds its own well, and should it become diseased it may be removed without serious loss of crop. There are few larch plantations now in which the disease is not more or less prevalent, and on some estates where the original plantations of larch are still sound, and all the conditions are favourable, the young plantations have been ruined by the disease. The wood of the larch is used for a great variety of purposes where strength and endurance are required, but it is not so well known that it also makes excellent furniture and may be both carved and polished, when it is equal in appearance to pitch pine. We have seen articles of this description that have lasted without warping or shrinking for nearly forty years, but for such purposes the wood of course requires to be seasoned.

JAPANESE LARCH. *Larix leptolepis.*—This larch, which covers mountain tracts in Japan, has hitherto been described as a small tree between thirty and forty feet high, and next to worthless as a timber-tree. It has, however, been extensively distributed since the first edition of this work was published, and become better known. The author believes that he was the first to recommend the species as a useful timber and ornamental tree, in the "Field," some years ago, which led to inquiries, and he planted it both pure and mixed at Wortley about the same time. Before then it was not quoted in nurserymen's lists, and Messrs. Dickson & Co., Waterloo Place, Edinburgh, were the first to raise and distribute stock of it, through the enterprise of Mr. W. H. Massie. The tree was introduced from Japan by Veitch in 1861, but was wrongly described in Veitch's "Manual of the Conifera" as attaining to less than half the height of the common larch, and inferior to the latter both as an ornamental and timber tree ;—whereas examples growing at Blair Drummond, Perthshire, Munches, and Kirkennan, Galloway, now thirty feet high, or thereabout, and many younger examples, show that it grows as fast as the European larch and is more ornamental. The Japanese larch is not mentioned in Nesbit's edition of Brown's "Forester," nor in Schlich's "Sylvicultural Notes on British Forest Trees," but it has been very favourably noticed by planters during the last few years as a good grower and disease resister. In Professor Schwappach's recent report on Prussian experiments with exotic trees he thus speaks of the Japanese larch :—

"Growth in youth is more rapid than in the case of the

common larch, in fact, it surpasses that of any of our more valuable indigenous trees. On the average it is found that at five years the trees are three feet six inches high, at ten years ten feet, and at fifteen years nearly twenty feet. In certain cases trees of nine years of age have reached the height of thirty-seven feet, but this is quite an exceptional rate of growth. Height-growth appears to continue right through the summer, and on till the end of September. It is found that the Japanese larch does not curve over on the top to the same extent as the common larch. It is very important to note that the Japanese larch possesses *very great power of resistance in regard to both the larch moth and the larch disease.* This tree also recovers very much more rapidly from injuries than is the case with the common larch. When it loses the main shoot, it produces a fresh leader in a very short time."

The trees in Perth and Galloway were raised from seed collected by the owners of the estates named, in Japan, and sent home by them, and the trees have now passed the critical stage at which the disease usually shows itself, though growing near diseased larch of the European kind. I have inquired into every case of reputed disease of the Japanese variety, including those reported by Colonel Bailey in his Novar pamphlet, but in no instance have the cases reported been confirmed. If the Japanese larch proves disease-proof its value as a substitute for the common larch can hardly be over-estimated. Five years ago I formed a small plantation of the Japanese larch and Corsican fir, in equal proportions, on a very exposed north-east aspect about 800 feet above the sea level, on naturally well-drained ground and thin soil. This was, I believe, the first regular plantation of the Japanese larch planted in Britain. The trees were from the first batches raised by Dickson & Co. I bought them in one year's seedlings, and after giving them one season in the home nursery, I planted them out alternately with the Corsicans when about six inches high. Very few of either failed, and when I visited the plantation last I found that the larch were the dominant trees, running from seven to twelve feet in height and over-topping the Corsicans. This may be considered good growth in the time on one of the bleakest spots in Yorkshire.

DEODAR. *Cedrus deodara.*—This tree has not been as yet tested as a timber-tree in this country, but in its native habitat it is known to produce timber of the best and most enduring description, and examples of the wood that we have seen in this country were harder and heavier than good examples of larch grown under the same conditions. Dr. Masters, in his "Notes on the Taxaceæ and Conifera," says, the resemblance of the cedars to the larch is striking botanically—a remark that applies to the habits of the two trees also. The deodar, in a plantation, grows a little slower than the Scotch fir and succeeds in a great variety of soils, provided they are naturally or otherwise well drained, and it also prefers an upland and open, or even exposed, situation. In warm, damp valleys it becomes sickly, but is extremely hardy in situations that suit it. During the unusually severe winters of 1860 and 1894 it did not suffer in the slightest degree, where the common English yew and holly suffered severely. Magnificent examples are to be seen at Murthly Castle, in Perthshire. It is well worth planting with the larch and Scotch fir on dry soils, which suit all the three.

WELLINGTONIA. *Wellingtonia gigantia.*—We have seen numbers of this tree between thirty and forty-five years of age felled, and in every case the wood was rather soft and white, with a very large proportion of sap-wood. The timber is, however, quite equal to that of the common spruce, and from numbers of careful measurements and comparisons we have made, it seems to produce measurable timber at about twice as fast a rate as the larch, spruce, or Scotch fir. In cold, windy situations, isolated trees become branchless scare-crows, but in a plantation it produces an ideal pit-prop pole in an extremely short time, and does not lose its top like the Douglas fir. In the quantity of timber produced per acre it would, we believe, beat in a given time any other member of the conifera tribe except the Douglas fir. It should be planted along with the spruce, Scotch fir, and larch.

CHAPTER VIII.

PREPARATION OF THE LAND FOR PLANTING.

Cleaning.—Draining.—Fencing.—Roads.

SECTION I.—CLEANING.

ELABORATE instructions have from time to time been given on this head, but it cannot be too clearly realised that the financial returns from timber crops in this country are never likely to permit any great initial outlay in the shape of sub-soiling, trenching, or ploughing, etc.   Nor, except draining, is it often needful to disturb the natural soil.   In many cases even draining is not needed.   Indeed it would be a difficult matter on private estates in this country to find plantations where any expensive preparation of the ground had been attempted, and the condition of plantations generally show that no such preparations are as a rule needed.   Trees root too deeply to be permanently affected by any preparation of the surface soil that is practicable, at least in poor waste lands where the soil is thin.   Rough surface vegetation may have to be cleared away by burning or cutting previous to planting, and kept down afterwards till the young trees meet and smother under-growth, but it is seldom necessary to do more. Hitherto British woodlands have generally been planted on the natural surface, and the same remark applies to Continental forests.   In some few instances proprietors have, on the advice of their foresters, gone to the expense of deep steam-ploughing previous to planting, but it is held by many experienced planters that little or no equivalent advantage is gained thereby; that in a pulverised soil the roots sooner reach the inferior sub-soil; and that on bare fallow young forest trees make less progress during the first year or two than they do when planted on the natural grassy surface. It is certainly a fact, that bare ground, once it hardens on the surface, suffers much more from drought in summer and cold in winter than grass land does. So marked was this, in a case that came under our notice, where a crop of potatoes was succeeded by plantation of young larch, that the forester, instead of keeping the weeds down by the hoe the second year, simply trod or cut them over and left them lying as a mulching, and with advantage to the trees

Land from which a crop of timber has been recently removed is considered the most unsuitable for planting, particularly when the previous crop has consisted of any of the pine tribe, which may leave the seeds of disease and insect pests behind them. Even stubbing up the old stools does not get rid of these dangers, and that is expensive work ; while trenching the ground, owing to the cost, is prohibitive. The best plan in such a case is to leave the ground vacant for a few years, exposed to the frost and weather, and it is also an excellent plan to burn the surface vegetation frequently. Fungus from the old stools, such as the dangerous *Agaricus melleus*, are to be feared, especially when the succeeding crop consists of the same species as the preceding one ; and under such circumstances a change of crop is advisable. Still, re-planting old woods without any preparation is a common practice, and failures are not common after the trees are fairly established.

SECTION II.—DRAINING.

As to drains, soil that does not in winter remain sodden or spongy after rains or indicate stagnant water does not need draining, and where these signs are present, open drains from two-and-a-half feet to three feet deep, nine inches wide at the bottom, three feet wide at the top, and about thirty feet asunder, will carry off all superfluous water from heavy rains. The trees themselves absorb much moisture from the ground during the season, but, on the other hand, the evaporation from the ground is considerably less in woods than in the open fields. Spongy peat-lands and morasses require deeper and wider drains to render them fit for trees. According to the "Highland Society's Transactions," vol. v., p. 96, in draining extensive peat morasses near Moy, in Ireland, an arterial drain, thirty-three feet wide and from eight to ten feet deep, cut with a slope of forty-five degrees, was first made, and into this sub-mains eight feet wide, five feet deep, and two feet wide at the bottom were led, and into these again the smaller surface drains.   Draining on this scale, as found in the Fens, takes time, and the work can only be proceeded with as the water is gradually drawn off.   In the case mentioned, Mr. Webster, author of the paper, states that after draining, the bog sank two feet, becoming dry and firm and fit for planting.   Timber and other crops grow freely in pure peat soils, thoroughly drained as described, but as such soils consist to a large extent of vegetable matter, they are much benefited by heavy dressings of lime laid on the surface.   All drains should have an incline to a deeper main drain of sufficient capacity to carry the water readily off to the nearest outlet.   This work should of course be completed before planting is begun, and as drains in woods soon get choked by fallen leaves and branches, and become overgrown at the edges by coarse vegetation, they should be cleaned out at intervals. The general preparation of the land for the raising of plantations from seed is the same generally as for planting, but other operations connected therewith will be more properly dealt with in a future chapter on the subject.

SECTION III.—FENCING.

Fences for plantations are of various descriptions.   On most estates all fences abutting on woods are kept up by the proprietor, and as on many estates the fences extend to many miles, their maintenance is one of the most expensive items connected with the woods.   In German forests there are few or no fences along either wood-roads or highways, or indeed anywhere where they can be dispensed with, and where they do exist they are made chiefly of materials from the forests close by.   The quick thorn hedge is the most popular live fence in this country, sometimes mixed with privet, beech, holly, or elm, but the beech makes the best live fence round woods.   Hedges are, however, going out of favour owing to their cost.   The state in which live fences are generally found after a few years, especially in England, shows great neglect, due mostly to want of time to attend to them.   Such fences get thin and scraggy, owing to the shade cast by the trees, and being left uncut, perhaps for years, they get too high and consequently thin at the bottom, and in many places die off altogether. To mend this state of things, the live portions are slashed and laid anyhow and the gaps made up with stakes, dead brushwood, or bindings, which have to be renewed often. Young live fences also need protection from rabbits by wire-netting, and from cattle by wooden palings, which is another objection to their use. Of all live fences for woods the beech hedge is the best, because it is more easily and quickly got up than a thorn or mixed hedge, endures shade well, is dense and close in winter as well as in summer, as the leaves, though dead, remain on the branches, and it can be grown to a height of twenty or thirty feet without losing its density at the bottom. In some parts of Perth and Forfar the sturdy beech hedges, growing under the almost continuous shade of the hedge-row trees that line the roads there for miles, are a feature. Some of these hedges are very old, but still stout and strong. (See Plate 12.)

The general management of hedges consists in trenching a strip about three feet wide and eighteen inches deep, where the hedge is to be, planting the quicks or beech closely together in the centre of the strip, as forest trees are planted in the nursery (chapter xi.), and afterwards keeping the hedge trimmed by the hedge-bill till it has grown to the desired height. There is no need for a ditch alongside a hedge where the ground is dry or has already been drained, and digging along the bottom of the hedge on the plea of killing weeds should never be allowed. Many of our railway hedges present a sad spectacle from having had their roots mutilated by the spade by annual digging in that way; but some railway hedges are examples of good management, and all are usually planted on the flat on all soils.

The difference in the cost between hedges and wood or iron fences is great. A wire, iron, or wood fence may cost from eightpence to two shillings and sixpence per yard run, and a hedge will cost two shillings and sixpence, including the protecting fence on each side and constant attention, while iron and wood needs little attention except painting with gas tar or pitch at long intervals.

Furze and turf fences are serviceable. A bank of turf, skinned from the land on each side, is thrown up to a height of three or four feet—the base being about three feet wide and the top about one foot. The furze is sown on the top and sides, in furrows or holes, and if protected from cattle and sheep, which eat the furze, a formidable fence is formed in two years, after which browsing does little or no harm but rather helps to keep the furze close and dense.   Turf and furze fences look picturesque, and if the sods be thick and well piled up they last long and need little attention.

Dead fences are constructed of iron, galvanized wire-rope, annealed wire, wood, and stone, and sometimes of iron and wood combined.   They may be ornamental or plain, but plain fences only, for the protection of woods, will be referred to here.   Of iron fences the continuous bar fence is very service-able and strong, and costs about two shillings and sixpence per yard set up.   Strained wire fences are cheaper, while the barbed wire fence is the cheapest of any because it is rarely disturbed by cattle, while bar iron and galvanized wire rope are often bent or slackened by cattle rubbing against them. For iron fences the posts should be of angle iron with strong straining terminals, but oak or larch posts are best for wire fences, and the wire can be nailed to the posts by staples very securely.   The iron fencing business is in the hands of the manufacturers, who supply estimates and usually execute such work.   Wire-rope and annealed wire is supplied cheap, by the hundredweight, and if the wooden posts are provided by the estate, a handy labourer may soon erect a wire fence, which should be about four feet high, tightly strained and stayed, with the strands put on close enough to stop sheep and lambs. Barbed wire fences should be erected in the same manner. The objections to barbed wire disappear to a great extent where it is only applied to fences against plantations, and there can be no doubt about it being the most effective barrier against cattle ever yet invented.   Cattle and horses soon get acquainted with it, and one or two strands put along the top of a weak fence will often make it as strong as the strongest at the cost of about one penny per yard.   In the writer's experience of barbed wire on an extensive scale against woods, very few accidents, and these slight, have occurred to cattle from it; while accidents are frequent with smooth wire fences, owing to cattle getting their legs over the wires and their heads through between the strands.   Such accidents rarely happen with barbed wire, because the first prick drives the animal off. Both barbed and annealed wire fences of a cheap but effectual description are now very common in Scotland everywhere. In fact, the extent to which barbed wire is now used by farmers and others is sufficient evidence of its utility and harmlessness. The various kinds of wire fences look light, and if the posts, when of wood, are painted a dull green, they are practically invisible against a wood, a little way off, and allow the natural margin of the wood to be seen. On some estates, within recent times, many miles of hedges in parks have been removed and invisible wire fences substituted with excellent effect.

The dry stone-wall fence makes a good durable fence for a plantation, and if the first cost is considerable, it is perhaps the cheapest in the end where stone is readily procurable. From a landscape point of view, however, they are even more objectionable than hedges. In all cases the regular " dry-waller " should be employed by contract in the erection of such fences, as an unskilled hand cannot do such work properly. The cost of such fences depends on the suitability of the stone employed, the distance it has to be brought, and the rate of wages paid in the locality.

Wooden fences or pailings are of various kinds, but for the protection of plantations only, the fence may be plain and made out of the most suitable timber on the estate, or such as can be got at the nearest timber yard or saw mill, where fencing materials are usually in stock, the railway companies using great quantities of such materials. Larch or oak make the best fence, and the one or the other should be used for the posts at least. Scotch fir or spruce will do for the rails, which should be about four-and-a-half inches wide and one-and-a-half inches thick. The top rail should be about four feet from the ground, and the others should be close enough to each other to prevent lambs getting through. This is the common Scotch pailing, consisting of stout riven or sawn stakes driven firmly into the ground and a continuous bar nailed to them. Whatever kind of fence is employed to protect plantations, they should be set up at a sufficient distance from the trees to prevent cattle and horses from reaching them.

SECTION IV.—ROADS.

Good roads increase the value of plantations because of the facilities they afford for the removal of timber, always the heaviest item of expense in disposing of timber, and generally borne by the vendor, because it must come off the price in the wood. " Easy to get away " is always a recommendation to a sale of timber and one the vendor rarely omits in a notice of sale. Forest roads should be laid out not more than two hundred or three hundred yards apart in extensive woods, and in a direction to afford the easiest and quickest means of exit to road or rail. Access should also be provided, as far as practicable, to interesting spots and pleasant prospects; but in a hilly or undulating country the main roads should, as far as possible, be laid out in easy gradients with a continuous ascent to the highest parts of the forest, and not in the uphill and downhill way so often seen on estates. Highways and railways usually traverse the lower slopes of hills, or the valleys, and the advantage of having forest roads laid out as described is that timber waggons go *up* empty and come *down* loaded. Alternating steep ascents and descents greatly lengthen a journey and add enormously to the cost of haulage and road repairs. Horses have, of course to be employed in hauling timber, and in Yorkshire, where this work is well understood, six horses are, as a rule, employed to draw two waggons, each waggon usually carrying from two to three tons of timber, or from eighty to one hundred and twenty cubic feet. The reason of so many horses being required is generally the uneven nature of the roads and their being laid out in the wrong place, as, for example, when a road through a wooded valley traverses, with many ups and downs, the hillside half-way between its summit and its base, instead of the bottom of the valley. In a situation of this kind the timber from the underside of the road has to be dragged up from the ravine to the road by heavy tackling of blocks and pulleys attached to standing trees, which are often injured thereby. Work like this takes up much time, is arduous and expensive, and very trying to horses. Then when the waggons are loaded and despatched, one has to be unyoked at every incline and the six horses attached to one waggon to pull it to the top, and then unyoked again to return for the second waggon, and so on, as often as may be necessary. The road gets torn up also by the horses' feet in the ascent and ploughed up by the slipper or brake in the descent, entailing extensive road repairs. In Germany, on the Hartz Mountains, the roads have, as far as practicable, a continuous winding ascent, and the trees are not dragged up to the roads, but are slid down to them and loaded on to timber waggons drawn by oxen—the loads equalling those drawn by the same number of horses in England, only the road being downhill the work is easy.

Shooting rides we have elsewhere recommended to be twelve feet wide, but main wood-roads should not be less than sixteen feet wide, in order to allow vehicles to pass each other, and they should have a twenty-four-inch deep drain at each side on soft or retentive land. Main roads do not require to be deeply macadamised, as heavy traffic is not frequent on them, and experience shows that the traffic is almost where the horses and the wheels travel. Breadth of wheel makes much difference to the traffic. No heavily laden vehicles should be allowed on wood-roads or ˏdrives with wheels on which the tyres are less than six inches wide, and nine inches is necessary on heavy, soft lands. Much road mending will also be saved by judicious management in seeing that advantage is taken of frosty and dry weather to remove timber. Road-metal, consisting of rough cinders or broken stones, should be spread principally on the wheel track, and particularly in the wheel ruts. In time the traffic will harden the track, and when it does get cut up the ruts are soon filled in and rolled smooth, becoming green and pleasant again in a short time.

In addition to main roads, narrow paths or shoots should be left in the plantation communicating with the main roads, where men and horses can enter to drag felled timber out from where it has been felled. Good or large trees should not be cut merely to facilitate their easy removal, but only when too heavy to be removed otherwise ; and care should be taken to cut in judicious lengths so as not to spoil the timber for the consumer's purpose.

CHAPTER IX.

SEASON TO PLANT FOREST TREES.

Conifera—Hardwoods.

SECTION I.—CONIFERA.

No question connected with forestry has exercised the minds of foresters and their employers more than this. Which is the best season for transplanting—spring or autumn—has been a much debated subject. The vague meaning generally attached to the terms "spring" and "autumn," the frequent failures at all seasons, often from causes not attributable to the seasons at all, and the mistake of treating evergreen and deciduous species alike, has been at the bottom of much of the difference of opinion that exists. Writing on this subject in his "Theory and Practice of Horticulture," and on the failures and successes of planters, Dr. Lindley says that transplanting is too generally practised as an empirical art and taught dogmatically. "One hardly knows," he observes, "how to draw any other conclusion from the opposite opinions held by planters, and the dogmatical manner in which they are too often expressed." In discussing the planting of evergreen and deciduous trees, Lindley lays stress on the fact that excessive evaporation from the foliage, thereby overtaxing the mutilated roots and causing the plant to wither up and die, is the chief danger to be feared—quoting with approval from McNab the words "half a day's sun in the spring and autumn will do more harm immediately after planting than a whole week's sun from morning to night in the middle of winter." The reply to the last argument is, that experience has shown that the sun of autumn and spring is infinitely preferable to the cold of winter, for all kinds of conifers at least. Foresters hitherto have generally recommended the months of November, December, February, March, and April, which, with the exceptions of April and the end of March, are the worst months in the whole year. All the species of conifera may be transplanted at the same season, but the species usually grown for timber in this country are not numerous, and the best season to plant any of them is undoubtedly the autumn, from August till the end of October, and what cannot be got out during these months should be held over till April and May. In the south, planting may be begun in March. The month of August is early, some may think, but it must be remembered that where large areas have to be planted it is necessary to begin as soon as possible. The only objection to planting in August or September is the condition of the soil. If it be sufficiently moist to work it will do, and there is little fear of failure. We have purposely tested autumn, winter, and spring planting on a large scale and often, both in the nursery and in the woods, and we have recommended autumn and late spring planting to nurserymen and foresters who have tried it, and their experience has been the same as our own, viz., that these two seasons are by far the most favourable, and winter, from November to March, the worst. Some of the pines, like the Corsican fir and *Pinus pinaster*, are bad transplanters—the first-named especially, which often dies off wholesale, and always fails to a greater or lesser extent when planted at the dead seasons of the year, just as the common holly does; but in early autumn, or late in spring, it is quite equal to the Scotch fir as a transplanter, and the Scotch fir is one of the best, although it too fails at times. Danger of excessive evaporation from the foliage in autumn and spring is not so great as Dr. Lindley seems to think. We have repeatedly transplanted large breadths of Scotch, Corsican, and Austrian firs in the home nursery, throughout the whole of May, and sometimes far into June, when the young shoots were from two to three inches long and very soft and tender, and lost hardly any plants. The young leaves and side shoots became limp and drooped for a few days, but one good watering as the rows were planted was sufficient to tide them over the first few days, when all danger was over. Some of the Edinburgh nurserymen who saw our stock annually have repeated our experiments on a larger scale with the most satisfactory results. Large plants, two years transplanted, will move equally well at the same season provided the roots are well "puddled" at planting or watered afterwards. Very early or very late removal from the nursery to the open land is not, however, to be recommended if the ground be dry, as watering extensive young plantations is out of the question unless labour is plentiful. It was our experience in late spring

planting that first led us to begin a month earlier, in autumn,
soil conditions being favourable.   It is well known that the
soft young shoots and leaves of firs and other evergreens
suffer far more severely from drought and evaporation than do
the older leaves, and we concluded that if young plants started
into tender growth could stand moving and resist the bright
sunshine and drought of May, the more mature plants of
August and September would transplant equally well or better,
and it was found that they did so.   Our guide, therefore, now,
is not dates, but the condition of the current season's growth.
If the terminal shoots have ceased to lengthen and have
plumped their buds they may be transplanted in August, or
even earlier, with every prospect of success, always provided
that the soil is workable and moist, or that watering is practicable.   Of course, pit-planting only should be the method
adopted in the woods, and the pits should be made as the
planting goes on.   There is no advantage whatever in digging
the pits long beforehand ; the soil is never in better condition
than when newly turned up for planting all kinds of plants.
Gardeners have long acted in this belief.   The main advantage
of early autumn planting is that the plants get established
before winter and make a good growth the following year ;
whereas in winter and early spring planting those that survive
make hardly any growth, only expanding their buds but
remaining practically at a standstill for one whole year.   This
loss of a year's growth, during which there is no increment to
the stem, means more than might be supposed.   It will be
apparent that whether the tree be planted in autumn or the
spring following, the ensuing summer's growth will be the
first year's growth in either case ; hence by planting in
autumn, and getting the trees established before winter, a
season's growth is gained the first year, against none by
planting in the spring.   Supposing a tree to contain one
hundred cubic feet at the end of one hundred years, when
felled and sold, that would represent an average annual increment to the stem of one cubic foot.   But if the tree stood still
one year, the first year, instead of adding to its growth, the
actual growing period of the tree's life would be ninety-nine
years, the contents of the stem proportionately less, and the
loss in money over an extensive plantation might be represented by hundreds or perhaps thousands of pounds.   This
question of increment is much more intelligently studied on
the Continent than with us, as in the case of large areas it
is perceived that anything tending to check the regular pro-

gress of growth assumes importance. The older and larger a tree gets the greater the ratio of annual increment. In the earlier stages of growth the increment is fractional, by comparison, with that added in the later stages of the tree's life, and which may then amount to several cubic feet every year. For example, a tree trunk forty-five feet long, the quarter girth of which is eighteen inches, contains 101 feet 3 in. 0 pa.; but if in one year the quarter-girth of the tree increases one quarter-of-an-inch, the bulk rises to 104 feet 0 inches 11 pa., and that is only a moderate increase. We have seen sections of the Douglas fir, oaks, and other trees showing a very much larger annual increase than the above; and Dr. Lindley states in his "Theory and Practice" that the annual rate of growth of oaks on the Duke of Wellington's estate, computed in tenths of an inch, was ten, which in a large tree means many cubic feet annually. Some may think that it is superfluous to mention facts like these, which should be known to all practical men, but it is a fact that they are not sufficiently realised by owners of woods, or the valuation, for sale, of standing timber made one year would not be held to be sufficient for several years to come, as has often happened. It is well known that the period allowed on estates to purchasers to clear lots off the ground depends on the size of the lots; and we have known six years granted, where there was nothing urgent, the purchaser paying cash down at the beginning, but trusting to the increment gained during the time to pay interest and also compensate him for incidental expenses connected with felling and hauling, etc.

When autumn planting cannot be carried out, then spring is the next best season, extending from March till the end of May, provided the soil is sufficiently moist. Even so late as May, with trees that have been transplanted the previous year, or two years before, there should be few failures if the roots are well puddled and pit planting is adopted, taking out the pits as the work proceeds.

In any case, none of the conifera tribe should be planted after the first, or at the latest, the second week in November, nor between that period and the middle of March. This period is condemned alike by the theorist and the experienced forester. The roots of evergreens are said never to be quite inactive, even in winter, but for all practical purposes growth is at a standstill in the case of plants lifted with mutilated roots and transplanted in winter, and it is well known that by far the greatest losses are sustained under such conditions.

SECTION II.—DECIDUOUS OR HARD-WOOD TREES.

These are much more easily dealt with in transplanting
than conifers, there being next to nothing to fear from excessive evaporation after the fall of the leaf, and between that
period and the expansion of the buds in the spring, nearly all
the hard-woods may be transplanted in mild open weather ;
but autumn is the best season, for the same reasons as those
given in the case of conifers, viz., that the trees get established
before winter sets in and make a much better start in spring.
The fall of the leaf is usually given as the proper time to begin
planting, but where much work has to be done, planting may
begin weeks before the leaves fall from the trees.　　There
may be as much as a month's difference in the time of the
general fall of the leaf, one year with another, so much depends
on the weather.　　The real test of the fitness of the trees for
removal is the hardness and maturity of the current year's
wood, and these conditions exist long before the leaves fall.
We have transplanted deciduous species successfully in large
quantities while the leaves were still green, in autumn, the
leaves usually turning yellow and falling off soon after planting.
We refer to this matter more particularly because the " fall of
the leaf " is the guide usually given by foresters for
beginning planting operations, and it means useless delay, as
most of our deciduous trees often retain their leaves till
November, and some, like the oak, even till the middle of
that month, or later.　　Gardeners have long disregarded this
rule, and often transplant without risk large deciduous fruit
and other trees in early autumn while the leaves are still green,
and severe root pruning operations are often begun in July
and August.　　The advantages of transplanting or root pruning
early in the autumn, before the fall of the leaf, are demonstrated by the fact that the fruit trees so treated will often bear
a crop of fruit the following season—a thing which rarely or
never happens after winter or spring planting or root pruning.

CHAPTER X.

THE HOME NURSERY.

Advantages.—Stocking.

SECTION I.—ADVANTAGES.

ON all large estates where planting is carried on a nursery is necessary for economical and other reasons, the most weighty of which are that the trees can be prepared more cheaply in the home nursery and transplanted from there to their final quarters far more successfully than they can be from a distant nursery. Without attaching blame to nurserymen, who are, as a rule, anxious to serve their customers well, it is a fact, that the percentage of failures in young plantations is much greater with trees direct from a public nursery than it is when the trees are moved from the home nursery to the woods. The reason of this is that in the latter case the planting can be begun at almost any day or hour when the weather is favourable, that the trees can be more carefully lifted, need not be long out of the ground, and suffer but little check from a change of soil or climate. Trees from a distant nursery, and probably different soil, on the other hand, may be days out of the ground and exposed before being delivered, and may have to lie for weeks after that only "sheughed" in by the heels should snow or frost come and suspend planting operations. Nor is the lifting of the trees always done so carefully as at home, and from any of these causes failure may result. Many planters are, however, obliged to buy from the nurseryman, and when that is the case the purchaser should see to the careful lifting of the trees and their speedy delivery to his own care. It is not the price of the trees, in the catalogue, that affects the cost of planting so much as the losses sustained after the trees are planted. A word must, however, be said for the nurseryman here, because it is not by any means his fault always that the trees fail. There is much competition in the trade, and the wonder is that trees of the size and quality usually supplied can be turned out at such moderate prices. In fact, on small estates a home nursery is not necessary when satisfactory arrangements can be made with the nurseryman, so far as cost is concerned, and no doubt public nurseries will continue to supply a very large proportion of the forest trees planted in this country, especially broad-leaved deciduous species, which are much more easily and safely handled than the fir and pine species.   The losses sustained among broad-leaved stock are often great, because, even when frequently transplanted, they grow up quickly, and becoming crowded in the rows, numbers of the weaker plants perish ; whereas, trees from a public nursery can be had as they are required of a suitable size for planting out in the woods at once.   The main danger to conifers got from a distant nursery is injury from exposure and delay between the lifting of the plants and their delivery to the buyer, and the remedy for this is to give orders in good time, and, where practicable, to see them executed.   Nurserymen are always pleased to afford every facility in that way to customers.

The home nursery should be large enough to hold a sufficient stock of trees of the species intended to be used on the estate, and which should always be coming on in successional batches from one year's seedlings up to the planting-out stage, which is from two to four years of age, as a rule, according to the kind of ground to be planted and the species. The position of the nursery should be open and exposed on all sides except the north, as young trees removed from a sheltered spot to the open country, or perhaps a bleak hillside, suffer a severe check and often die outright.   The mere removal from the sheltering nursery lines, though the nursery may be exposed, is of itself always trying to young trees the first year.   Coddling of the trees in any form should be avoided.

SECTION II.—STOCKING.

As regards the stocking of the nursery, it is hardly worth the forester's while to raise his comparatively small quantities of the commoner trees from seed, because he can purchase first year's seedlings better and cheaper than he can raise them at home.   The nursery trade know this, and not a few of our large nurseries are supplied in this way by other nurserymen whose speciality is raising seedlings for the trade.   These one-year seedlings, which, in the pine class, are very small, and in the broad-leaved species only two or three inches high, can be quickly lifted and delivered anywhere with little, or no risk, and very few need fail in the nursery lines. The commoner species cost from about two shillings and sixpence to five shillings, and scarcer species about seven shillings and sixpence per thousand. At this rate a home nursery can soon be stocked, but unless the forester has gauged his wants pretty accurately, he may in two or three years' time find himself in possession of more stock than he can handle and get out in due course, and the trees then get above the planting-out size and become useless. Frequent transplanting will, of course, keep the trees in check and fit for moving, but every time the trees are handled in this way, before they go to their final destination in the woods, adds to their cost. For this reason the nursery should be roomy, so as to avoid crowding, which is the chief danger in home nurseries, particularly where those in charge are not familiar with nursery work. Where the room is limited, preference should be given, as before stated, to the pine class, as these are the most difficult to deal with, and the deciduous species may be bought from the public nursery. Young forest trees of the same kind, in nursery quarters, do not all grow at the same rate, and when the plants become thick in the row, and the rows are near to each other, the weaker trees are smothered and die out before the rows can be transplanted. One half of the stock may be lost in this way in a short while. The ash, alder, sycamore, and other broad-leaved species suffer in this way, as the second year after planting in the nursery the strongest seedlings will often make growths from three to five feet long, and, overtopping the weaker trees at an early stage, the latter make no headway and finally perish. The writer has seen what appeared to be a fine even quarter of ash or sycamore, when lifted, reveal losses from smothering to the extent of nearly thirty per cent. Such losses can only be prevented by giving the plants the room they require. It is not the crowding of the plants in the row that does the mischief so much as the crowding of the rows so closely together that the tops of the strongest trees meet and exclude the light from the weaker ones. At all stages the rows should stand clear of each other so that the light may reach the ground between them. The weaklings at the bottom of the rows will then receive sufficient light to keep them alive till the next transplanting, when the tall and the short plants should be separated.

9

The main objects to be kept in view in a home nursery of forest trees are, not to overcrowd it with more stock than can be handled in time ; not to have too many trees of any one species ; to keep up a regular succession of all the species to be used on the estate from one year's seedlings to the final transplanting stage ; to keep the rows clear of each other ; and to transplant, or severely root-prune with the spade, every two years at least, all those trees that are intended to go out to form plantations. The transplanting of nursery stock, the object of which is to keep the roots in check, is expensive work, but we find that the same end can be as successfully attained by simply cutting in the roots with a spade in spring or autumn. This work, if done carefully, is far more expeditious than transplanting, and few or no trees die. Two men, one on each side of the same row, should go opposite each other and insert their spades, a few inches from the trees, in a slightly slanting direction, on each side of the row, till their spades meet beneath the row ; then, pressing down the handle, the trees should be given a hitch up till the roots are heard or felt to give, and that is enough. Afterwards a man may go along the row with a foot on each side and press the loosened soil slightly down again. Corsican firs, which could not have been transplanted without loss, we have often treated in this way with complete success. The advantage of the plan is that the roots are checked without being mutilated or exposed, and when the trees are transplanted the following autumn or spring the roots are a fibrous mass close to the stem.

The instructions given here are general only, because it is presumed that where an estate is large enough to require a home nursery the forester will understand the ordinary details of nursery work. We may add, that the quarters of the nursery should be large and the roads and paths roomy and convenient. The main points are not to over-stock nor neglect transplanting and cleaning.

In Germany the nurseries are very unpretentious affairs, situated here and there in the forests where they are wanted, and are kept clean and in good order—the trees never being allowed to get large before they are put out. Such small plots are soon made in any small clearing, and fenced round with the materials at hand, and, as regards efficiency and usefulness, often surpass expensively laid out and injudiciously stocked nurseries on private estates in this country.

CHAPTER XI.

RAISING PLANTATIONS BY SOWING

AND PLANTING.

Forest Tree Seeds.—Sources of Supply.—Collecting.—Storage.—Germination.
—Sowing —Methods of Sowing.—Planting.—Size and Age of Plants.—
Nursery Preparation.—The Wrong Way.—The Right Way.—Final Trans-
planting.—Notch Planting.—Pit Planting.—Dibber and Trowel Planting.—
Tending.—Cost of Planting.—Planting uneven-aged Woods.—Extending
Plantations from Thinnings. — Transplanting Large Trees.— Sea-side
Planting.

SECTION I.—FOREST TREE SEEDS.

FOR the portion of this chapter devoted to sources of supply,
collecting, storing, and germination, etc., we are indebted to
the able paper on "Forest Tree Seeds," delivered by Mr. W.
H. Massie (of the well-known firm of Messrs. Dickson & Co.,
seedsmen and nurserymen, Edinburgh), to foresters and
gardeners, at the Royal Botanic Gardens, Edinburgh, in 1895.
The subject embraced under these headings has not been fully
treated hitherto in forestry books, but is sure to assume
importance should any comprehensive system of forestry ever
be adopted in this country.

SECTION II.—SOURCES OF SUPPLY.

"Speaking broadly," says Mr. Massie, "there are few
quarters of the globe from which seeds of some species of our
forest trees do not come, but it will suit our purpose to glance
shortly at those countries where the forest tree seed trade
forms a not unimportant branch of commerce. Chief among
these is Germany. The Germans not only collect tree seeds
in large quantities in their own extensive forests, but through
the enterprise of their merchants and their improved methods
of cleaning they draw to themselves large supplies in the rough
condition from other countries in Europe, such as Austria,
Norway and Sweden, etc., and become the distributors to the
rest of the world; so that from Germany almost every variety
of forest tree seeds can be had—Hamburg and Erfurt being

the chief depots of distribution. France collects on a smaller scale than Germany, but is the principal source of such species as oak, Spanish chestnut, hazel, maritime pine, broom, turze, etc.   Italy is also now collecting considerable quantities of the seeds of many of the firs and rarer pines, and America sends Douglas fir seeds and a few other species, while Japan sends not only seeds of larch and many pines, but also a greater variety of shrubs than can be had from any other source. Our home supplies are, however, to us, for good reasons, the most important.   In Scotland we can procure seeds of every variety of the common forest trees, if in some cases to a limited extent, owing to unfavourable seasons.   The principal collecting districts seem to have been fixed, not because the best and largest extent of certain trees are found there, but because collectors once set agoing with one special article naturally extend their operations to other species for which there is a demand.   Scotch fir and larch come principally from Perth, Forfar, Inverness, Moray, Ross and Deeside; and deciduous species come principally from Perth, Moray, and Dumfriesshire.   From England we get our best acorns, chestnuts, beech, and such like."

SECTION III.—COLLECTING TREE SEEDS.

Where seeds are produced in sufficient quantities to make gathering a paying business there are professional collectors who go about their work in a systematic way, and the work is often of a hazardous nature, as the collectors have to climb the trees to their highest points and hook in the branches and gather the seeds the best way they can.   In Germany, where the trees stand more closely together, the collector frequently swings himself from one tree to another, like a squirrel, and thus saves himself the labour of descending and climbing up again.   Seeds of deciduous trees and such as shed their seeds on the ground are, of course, more easily collected.   It is of the highest importance that seed should be only collected from healthy trees, but intense competition has had the effect of driving collectors to the trees where the seeds are most numerous and most easily procured and often of inferior quality.   It is a recognised fact that an excessive crop of seed, especially on young trees, is a sure sign of weakness or ill-health.   If it be so important for the gardener and farmer to select his seeds with care, how much more important should it be for the forester to do so in the case of crops that take perhaps a hundred years to come to maturity.

SECTION IV.—STORAGE.

Airy lofts and cool, dry cellars and sheds are required for this purpose, but the seeds of some species are best kept in pits or in heaps in the open air. The greater part of our forest tree seeds endure severe frost without injury, but there are exceptions, and those are such as retain much moisture, like the acorn, chestnut, and beech, which are rendered useless by ten or twelve degrees of frost, hence require protection, but should be kept cool and not too dry. Seeds of species that have sometimes to be kept for several years, like the larch and Scotch fir, are best stored in their cones when those have been dried. In this way the seeds retain their vitality unimpaired for years, which enables seedsmen to take advantage of a fine season and fine crop of sound seed. Cases have been known of Scotch fir cones having been found in a peat moss several feet below the surface, the seed from which produced healthy plants. Fleshy seeds of the nature of the hawthorn and holly are best kept in pits covered with straw ; after they have been turned several times and fermentation has subsided.

SECTION V.—GERMINATION.

Germination depends on the seeds being well-matured and carefully handled and cleaned. Not only the value of the seed but the thickness at which to sow depends on the percentage of good seed in any sample. The usual mode of testing the seed is to grow them, but in many experiments I have made I have come as near the mark by cutting and examining the seeds as by growing, and the latter is by far the most expeditious method. Other things being equal, large and fully developed seeds invariably produce the strongest and healthiest plants.

Mr. Massie makes the following interesting remarks about the larch also :—" Of the common larch there are several varieties, among which we find two well-defined varieties distinguished by the colour of their catkins, which are red in one and white in the other. The red prevails among the older larches in Scotland, and all the finest specimens of the tree throughout this country are of the red flowered variety, while the produce of imported seed from the Tyrol and Germany are found to be, to a large extent, of the white variety. Observation has also shown that the red is the hardiest variety, and it has been repeatedly found that the produce of the white variety fail to ripen their tops in time to resist early frosts in autumn. The Scotch-saved seed of the white variety also produces plants of a less hardy constitution than is produced by seed from the red variety."

SECTION VI.—SOWING PLANTATIONS.

It is undoubtedly by far the best plan to raise plantations from seed sown direct on the spot wherever the ground and natural vegetation will permit that to be done. It is incomparably the quickest and the cheapest plan, and trees raised from seed where they are to grow acquire a hold of the ground that transplanted trees never do, and are hence much less liable to be blown down. The conditions favourable to sowing are, however, exceptional in this country, hence planting is resorted to as a rule. No doubt all our old British forests were naturally produced from seed, just as great tracts of forest on the Continent of Europe are now, and no doubt, like the latter, they were dense and unlike our " cultivated " woods and plantations of the present day. Practically, little or no natural regeneration goes on in our British woods because the conditions are unfavourable, the underwood and rank undergrowth being too dense and thick to permit seedlings growing up. It is a well-known fact, at anyrate, that in what are considered fairly well managed woods of broad-leaved and conifera species, mixed or pure, that seed freely, the natural seedlings are very scantily produced, hence the common practice of replanting thin old woods with transplants from the nursery. The seeds of a number of species are shed abundantly, and vegetate, but the young plants perish in the struggle with the coarse natural herbage and weeds during the first and second years of their existence, or, if they do get up, it is only in scattered patches where the surface is favourable. The common bracken is one of the worst enemies of young forest trees and everything else, as wherever it abounds in unbroken tracts it kills even the grasses. We know of extensive woods where the bracken has done this, and where even sturdy transplanted forest trees, eighteen inches to two feet high, are smothered and killed by it unless it is beaten down for a year or two at the beginning. These are the obstacles to reproduction by seed at the present time, but they would to a large extent disappear under a proper system of rotation and culture, as on the Continent, where such unfavourable conditions do not exist to the same extent, the forests being comparatively free from undergrowth and the surface of the ground in a receptive condition for the seed. It is, however, in the beech forests that natural reproduction is most relied upon, planting being resorted to extensively in the case of firs wherever sowing is doubtful. These remarks refer more particularly to land already under timber, but getting thin or approaching a final clear cut. Seed may be sown on the natural surface wherever the vegetation is thin or scant and not likely to choke the young seedlings—as, for example, on sandy commons, moors, or mountains where there is only heather or thin grass—if the heather has been burned not long before all the better. Heath does not smother young seedlings as coarse grasses and weeds do, even when it is rank and tall, and we should not hesitate to sow amongst it at high altitudes in preference to planting. A large per centage of forest tree seeds germinate, and, with the exception of the mast bearers, like the oak, chestnut and beech, one pound of seed represents an enormous number of seeds, and the price per pound is not great. In fact, a forester can buy his tree seeds cheaper from a respectable seedsman than he can gather them himself, except in the case of easily procured sorts, like the oak, beech, or sycamore, etc. The season to sow tree seeds is from October till May, but spring sowing is usually preferred, by nurserymen, at least. On private estates, however, where the purpose is to sow the plantations direct, we would advise sowing in autumn, or as soon as new seed can be got, using plenty of seed to make up for losses from birds and vermin. Except in skilled hands, keeping tree seeds for any length of time is difficult. They are apt to germinate prematurely or to lose vitality unless preserved under proper conditions, as described elsewhere in this chapter.

SECTION VII.—METHODS OF SOWING.

Nature scatters the seed broadcast on the ground, where it is beaten into the soil and surface vegetation by the snow and rain, germinating, even in the case of large seeds, like the acorn, though barely covered. In artificial sowing, however, nature can be improved upon by making the seeds go further by regular distribution, and covering them sufficiently to quicken germination and protect them from exposure to the weather and vermin.   Assuming that the ground is suitable for sowing, as described above, light seeds, like the birch and alder, for example, may be scattered broadcast, but larger seeds, down to the size of a small pea, like some of the pine tree seeds, may be planted in twos and threes together by hand, pressing the seed just into the surface and no more, except in the case of the larger species, like the oak, the acorn of which should be buried.   For smaller seeds, on a grassy surface, little more than contact with the soil is needed, as the grassy covering will afford sufficient protection.   Far more danger arises from burying too deeply than from not covering at all.   In planting tree seeds, by hand, a few men can soon go over much ground.   The men starting in a line, about one yard apart, with the outside row set out with flags, as a guide, at each end of the line, one or two seeds should be deposited at every step or thereabout, until one section is finished, then the line of men wheeling round again takes up another section, and so on till the ground is sown.   In filling up vacant spaces in woods the ground should first be cleared of all rank surface vegetation by mowing or burning strips about one foot broad and three feet apart, dug by the spade, and on these the seed should be sown thinly in shallow furrows.   Such strips are afterwards easily found and kept free from weeds, and should the seedlings come up too thickly they can be thinned out and transplanted to make up deficiencies elsewhere.   Sometimes, in re-planting ground from which a crop of timber has been removed, expensive preparations are made in preparing the ground by stubbing up the old roots and trenching, etc., which is, no doubt, beneficial to the next crop of trees, but in this country such work is very expensive, and we doubt if it be worth the trouble, while it is quite certain that many old woods have been re-sown or re-planted where numerous old stools were left in the ground without any harm resulting.   In such cases a change of crop, as regards the species, may be advisable, but as much that trees take out of the soil is restored to it again in the fallen foliage, even a change is not urgent.   In forming plantations by sowing on good land the ground is sometimes ploughed, cleaned, and fallowed, and sometimes even steam ploughed, previous to sowing, but we do not think such expensive preparations are necessary, seeing how well both seedlings and plants thrive on poor ground that has never been subjected to any preparatory treatment.   It is, perhaps, better to plant even good land than to sow it, but if sowing is desired it is only needful to plough a couple of furrows, where the rows are to be, and sow on these. Two furrows are turned over and the seed is sown in the shallow furrow formed where the second sod laps over upon the first. The seed may be then covered in with the back of a rake, and the work is finished. The first year weeds will not be troublesome, but in the second and third years the rows should be looked over and the grass and other herbage pushed off the young trees so as to give them light. We much prefer this plan to sowing broadcast.

SECTION VIII.—PLANTING. SIZE AND AGE OF THE PLANTS.

Where any doubt exists about sowing, recourse must be had to planting properly prepared young trees of a suitable size. The younger the trees are the less they cost to buy or raise and to plant, and the better they succeed, but the same objection applies to very small plants that applies to sowing seed, viz., their inability to struggle successfully against coarse weeds and tall grass, etc., during the first year or two. For this reason, established plants, from three to four years of age or thereabout, that have been transplanted at least every two years, and which are from one foot to twenty inches high, are usually preferred. Young (one or two-year-old) seedlings cost from two shillings and sixpence to seven shillings and sixpence per thousand, and may be planted by the dibber or trowel, under the conditions before described as suitable for seed, and with every prospect of success, but not otherwise. Such trees, though not usually transplanted, move safely and suffer but little check, but not so trees above that age— pines more particularly. Hence the practice, in all good nurseries, of transplanting every second, or at most every third year, in order to check luxuriant growth and keep the roots short and bushy, so that when the trees are finally removed to the woods they make a good start. If transplanting has been neglected failures may be expected. Of course, frequent transplanting adds to the price of the trees, and in justice to respectable nurserymen who transplant their stock frequently, it should be stated that when plants of large size are offered much under the market price it may be suspected that transplanting has been neglected and that the trees may prove dear to the purchaser on that account. Thirty shillings

per thousand is about the average price
for trees from three to five years of age.
As has been said before, preparatory
transplanting in the nursery is of most
importance in the case of the conifera
species, because all of them are more
sensitive to removal than the broad-leaved
species that grow quickly, even after
transplanting, and may be cut down to
the ground without injury, while young
conifers cannot be so treated. Any competent gardener or forester can tell, by
their appearance, if forest trees have been
transplanted as often as required, because
such trees are short and sturdy for their
age and much shorter jointed both in
stem and branch than trees of the same
age that have not been moved, and which
are usually tall and spindly, with long,
straggling roots. A Scotch fir, for
example, five years of age, that has never
been transplanted, will usually be twice
the height of one that has. Moreover,
there is a right and a wrong way of transplanting in the nursery that should be
here described for the benefit of the
planter.

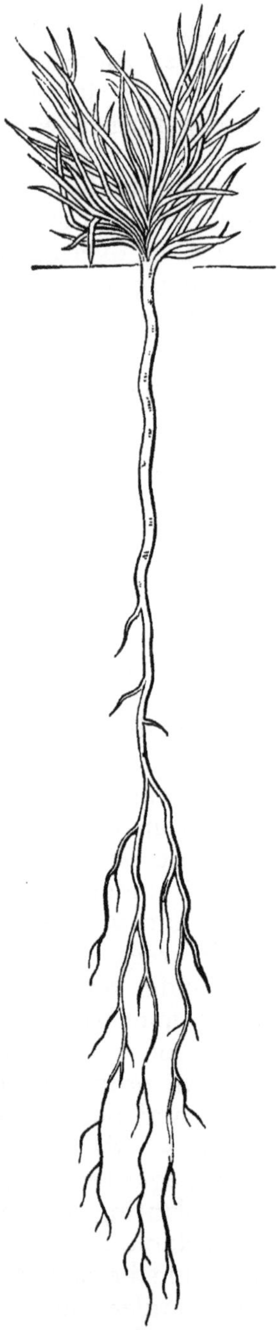

SECTION IX.—NURSERY PREPARATION.

THE WRONG WAY.

This method is, we believe, confined
to Great Britain, and is condemned by
Continental foresters as thoroughly bad
in principle. Whether the method
originated with the nurserymen or the
foresters we cannot say, but it is extensively practised by both, and as it lends
itself to the bad "notch" system of
planting out, it may be favoured on that
account. Figures will best illustrate our
meaning as regards right and wrong

Fig. 1. One Year's Seedling.
Corsican Fir.

methods of preparation. Figure 1 is a
portrait of a one-year-old Corsican fir, and is fairly representa-
tive of the conifera generally, and hard-woods also.

In all seedling forest trees the tap-root dives straight down into the earth, if it can get, and is much longer than the top of the tree. Figure 1 is a fair example. It is six inches long from the top of the tuft of leaves to the extremity of the root, and one inch at least was lost in the lifting—the root being actually six inches longer than the top. The second year the disproportion increases, the top usually developing a short node of leaves of the normal size, while the tap-root will often be eighteen inches long and the tendency still downwards. After this the disparity decreases rapidly; but the tree has got a hold of the ground that the transplanted tree never acquires. In hard-woods the roots of young trees go much deeper. In a permeable soil we have seen two-year-old seedling oaks with perfectly straight tap-roots four feet long when the tree tops did not exceed fifteen inches in height. At the end of the second year the young plant, Figure 1, would, in the usual course, be transplanted, and have its long maiden root shortened considerably. In the usual transplanting operation, an L-shaped furrow is made in the soil, against a tightly-stretched line, and in this furrow

GROUND LINE.

the young plant, by the wrong method, Fig. 2, is set with the lower portion of its roots bent outwards at right angles to the upper portion, and corresponding with the section of the furrow; the root is then covered in, and so on with all the plants in the row, and every row, all the roots in the plot pointing in the same direction. When the tree is lifted the second time, perhaps two years later, to be again transplanted, the root has lost its natural shape, and become permanently " set " in the form in which it was bent in the furrow. This goes on for several years till the tree is old enough to go out, when it becomes like Fig. 3—another portrait of a Corsican fir from among a number of the same shape in a large nursery

Fig. 2. Section of Furrow.
Wrong Way. Nursery Transplanting.

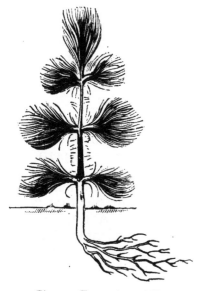

Fig. 3. Transplanted Tree.
Wrong Root Form.

quarter. The tree cannot now be easily planted with its roots in a natural position, and, as a matter of fact, that is not attempted in notch planting, the roots being simply drawn under the sod at a right angle with top in the position they have been trained in the nursery.

Judging from the vast quantities of young forest trees of this shape that have been turned out in the past, we should say that a very large proportion of English, Scotch and Irish plantations have been furnished with plants prepared in this way. It is a practice solely confined to forestry, as gardeners never practise any other method of planting than that of inserting tap-roots straight down into the soil, and, in the case of trees desired to root near the surface, of spreading the roots regularly out in a circle equally round the stem. Professor Schlich, in his " Manual of Forestry," vol. xi., p. 113, speaking of raising plants for sylvicultural purposes on this one-sided plan, says, " the result is that the plants develop a lop-sided root ;" that " it may be easier to put out such plants, but the system is certainly not favourable to the development of the trees grown from them." He had " observed that in many cases trees thirty to forty years old had not yet established a normal root system, and that numerous trees are blown down for this very reason." This subject has also been referred to long since in the horticultural papers, and more than forty years ago, Lindley, in his " Theory and Practice of Horticulture," referred to the danger of giving tree roots an unnatural shape, which they are apt to retain during their life, citing the case of certain pines nursed in pots in the nursery, for sale, and which were continually being blown down in plantations because the roots never lost the corkscrew habit which the pots gave them. The subject is an important one, and we allude to it at length here for that reason.

SECTION X.—THE RIGHT WAY.

The right way to transplant a young forest tree needs but a short description. Whether in the nursery or in the wood the top and root of the tree should be in the same perpendicular line, like Figure 1. Of course, when trees have to be transplanted several times the roots have to be shortened to keep them within convenient bounds for lifting, but that is a necessity of the practice and no advantage. A tree raised from seed in a plantation, and never transplanted, has a natural and strong grip of the ground which the transplanted tree never acquires, but the planter may imitate nature to a

considerable extent if he chooses to try. The much deeper
and stronger grip of the ground which the perpendicularly
planted or undisturbed seedling tree has from the beginning
gives it an immense advantage at the start, and it will keep
the lead and resist vicissitudes of wind and weather far more
successfully than the other. Figures 1 and 2 show the difference of root-hold in the two trees very clearly. The top-
weight alone of the transplant, Figure 2, places it at a disadvantage at a period when the seedling, Figure 1, would have
become firmly established. In transplanting young trees in
the right way, while still in the nursery, the planter will see
from the foregoing remarks that what he has to do is to make
the furrow, dug out by the spade, deep enough to allow the
roots of each plant to be placed in the natural position, that is,
straight down into the soil. The ground is prepared in the
usual way, planted as dug, and the line stretched for the rows
at a distance apart according to the size of the plants. The
soil is then patted above the line to firm it for the cut, and

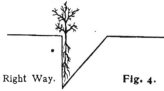

Right Way.   Fig. 4.

that done, a furrow is cut out with the
spade of the shape shown in Fig. 4.
The side next the line, shown by a
dot, should be perpendicular, and
against that side should be placed
the young tree with its roots hanging
straight down against the soil. The man takes the plant in his
left hand, and placing the root in position, the same depth
from the collar as before, with his right hand pushes a handful
of soil from the opposite sloping side of the cut against the
roots to hold them in their place, and so on till the row is
completed. Then he digs on for the next row, levelling down
smoothly and neatly as the work proceeds. In transplanting,
but few plants should be exposed at one time, as the roots
are easily injured by exposure to the air and sunshine.

In the garden and forest tree nursery we have never raised
young trees or shrubs in any other way than this, and in the
case of forest trees especially the roots have always lifted in
an evenly balanced shape and been planted on the pitting
system easily and successfully. In planting young forest trees
we never attempt to spread out the roots, but always aim at
giving them a good "tap-root" hold of the soil. We find
from very careful experiment and observation that the young
tree, in due course and before long, pushes out horizontally
roots of its own accord as soon as it gets hold of the soil.
The most important point is to let the extremities of the roots
down deep and straight so long as the collar of the plant is not
buried.

Figure 5 is a portrait of a tree such as Figure 1 becomes after it has reached the age of about five years and been several times transplanted in the right way. Had the tree never been transplanted, the roots in Figure 5 would probably have extended to a greater length than the top, but frequent transplanting has kept them short. Unlike Figure 2, however, the roots have grown in a natural position, and in pit planting can be easily inserted in the hole in the right way.

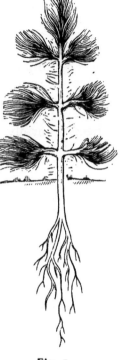

Fig. 5.
Transplanted Tree.
Right Root Form.

SECTION XI.—FINAL TRANSPLANTING TO THE WOODS. SETTING OUT THE LINES.

The first work consists in clearing the ground of all rubbish and surface vegetation by cutting or burning. That done, the lines should be set out not more than three feet apart in favourable situations, while two feet is not too close at high and cold elevations. There is no objection to thick planting, except the cost of the plants, and the advantages of getting the trees to meet and cover the ground quickly is unquestionable. The greater warmth and shelter afforded, when this stage is reached, is exhibited in the quicker growth and general well-being of the trees. It is understood, of course, that the distance between the plants in the rows is the same as the distance between the rows. The lines should be set out broadside to prevailing and cold winds for the sake of shelter, and not end-on to the wind, and so admitting cold currents between the rows. Some object to straight rows because of their formality, but the formality disappears when the trees meet, particularly in mixed woods, and there is hardly any other method of planting that does not resolve itself into lines in some shape or other. The straight line system is almost universal, both at home and abroad, and is most easily executed. In planting, the trees should alternate with each other in the opposite row, and in mixed plantations the different species should follow each other in regular order in each row. The subject of mixtures and nurses is dealt with in other chapters.

SECTION XII.—NOTCH PLANTING.

This system is described here but not recommended, although it has been much favoured in the past because it is a cheap and easy way of planting, but that is all that can be said in its favour. The failures that occur in notch planting, even when done carefully, are often excessive. Notching is usually practised only where there is a sod. The workman makes a T-shaped slit in the sod with the spade or notching tool, then inserting the spade at the head of the " T " he pushes it under the sod, down the leg of the " T," and folding the sod back right and left draws the roots of the tree under, puts back the sod on the roots, treads it firm, and the operation is completed. The bad features of notching are that the root of the tree is inserted in a lop-sided, unnatural position, close to the surface, where it is certain to suffer from frost in winter and drought in summer ; the thin sod being an insufficient protection. Indeed, in dry summers we have seen the sods shrink widely at the slit and expose the roots, causing the death of the trees in a short time.

SECTION XIII.—PIT PLANTING BY THE SPADE.

There is more than one way of pit planting, but the best method consists in making a pit or straight-sided hole, the width and depth of the spade, for the roots of the tree to be dropped into perpendicularly at one side and wedged firmly up to the collar. The other method of pitting may be called the " spread-root " method, and as it is much insisted upon by Brown, Grigor, and others, extensively practised, and very expensive and useless, we propose to describe it fully. Grigor, in his " Arboriculture," p. 65, recommends the most extravagant method of any. For two-year transplanted hard-wood trees he recommends the pits to be eighteen inches wide and fifteen inches deep, but says that the more capacious the pits are formed the roots of the plants can be better spread. For trees beyond the age of two-year transplants, the pits, we are advised, must be larger still. The pits having been dug out, the top sod is chopped up and put in the bottom of the pit and the remainder left to cover the roots. This spread-root method of pitting is based upon the erroneous assumption that the roots of the tree, instead of going down, will spread out laterally and take possession of the soil in the hole first and then spread from there into the adjacent soil. But the roots do not behave like this at all, and the forester who plants in this way defeats his purpose and causes his employer needless expense. Every gardener of experience knows full well that in the case of young trees the roots, in a soft open soil, strike down, and the practice of lifting, root-pruning, and concreting, etc., is based upon this well-known fact; these operations being intended to prevent the roots going down and make them spread out near the surface. Forest trees behave in exactly the same way, particularly when young and newly planted, and the wonder is that foresters have so long followed the useless practice of wide pitting without discovering the fact. No matter how good the soil in the large hole may be, the roots of the tree strike down to the bottom, and more readily in soft than in hard soil. These facts may be verified in any plantation. The young tree root behaves like the seedling, as shown in Figure 1. In fact, the tree wants but little from the soil, and nothing is better known to planters than the fact that, in young plantations, on good land even, of moderate depth, the roots make straight for the subsoil beneath, and after a few years are chiefly found there, permeating the poor, rocky strata in all directions. What led us first to test the wisdom of wide pitting, was the expense. According to Brown and Grigor, digging the pits alone, by contract, costs from fifteen shillings to twenty shillings or thereabout per thousand where wages are low; and we know estates in England where thirty shillings was the price paid. These figures may have to be nearly doubled before the trees are planted and the holes filled in again, thus adding enormously to the cost per acre. By the system of narrow pitting and planting at the same time, we have had the work completed for less than half the above price, viz., for twenty-two shillings and sixpence per thousand, and this sum included the lifting and sorting of the plants in the home nursery. In the two cases the conditions were all equal. Grigor was a great raiser of forest trees, and no one should have known better that, apart from the objections to wide pitting stated above, frequently transplanted trees from a nursery and of the right age have practically no roots fit to spread. Not long since, on a well-known estate, wide pits were made where a plantation was to be, the trees having been ordered from a nursery. We saw them being put in, and to all appearances there was not a tree in all the many thousands delivered whose roots could not have been got into a pint pot or even a smaller vessel: they were simply lost in the large holes, and the soil, being soft round the necks of the trees, got worked into a puddle by the trees being blown about by wind. We tested this matter severely over the whole of a large plantation. The plants were mostly four-year-olds, some older, raised by ourselves. The soil lent itself to the experiment, being a stiffish loam. Narrow planting spades, a little broader than a good planting trowel, were used; and the holes were the depth of the spade and just wide enough to get the roots in suspended perpendicularly on one side of the hole. Roots that were more bushy than usual were gathered together and inserted into the hole in a bunch and wedged up like the rest. This plantation is one of the few in this country that has been planted and grown on so far, on the dense system of culture. The trees have now reached the stage when the grass and weeds begin to die out and the lower branches to die off, and few more regular or healthier plantations could be found. A large proportion of the trees being Corsican firs, the worst transplanter among the conifera, many who have seen the plantation have expressed surprise at the remarkably small proportion of failures, as indicated by the plantation generally, and more particularly by certain marked, unbroken rows planted as a test. Every tree in the plantation was practically dibbled in, the whole bunch of roots being treated as one tap-root, and being home raised they had bushy straight roots, and could therefore be better dealt with. The cost of labour, in both pitting and planting, was less than the cost of simply digging the holes in another case where big pits were made. We have planted still larger tracts with equal success in the same way, on very rocky, poor, hilly ground, where the pits were difficult to make; but the progress of the trees from the first has compensated for the trouble. Narrow pits, then, we believe to be the best for trees several years old, and the trees should be put into the pits as shown in Figure 4 and made firm from the point of the lowest root to the collar of the plant. The pit should really be of the same shape sectionally as Figure 4.

Since the first edition of "The New Forestry" appeared, the two methods of planting have excited some interest among owners of woods, and at the Highland Agricultural Society's show, in July, 1902, at Aberdeen, Colonel Innes sent some examples showing the superiority of pitting over notching. I am indebted to Mr. James Wilson, agricultural lecturer at

10

the Aberdeen University, and who had much to do with the arboricultural exhibits there, for particulars about these exhibits, the first of their kind.   He writes:—" Colonel Innes planted a wood, partly by notching and partly by pitting. He sent us two fair samples from this wood, each of Scotch fir and larch.   The pitted larch was three or four feet longer than the notched, the pitted ones being from twelve to thirteen feet high, and also slightly thicker.   These statements apply also to the Scotch fir."   No doubt such trees would keep their lead, and at maturity, or even earlier, the pitted plantation would be the gainer by thousands of feet, according to its extent.

Some planters recommend the pits to be taken out weeks, and even months, before planting time, on the plea that exposure to the air benefits the soil in some way, especially in bad soils.   The reply to the last-named plea is, that when the soil is so unsuitable that the soil from the pits has to be ærated, the ground is unfit to be planted altogether, seeing that the roots will quickly extend beyond the limits of the pit.   Generally speaking we have never seen the least advantage in digging the pits long before planting, and the experience of garden culture is opposed in principle to the practice, and garden practice deals with a far greater multitude of subjects than forestry.   If there be one practice more than another that the gardener has proved to be a wise one, it is that it is always best to sow or plant in freshly turned-up soil, and rather than do either, in a soil that has been thrown up for some time, he will fork and harrow again and again, if accidents of weather or anything else interferes with his operations at the first digging.   The forest tree is no exception, and trees that are planted in the newly turned-up soil as soon as the pits are opened will be found to succeed in a perfectly satisfactory manner.

SECTION XIV.—PLANTING WITH THE DIBBER AND TROWEL.

These tools are only used for planting forest trees at the first and second years seedling stage, and they are used on the same principle as the spade in pitting.   Sometimes in hard soils a crowbar is used.   The dibber ought to be heavy, thicker than an ordinary garden dibber, and shod with iron. In planting, the dibber should be inserted straight into the ground, and deep enough for the roots, which should be dropped straight into the hole as the dibber is withdrawn. The dibber should then be pushed down a second time, close to the first hole, and pushed forward so as to wedge the plant firmly into position up to the collar, the second hole being afterwards filled up with the dibber point. The trowel is used in the same way, and is useful in rough stoney soils, where a dibber cannot be employed.

In planting by any of the methods described, the roots of the plants should not be long exposed to the air, and in dry weather they should be puddled before planting. The head forester or his foreman should overlook every operation and make sure that the men understand their work and execute it properly. Should the trees have to come from a distant nursery, care should be taken to see that they are got up carefully and quickly, and delivered as speedily as possible at their destination. The dilatory process of counting, bundling and sorting in the nursery is the cause of much delay and injury by the exposure of the roots. We prefer to buy by the row or quarter, and to send our own men to superintend the getting up and despatching of the plants by road or rail with all speed.

SECTION XV.—TENDING NEWLY PLANTED TREES.

Some attention is needed by young plantations for the first two or three years, or until the trees get their tops fairly above the surrounding rank growth of grass and weeds, which should be trodden, beaten or cut down during the summer. A few weeks' neglect in this matter may cause great injury to the trees, as the heavy tall grass, weeds or bracken get laid over the smaller trees and smothers them. It is very important that this should not happen towards the end of the season, covering the trees over during the winter. One man with a few boys under his charge armed with sticks or sickles may soon go over a plantation and relieve the trees, each boy taking one row and beating down the grass, etc., round each plant. Strong winds do much injury to young plantations by blowing the trees to one side, and when left in that position they grow up with an awkward bend at the base of their trunks, which greatly detracts from their value when felled and sold. Their liability to be blown to one side or prostrated by gales, is one of the most serious objections to planting trees more than one foot high, as they get blown over by every gale and are difficult to set up again after they get loose at the neck. Thick planting is one of the surest preventives, especially in the case of top-heavy firs, which are prone to fall over any time before the rows meet ; after that they are pretty safe from danger.

SECTION XVI.—COST OF PLANTING.

It is next to impossible here to estimate the cost per acre of forest tree planting, so much depends on the price of labour, the size and price of trees, the number to the acre, the species used, and whether bought or raised in the home nursery. But no forester need be in any difficulty on this head. All he has to do is to decide what the species are to be planted, to ascertain their size and value per thousand from a price list, find his own rates for labour and preparation, and the total will give him the nearly exact figure.

SECTION XVII.—UNDER-PLANTING : UNEVEN AGED WOODS.

This is a method of planting with which British foresters are not familiar, as practised on the Continent, and we cannot say that it is a plan adapted to British woods on private estates, because of the danger of the work being suspended from any cause during the long interval of regeneration or planting required. The uneven aged system has been adopted in Germany, as yet on a limited scale, with the object of reducing the labour of tending mixed woods of species varying greatly in rate of growth, and in which the strong species may crush out the weaker. The method consists, practically, in planting the weaker species only at the beginning and following with the stronger species later, at intervals of years if necessary, so as to handicap the latter, to use a well-known phrase. In the chapters on mixed and pure forests, we have suggested a method of dispensing with the uneven aged system by selecting the species carefully, with an eye to similarity of habit, for mixed woods, and the reader is referred to that chapter. The most noteworthy example we have seen of an uneven aged forest was in the Hartz Mountains, near Lauterberg, where spruce was planted ten years after the beech, and had overtopped the latter by twenty feet, the trees being past middle age. Uneven aged woods, as the term is understood in Britain, consist of woods containing trees of various ages that have been planted from time to time in over-thinned woods approaching maturity, or trees from old stools in woods from which timber has been removed. There has been much aimless planting in this way, owing to the absence of any definite system of clear cutting or rotation on estates. Woods grow up till they have nearly reached maturity, and are over-thinned and filled up again with young trees. Later another fall of timber of the older trees is probably taken out of the wood, and the trees falling on the later planted ones injure and destroy many, not to speak of the damage done by haulage. This entails another beating up to make good the blanks created, and so on till the end, if that ever arrives. This is what may be called in England an uneven aged wood, consisting generally of an indiscriminate mixture of all ages, and usually forming as bad an example of management as could be found. There would be less objection to such woods if they were managed in a methodical way. When a wood becomes so thin as to need partial re-planting, the crops from the old stools should first be looked to and encouraged, and the vacancies afterwards planted, but in all such woods the fellings of the older timber should be at long intervals, in order that the young trees may have time to grow up, when the damage sustained in felling and hauling will be less and the blanks sooner filled up by the growth of the younger trees. In Germany the final cut is sometimes delayed till after the ground has been re-planted or sown, but the trees felled have such small tops and the young crop is so dense that less damage is done than happens when trees with broad spreading heads are felled over younger trees as is done in British woods.

Under-planting may be very usefully and profitably adopted in thin old woods consisting of oak, ash, and elm, etc. These do not bear shade, and are useless for under-planting themselves, but beech, silver fir and spruce are good shade-bearers, and may be used to under-plant with success—care being taken to plant not too close to the standing trees. Under-planting is much practised on the Continent, where we have seen it; but the following extract from " The North British Agriculturist " is interesting, as showing what is done as far north as Sweden in that way in Government woodlands :—" These consist of oak and Scotch pine chiefly. The oak is seventy years planted, and it has been under-planted with spruce, silver fir and beech.   By far the largest area has been under-planted with spruce, but the silver fir seems to have been more successful, while beech has not been employed to a sufficiently great extent to enable one to form an opinion as to its suitability, though, no doubt, it would prove the most beneficial of all.   The undergrowth or soil-protecting crop of spruce or silver fir is introduced and cleared off again twice, or it may be even thrice, in the course of the rotation of the oak crop, which is 120 years, the poles finding a ready market for paper pulp spruce making, etc."

SECTION XVIII.—EXTENDING PLANTATIONS BY TRANSPLANTING THINNINGS.

A good way of extending young plantations with trees large enough to produce effect or covert at once, is to use the thinnings from young plantations by transplanting them elsewhere, instead of cutting them out when they are next to worthless for any other purpose.   We have seen considerable areas stocked successfully in this way, when the trees were eight to ten feet high, both conifers and broad-leaved species. Such trees should, however, not be planted thinly or as isolated specimens, because they will not stand gales or exposure, coming from a dense wood, and the plan is not recommended except for the purpose named, but in groups and plantations, and close enough to touch each other.   This plan is not so laborious or expensive as might be supposed, because large balls of roots and transplanting machines are dispensed with. The trees are prepared by a simple method of root pruning, about a year before they are transplanted, and in the following manner.   Suppose a young plantation needs to be thinned in the usual way, the trees to come out should all be marked, and every marked tree should then be gone round with a long sharp spade, and have its roots cut in to within about nine inches from the stem.   In doing this, the spade should be pushed in in a slanting direction towards the tree and right round the tree till the operator has made sure that every root is severed.   The root-ball should not be prized or heaved up, but the spade should be only pushed in and withdrawn again. A few unimportant roots may be missed under the stem of the tree, but all the main roots will be cut if the spade is long enough and well worked in.   In this way one man can root-prune many trees in a day.   This work should be done in early autumn or early spring, and if the operation has been properly executed the trees will show it during the summer by the check to their growth, which will be very short and stunted. By the following autumn the trees will be ready for moving, and they may be lifted each with about as much soil to their roots as a man can carry, or less. In lifting, the man should go round the roots outside the first cut made in root-pruning, and work in with a fork till the ball is sufficiently reduced, when the tree should be removed to the ground to be planted, and where the holes for the trees should be previously prepared. In planting, the roots should be spread regularly out and covered over about six inches deep, trod carefully but firmly, and well watered. Large trees may be moved successfully in this way, but almost everything depends on the root-pruning preparation beforehand. We have advised cutting to within nine inches or one foot, but a little judgment must be used. A very vigorous tree may be allowed a little more room, and a weak one less, and if the ground is too hard and stony to be simply cut by the spade, the tree should be dug round with the narrow planting spade and have its roots cut in in that way, filling in the trench again afterwards. We have cut many kinds of good-sized trees in this way very severely, with no more effect upon the tree than just a check for the following year. It is surprising the severe root-pruning that a tree will endure, so long as what is left of the root is not lifted quite out of the ground and shaken free of soil. Extremely few roots will keep a tree alive if they have not been disturbed, and in close root-pruning a few roots are always left untouched by the spade. We have noticed in fir trees, root-pruned as described, that the buds just expand or little more the summer following, and that the year after transplanting they make good growth, showing that the root-pruning of the established tree had more effect than the subsequent transplanting. Proof of what we state here about root-pruning is found in woods where firs have been prostrated by gales. In such cases the roots are nearly all torn out of the ground and exposed, only a few roots on one side remaining in the soil. Yet such prostrated trees live, and in some cases they have produced from their upper sides a crop of poles. A case of this kind was recorded in the " Field," by the proprietor, in 1898. The plan of extension here recommended has these advantages, that it is not expensive considering the size of the trees and the effect produced at once, and that the thinnings from the other plantations are utilised instead of wasted.

SECTION XIX.—TRANSPLANTING LARGE TREES.

This is a business that has little connection with true forestry, but it is one that usually devolves upon the forester and must be noticed here.   It is not advisable to transplant large trees on an extensive scale, to form groups, .as has been advocated in times past, because it is a most expensive plan and because such trees are very apt to be blown over by gales unless stayed by wire ropes, which are troublesome, requiring frequent attention.   We know estates where numbers of tall trees were transplanted successfully, many years ago, scarcely any of which now remain, nearly all having been prostrated by gales within the last twenty years.   Trees from ten to fifteen feet in height may be moved with a good prospect of their roots getting a sufficient hold of the ground and their top receiving but little check; but when trees from twenty to thirty feet are transplanted, disappointment may be expected, and some species endure moving much worse than others— thorns, oaks, ash and elms for example.   Moderate sized trees may be transplanted without previous root-pruning, and large balls of earth are not necessary, but still root-pruning the year before almost ensures success.   Trees from ten to fifteen feet high may be cut in to eighteen inches from the stem, which will leave a ball of earth less than three feet wide when the ball is reduced in lifting.   That size should carry successfully in a barrow, or on a skid made of boards and drawn by a pony.   We have moved many trees successfully, up to twenty and thirty feet in height and of all kinds, with no other appliances than could be extemporised on the spot.   However excellent transplanting appliances may be, they may be ren- dered useless by careless work with the spade and needless hurry.   It is much better to have a good fringe of roots to the tree than attempt to carry a large ball of soil which is apt to fall to pieces at a critical moment, carrying whole masses of roots with it.   Preparation by root-pruning the year before will, however, usually prevent all risk, and with trees of any value that course should always be adopted.   Copious water- ings should also be given to the roots, which should also be thickly mulched during the summer.

SECTION XX.—SEA SIDE PLANTING.

Pure sand, as is well known, is one of the poorest rooting mediums known so far as surface crops are concerned, but it is also a well-established fact that the poorest sand lands produce excellent crops of certain kinds of timber, and numerous examples are recorded on both poor inland sands and on sand banks at the sea shore consisting of pure sand. On the western coast of France great tracts of sand dunes, once barren wastes, are now clothed with fir forests that yield great quantities of excellent timber and other products, and on not a few places on the British coasts are now established thriving plantations, extending almost from high-water mark, consisting chiefly of *Pinus pinaster*, Scots, Austrian, and Corsican firs; these species being apparently the most suitable of any for sea side planting. There is indeed no doubt about timber trees thriving on sand banks—mostly worthless for any other purpose, and the only difficulty is getting the trees established on drifting sands which are apt to bury the young trees. The French set up wattle hurdles among the plants as screens, and Grigor recommends thinning of fir woods and furze to be stuck in or strewed among the plants, especially near to the sea, in order to break the sand drift for the first few years, after which the trees are well able to protect themselves, affording shelter also to the land in a way that greatly enhances its value for farming purposes. Probably the common willow would be as good a subject to plant among firs for their protection, as anything in such situations. The following extracts from the "Field" on the value of the willow is worth quoting. It states that:—"Between Blackpool and Southport it is extensively planted in belt lines to protect plantations and gardens from the breezes which sweep along that part of the coast with unusual severity. It grows well in the light, sandy soil of the district; indeed, in some places, it is growing on what were but a few years ago nothing but sand banks. In the well-kept public gardens at Lytham, which extend to within about fifty paces of high water mark, the willow again is planted near the sea for shelter; and though the soil is poor, the trees in three or four years have grown twenty feet or thirty feet high. The elm, beech, sycamore, oak, laburnam and other deciduous trees become as brown and withered in foliage during the summer as if a severe black frost had passed over them; but the willow towers aloft, and is green and luxuriant to its topmost branches. In the extensive park around Clifton Hall, and close to the sea, the plantations have all been protected in the same way from the blast. In some places the willows appear to be of good age, and are considerably taller than the spruces, oaks and other trees which they guard from the storm."

Grigor also, writing in the last edition of his " Arboriculture "
on sea side planting, says:—" that the willow has no rival
among deciduous trees for planting as shelter to other trees,
a statement which we can corroborate from observation.
We have not seen the experiment tried, but we have little
doubt, from what we have seen of the willow's behaviour on
poor sand banks, that it would be one of the best of nurses in
such situations, provided it was planted one or two years before
the permanent crop was put in and planted thick enough.
Good sized cuttings inserted deeply enough would answer
very well.   After the permanent crop became established, the
willows could be gradually removed.   On the bleak sand
dunes of Gascony, the French foresters sowed seeds of *Pinus
pinaster* and broom at the rate of two pounds of the former
to five pounds of the latter to the acre, and in a little over
twenty years many acres of thriving plantations were thus
established.   The broom was the nurse in this case.   Anything in the shape of low bush or grass, to bind the drifting
sands, or dead brush-wood or furze laid amongst the trees to
prevent the sand from blowing, appears to answer the purpose,
and in a few years the trees can take care of themselves.
These are the only difficulties to contend with, and once
overcome success is certain."   We would recommend planting
instead of sowing.

The preparation of the trees for sea side planting is,
however, an important matter.   They ought to be procured
when only one or two years old, and nursed for a year or two
in the locality and soil in which they are to be finally planted.
In sand bank localities there are usually plenty of spots on
which a nursery could be readily extemporised, and in which
the little trees could be grown till they are one or two feet
high and fit to plant out in the usual way.   Barring the few
difficulties described, we do not know any description of
land that may be so easily and so profitably planted as sand
banks near the sea coast, and on some estates there is plenty
of scope for the reclamation of such lands by planting.

CHAPTER XII.

THE THINNING OF PLANTATIONS.

German Methods.—Their application to British Woodlands.—Execution of the Work.—Pruning, &c.

SECTION I.—GERMAN METHODS.

GERMAN foresters copy nature within safe limits; and we may glance at nature's process first. In natural forests, at the beginning, the young trees usually spring up in far greater numbers than can find room to grow for any considerable length of time, with the result that the struggle for existence soon sets in, and a very large proportion perish at an early stage of existence, the weak growers being over-topped and smothered by their stronger neighbours. From beginning to end of the forest's existence this struggle goes on, the weaklings perishing at an almost wholesale rate while still young, the mortality becoming less and less as the years go on, until the trees reach mature age and the strongest only survive. In the natural beech forests of the Continent the number of young trees that spring up is prodigious, from eighty to a hundred being sometimes found on a square yard, over great tracts, at the end of three or four years, after which the smothering process sets in and they thin themselves out rapidly. In Plate No. 5 the mass of vegetation shown in the foreground consists wholly of young beech seedlings, knee deep, from seed shed by the previous crop—natural regeneration. Artificial planting is resorted to only to fill up blanks, which are not numerous, as the ground at the end of the rotation period is usually bare and covered with humous, and seedlings come up in abundance. During the whole period from youth to age the overhead canopy of foliage remains unbroken unless disturbed by accident, the tops of the dominant trees meeting over the tops of the weaker ones which succumb, leaving no gap in the leafy roof, which shuts out the light from above, causing that deep gloom underneath that always gives a dense forest its sombre aspect. The effect of these conditions are that the trees are drawn up more quickly in height than would be the case were they distributed thinly over the ground and had more light and room. The lower branches die off at an early stage, leaving the trunk clean and free from knots, straight and of a nearly uniform girth from end to end, compared to trees which have room to develop their side branches down to the ground. A very large proportion of the timber imported into this country from abroad comes from natural forests and is of this description. Whether it consists of poles or logs its general character is the same, the conditions of growth being the same in all regions and the results similar.

Such is nature's method of producing timber, and all that man can do to assist nature is to step in and shorten the struggle at the beginning by sowing or planting more thinly and regulating the crop afterwards, according to the species, so as to secure the best results in the shape of a crop of timber. What strikes the observer in a natural forest is the density of the crop, the height of the trees, their freedom from branches, their straightness and cylindrical shape of stem, all qualities of the highest value in timber trees, which it should be the aim of the forester to secure, and which he can secure by the same means as nature employs if he chooses to use them. The forest tree of nature is moulded into shape by external agencies, now recognised in scientific forestry, reduced to practice, and called " Sylviculture," that is to say the cultivation of woods or forests as distinguished from " Arboriculture " or the culture of trees—two very different things long confounded. Some of the most accurate descriptions of natural forests have been given by writers of fiction, without any reference to practical forestry. Fennimore Cooper's descriptions of natural scenery are noted for their truthfulness, and his picture in " The Pathfinder " is well worth giving here : —
" The elm with its graceful and weeping top, the rich varieties of the maple, most of the noble oaks of the American forest, with the broad-leaved linden, mingled their uppermost branches, forming one broad and seemingly interminable carpet of foliage, which stretched away towards the setting sun. . . . . . The forest, as usual, had little to intercept the view below the branches but the tall, straight trunks of trees. Everything belonging to vegetation had struggled towards

the light, and beneath the leafy canopy one walked, as it might be, through a vast natural vault, upheld by myriads of rustic columns."

To a large extent the Germans regulate their thinning operations by the shade-enduring power of the different species, a hitherto unrecognised factor in British forestry, but to which much importance is attached on the Continent. The greater the shade-enduring power of any species, the greater the density of crop may be, the greater the number of trees to the acre and the greater the number of cubic feet. German authorities, indeed, profess to give the shade-enduring power, or "light requirement" of most species, but for all practical purposes the forest trees requiring special notice in this respect may be divided into four classes, viz., the beech and hornbeam, as compared with the oak and ash, etc.; and the spruces as compared with the pines. That is to say, the beech being a better shade-bearer than the oak or ash, it will stand crowding better, as also will the spruces compared to the pines. But the practical results go further than this in computing the final crop. According to Schlich, vol. i., p. 168, an acre of beech at maturity contains a greater volume of timber than does the ash or oak, and the spruces a greater volume than the Scotch fir. In the case of the spruces and pines, Schlich gives the following figures, "which give the average growing stock per fully-stocked acre at the age of one hundred and twenty years, in localities of the first quality in each case ":—

Silver Fir	...	...	17,400 cubic feet per acre.
Spruce ...	...	...	14,500	„ „
Scotch Pine	...	...	9,780	„ „

These figures are suggestive, as regards the great advantage which shade-enduring power gives one species over another, and the comparative productiveness of the pine and spruce. They are also a guide for the thinner, whether dealing with mixed or pure plantations, showing him that the room required by each species need not be regulated by the rule-of-thumb practice of giving all the trees equal space, but by their power to bear crowding. A beech or a spruce in a mixed wood may be crushed, but an oak or a birch may not be to the same extent.

In German forests it is difficult to tell artificial from natural
regeneration. What British foresters would call crowding to
an injurious degree is, in practice, the rule. Our methods of
frequent and severe thinning are simply regarded as wasteful
and excite astonishment in German foresters who visit this
country. In the first place, so far as we observed over
a large extent of the forest lands, the Germans do not plant
wider than from three to four feet under the most favourable
circumstances, and this width is adopted to save expense and
not because closer planting is objected to ; and at high elevations the distance is reduced to two feet or thereabout, and
two and three plants are put in each hole. Of course, the young
trees are not bought, as in Britain, from public nurseries, but
are raised in the woods and put out when about six inches
high at small cost. . Where practicable, seed is sown on the
rough surface, and in large tracts, as in the case of the beech,
natural regeneration is trusted to, but the thinning afterwards
is the same in both cases. The first and great object is to
cover the ground as soon as possible, and establish an overhead canopy, which is maintained unbroken till the end, or
nearly to the end of the rotation period, when the final crop
is swept away. Density, or crowding, is aimed at from the
first in order to shut out the light and air from the lower
branches and cause their decay, and at the same time to hasten
height-growth, even if it produces attenuated stems in the
early stages of growth. In thinning, the operator looks up,
and if the removal of a tree is going to make a gap overhead,
it is left. The consequence of regulating the trees in this
way is, that although the trees may have been planted at
regular distances at first, they do not all progress at the same
rate, and after one or two thinnings, regulated by the condition of the tops, the trees become irregularly distributed
over the ground, standing in little groups of threes, fours, and
fives, not far apart, even at maturity. Plate No. 4 shows
this very plainly in the way the fine cylindrical trunks are
grouped together. In the best managed German forests a
comparatively small head of live branches is considered sufficient to build up a tree of useful dimensions, and trees of
great girth are not aimed at, and could not be produced in
rotation period allowed. The first thinning or " cleaning "

as it is called is usually deferred till the trees are from twenty-five to thirty years of age, in the case of firs, or even longer, and a considerably longer period is allowed for beech and other broad-leaved species. Before the first thinning is executed (see Plate No. 1), the forest looks just in that condition which foresters in this country would regard as utterly neglected and almost irreparably damaged by crowding, but which the German forester regards as perfectly satisfactory, pointing to his mature forest as proof of the excellence of the system. In the first thinning, only the wastrels and dead trees are removed, but the dead branches on the trees left are not interfered with. From this stage the growth is more carefully watched, and although little or no pruning is attempted, top-growth begins to assert itself sufficiently to add annually a sensible layer of timber to the attenuated stems, which eventually develop into tall, cylindrical trunks of good girth. We measured beech trees of mature age, growing at about sixteen hundred feet elevation, that had a circumference of sixty-eight inches at five feet from the ground, and at about ninety feet up a circumference of only about ten inches less, the trunks being clear to that height. This was in the Hartz Mountains, in a late and cold locality.

The degree of density varies a little according to circumstances and the species. Professor Schlich, in his " Manual," vol. ii., p. 209, speaking of the Black Forest, gives the number of trees, consisting of a mixture of Scotch fir, spruce, and beech, per acre, at different ages, as follows :—

Age of wood in years	Number of trees to acre.
20	3960
40	1013
60	449
80	346
100	262

We believe these figures to fairly represent the degree of density in German woods generally, and if the reader will refer to the plates taken from photographs in different parts of Germany, for this work, he may form some idea how such dense forests look compared to plantations in this country.

In some parts of the Hartz Mountains, in the neighbourhood of the Brocken, at high elevations, where " snow breaks "
are to be feared and deer are troublesome, we have seen the
above quantities considerably exceeded. Taking the foregoing figures, however, as they stand, a glance will show how
widely British and German practice differs.   At the end of
twenty years there are as many or more trees to the acre than
British foresters usually plant at the beginning.   The disparity
grows less as the trees grow older, but the disparity is greatest
at the crucial period between the first and fortieth year, when
the crowding is greatest in order to promote height-growth,
lateral growth being suppressed as much as possible by the
exclusion of light and air.   Grigor, who was, and still is,
regarded by some as an even safer authority than Brown, in
his "Arboriculture," p. 91, plants three thousand trees or less to
the acre at the beginning, and removes "fully half the number
inserted per acre by the time that the most valuable portion
is twenty feet high," or say from ten to fifteen years old.   At
thirty feet, about twenty years of age, his advice is that the
trees " should stand on an average fully seven feet asunder,
or about eight hundred per acre."   Here we see the extraordinary difference between German and British practices.
We have Grigor planting thin and thinning out fully half the
trees planted per acre, almost before they have met in the
rows, and at the end of twenty years or thereabout reducing
the number still further to just about one-fifth the number
given by Schlich for the same period in a climate certainly not
more favourable to growth than the north of Scotland.
Grigor's practice does not appear to have been regulated on
any other principle than that of " rule of thumb," and cannot
be regarded as anything but wasteful.   Taking almost any
species of forest tree, and considering the kind of exposed
and waste lands usually recommended to be planted, and
the rate of growth to be expected, on what rational principle
can the removal of fully half the crop—almost before the trees
have met—be defended?   Of course, the light and air theory
dominated Grigor as it did his contemporaries.   At the age
of forty years, Grigor's number stands at three hundred to
three hundred and fifty, against Schlich's record of one thousand and thirteen, and so on to the end.   The attention of

foresters is particularly drawn to Plates Nos. 1 and 3, showing the beginning and end of the rotation period. The idea held tenaciously by foresters in this country is that if a young plantation is allowed to become as crowded up to twenty or thirty years of age, as shown in No. 1, the trees can never afterwards produce good timber or be healthy. Yet the plate represents the general condition of a young fir forest of the above age, or older, and for that part of it, of hard-woods also, under good management; and No. 3 shows what such a plantation becomes at maturity, or at the end of the rotation period—one hundred years. The trees in No. 3 run from one hundred to one hundred and twenty feet in height, and average about one hundred cubic feet in bulk of trunk, producing fine, clean, white deal that is used for a great variety of purposes. The engraving shows the edge of a " clear cut," and the trees are not marginal specimens but grown up in dense forest from the beginning. What the exact weight of crop might be we did not ascertain, but a glance at the number of trees on the ground showed that it must be enormous. No. 3 shows but a short stretch of forest, throughout the same, and a practical forester will form a very good idea from the plate how much timber an acre is likely to contain.*

In proceeding to thin any forest compartment for the first time (Plate 2) the German forester simply clears out the dead and dominated or smothered trees, afterwards collecting the small and worst for firewood, and putting rails and small poles aside for stakes and fencing purposes. The second thinning is regulated on the same principle as the first, but it is seldom executed till the trees have reached small pole dimensions of from two-and-a-half to three and four feet—the firs being peeled by the axe in the forest and prepared for delivery to the consumer. The period between the first and second thinnings depends on the progress of the trees, but in any case a period usually elapses during which, in a plantation on an English estate, several thinnings would have been carried out, and the thinnings been of so little value as hardly to defray the expense of removal. Thinning repetitions are conducted on the same principle throughout until the end of

---

* Plate 14 shows a Scotch wood, of denser growth than usual, and affording a useful comparison with No. 3.

·the rotation period ; but after middle age, when height-growth has been attained and it is desired to accelerate trunk development, or thickness of bole, the tops of the trees are allowed more room in order to increase the leafage, which in turn increases the trunk increment. The aim throughout, however, is to preserve a uniform rate of growth as tending to improve the quality of the timber. It is held by German authorities that quickly-grown timber is best in, the case of broad-leaved species, and that the reverse is the case with the firs, the width of the annual rings being the test in each case. According to this, it would of course be best to thin hardwoods freely in order to encourage top-growth and so augment the width of the annual rings, and the reverse in the case of the firs, so a compromise has to be effected, in thinning each species, in order to secure the best general results as regards a crop.

As regards the weight of crop produced in these German forests, we are told that from eight thousand to ten thousand feet was a common thing in a final cut; and we readily believed it from what we saw. Some experiments, however, carried out in the Duchy of Saxe-Wiemar, and the results of which were given us by the forest officers there, showed that on one hectare the quantity of Scotch fir timber, one hundred years of age, amounted to eleven hundred and twelve cubic metres—equivalent to about twenty thousand cubic feet—per English acre. This was sold by auction at the rate of £475 per English acre; twenty-seven per cent. being disposed of for firewood. These results exceed anything recorded in Britain, where, however, they may be realised under the same system of culture and management. German foresters assess the productive capacity of soil and locality as closely as possible, and the following table, taken from Schlich's " Manual," vol. i., p. 156, is given to show the number of cubic feet per acre that may be reasonably expected from one acre of Scotch fir at the final yield, exclusive of thinnings, according to the age of the wood and quality of soil and locality, as indicated by the numbers—No. I. representing the highest quality, and No. V. the lowest. " The figures present the mean of very numerous measurements " in Germany.

GROWING STOCK OF SCOTCH PINE WOODS,

IN CUBIC FEET PER ACRE.

Age of Wood.	TIMBER AND FAGOTS. Number of Quality or Yield Capacity.					TIMBER ONLY, 3 INCHES AT THE THIN END AND UPWARDS. Number of Quality or Yield Capacity.				
	I.	II.	III.	IV.	V.	I.	II.	III.	IV.	V.
20	2,320	1,530	1,290	1,060	810	790	70	30	…	…
30	3,650	2,760	2,140	1,740	1,390	2,210	1,170	830	440	360
40	4,800	3,860	2,900	2,370	1,090	3,870	2,830	1,970	1,290	900
50	5,820	4,740	3,530	2,910	2,320	5,060	3,690	2,700	2,040	1,430
60	6,750	5,420	4,060	3,360	2,670	6,020	4,690	3,300	2,610	1,870
70	7,510	5,960	4,530	3,730	2,970	6,790	5,250	3,820	3,070	2,240
80	8,140	6,400	4,950	3,990	3,190	7,420	5,720	4,260	3,350	2,510
90	8,670	6,780	5,300	4,170	3,300	7,950	6,100	4,620	3,530	2,690
100	9,110	7,090	5,580	…	…	8,390	6,410	4,910	…	…
110	9,500	7,370	5,820	…	…	8,780	6,690	5,150	…	…
120	9,780	7,630	6,010	…	…	9,060	6,950	5,340	…	…

Taking the Scotch fir as a standard, foresters, knowing the rate of growth of different species, may calculate approximately, from the above table, the yield to be expected from the kinds of timber trees usually grown.

In Sweden, where the forestry is not quite up to the German standard, the crops are also good.   The following is a Scotch estimate of these as published in the "North British Agriculturist" report of the Scottish Arboricultural Society's excursion to Sweden, in July, 1902 :—Clumps of good larch timber were seen, the stems being tall, clean, and cylindrical, and the trees are said to be free from the dreaded *Peziza*.   The age of these larches is fifty-seven years, and the total height of the trees is about 75 feet.   The stems girth from nine to ten inches under the bark at breast height, and there are 190 stems to the acre, giving a volume of 3,700 cubic feet (quarter-girth measurement).   These larches have been under-planted with spruce and beech, the former being twenty years old, and the latter seventeen years.   Finspang is one of the largest forest estates in Sweden.   Nineteen million trees have been planted, and besides this nearly four tons of seed have been sown, while the cost of cultivation has been slightly over seven shillings per acre for the period since 1860 to date.   The pine forests are thirty-eight years old, and are now about sixty feet high, and contain 2,800 cubic feet per acre, and they are worked on a rotation of ninety years."

Mark the age, height, under-planting, and number of feet to the acre here.   In one case the trees are about middle age, and in the other only thirty-eight years old, yet the yield per acre is nearly 3,000 and 4,000 feet.   After these ages the rate of annual increment increases rapidly, being doubled, trebled, and quadrupled towards the end of the rotation—amounting probably to from 10,000 to 15,000 feet per acre.

As regards the climate where these forests grow, we feel sure, from a critical inquiry into the subject and from observation, that it has nothing to do with the quality of the timber produced as compared with that produced in Great Britain and Ireland.   The conditions of temperature, rainfall, soil, gales, etc., are much the same as in this country.   The fine level lands are not, as a rule, planted in Germany, but the mountain ranges are usually unbroken forest of a density unknown with us.   The principal timbered regions of Germany and North Europe lie in the same parallel as the British Islands, or further north than that, and in Central Germany the mountains are clothed with timber up to three thousand feet and upwards.

In Britain it is not considered worth while to plant to nearly such a high elevation, and over-thinned woods, one can believe, are not likely to succeed under such conditions. The system of culture adopted alone explains the main difference between the forests at home and those on the Continent.* In Germany the cost of planting, or regeneration in any form, is very much less than with us. In the first place, very few species are grown, and in the second, the trees are raised in the forest and planted out very small. Failures are consequently few, and the cost of planting is fractional compared to the cost of planting on estates in Britain. In fact, buying trees is almost unheard of, but seed is sometimes purchased. Strict economy is the rule from beginning to end of the rotation period, and accounts are kept with care and exactitude.

Under some circumstances, in Germany, they have what are called " two-storied high forest," which resembles woods, in this country that have been under-planted, with this difference, that in Germany the second or later crop is allowed to grow up with and between the older crop, so that, practically, two distinct even-aged woods exist on the same, area, and the two crops are cut over at the same time. (Schlich, vol. i., p. 220.) This system may be likened to the practice of growing regular crops of underwood in woods and cutting them down when the trees are cut; but in Germany two-storied forest is only adopted when the first crop has from any cause become thin. Even-aged woods are most common, and final clear cutting the rule. In British woods, however, a second, or even a third crop of trees or poles might often be secured, if crops from old stools were taken care of and thinned and regulated instead of being left to produce what is little better than brushwood.

SECTION II.—THINNING BRITISH WOODS AND PLANTATIONS ON THE CONTINENTAL PRINCIPLE.   AGE AND SIZE.

In this we shall first endeavour to explain to the forester or his man how to carry out the rules to be observed in thinning on the above principle. From what has been said before, he will understand, it is hoped, that the object of thinning is not to give every tree in the plantation a clear space to itself, or to admit the light and air down to the ground

* Colonel Pearson, in his evidence before the select committee on forestry, stated that even in France, climatic conditions were much the same as in Britain, as far as related to forestry.

round every tree, but (after thinning, at any stage), to leave the trees so judiciously crowded together that their lower branches will meet and interlace so closely as to shut out the light and air from above and cause them to die off and be shed naturally at an early stage; the process to be continued until the plantation has reached maturity.   At the same time, on every tree a leader and head of live branches of sufficient size to sustain vitality and promote healthy growth must be preserved.   These are the main points to be kept in view, viz., the early and continuous decay of the lower branches as the top-growth progresses, and the preservation of a healthy growing top.   This is " density," and it must not be forgotten that those conditions must be maintained from beginning to end.   Once dense always dense.   According to Hartig, trees " that are reared in a very dense wood and then suddenly isolated in later life, suffer from sweating of the cortex," or top-drought, are checked in growth, becoming bark-bound, and finally stag-headed.   This is very noticeable in the ash when over-thinned, also in the larch, in which we have seen the annual rings decrease greatly in width after a severe thinning when the trees had reached middle age.   These facts must, therefore, be borne in mind when plantations approaching maturity are thinned with a view to augmenting the annual increment—a subject referred to elsewhere.

A difficulty which the forester has to contend with in this country, and one almost unknown on the Continent, where pure forests are so extensive and mixtures restricted to a very few species of similar habit, is our mixed woods.   The species planted are so numerous, and these of such wide disparity of habit, that any forester might well be puzzled what to do in thinning, where a portion of all the species had to be retained. Indiscriminate mixture is one of the worst faults of forestry in this country.   We shall here, however, try to point out what course the forester should choose under such circumstances.

Age has really very little to do with the matter, and no safe rule can be laid down on that line.   Situation and exposure makes so much difference to the growth of the trees that it is quite a common thing, even on the same estate, to see plantations of the same age differing so widely in height and density that one might suppose there were years of difference in their ages.   The height and condition of the trees should be the thinner's guide. · Supposing that we have to deal with a plantation of any kind in which the trees were originally planted three or four feet apart, no thinning should be needed till the trees have met and quite covered the ground, grown, say, to a height of from twenty to twenty-five feet, and become crowded. The guide in thinning should then be first, to preserve, in regular distribution, the species intended for the main crop; and, second, to preserve an unbroken overhead canopy of branches in every part of the plantation, while, at the same time, every tree left should have its head and shoulders clear up to the light. By "head and shoulders" the woodman will understand is meant the leading shoot and two or three tiers of branches below that. In a tree twenty feet high, for example, the head and shoulders may represent about five feet, or a quarter of the tree's total height. This is ample, at this early stage, to sustain healthy growth, for it must be remembered that the trees will still, at this stage, be furnished with live branches more or less down to the ground; and, although these may interlace and be crowded, sufficient light will still filter down to keep them alive as long as they are wanted. The fear of not giving the tree sufficient room is the bugbear that haunts the forester accustomed to severe methods of thinning. There is, however, no danger whatever, especially in healthy growing young plantations, because should the thinner err on the side of leaving too small a top, the tree will right itself in a couple of years or so. On the Continent great tracts of forest are to be seen of Scotch fir, spruce and beech, etc., in which the trees are one hundred and twenty feet high and upwards, and of proportionate girth, that never had more than a tuft of branches at their top from first to last. Plate No. 3 and frontispiece represents mature forest of splendid timber of this description, and it may be explained here that the spray seen between the firs (No. 3)* and below their tops is not composed of dead snags left on the firs, but is from the beech trees sixty feet high growing in the dense shade. Whether, therefore, the thinner is dealing with a conifera or hard-wood plantation, he will find the above rule a safe one to go by. In pure woods, or woods composed of a few species of similar habit, he will not have much difficulty in thinning, but in indiscriminate mixtures of any species, such as are often found on estates, he will have trouble if the number of species has to be preserved in any proportion. In such a case he must make up his mind to one of two courses. Either he must give up the ground to the stronger growing species and sacrifice the weaker as they get overtopped, or he

---

* Plate 14 represents an accidental example of a Scotch wood very much resembling a German forest, and which has not been too severely thinned.

must be constantly on the watch to prune the dominant species in order to equalise the struggle; and this means trouble in tending and a considerable loss of crop in the end. Mixtures of the conifera species alone, or broad-leaved species alone, are bad enough when they differ greatly in habit and rate of growth, but mixtures of both classes are worse, because the pinus family of the Scotch fir type cannot endure much shade, and there are a number of hard-woods that soon smother them in a mixed wood. In all cases, the margin of the plantation, especially on exposed sides, should be left dense in order to shut out cold currents. The width of this margin will depend on the kind of plantation, firs of the Austrian species being the best, as regards habit, for a close fence; but as a rule it will suffice if the trees are the same at the sides as in the rest of the wood, provided the margins are not thinned. Where it will grow, the Douglas fir, planted close in one or two lines, forms a high and close barrier against winds; and near the sea the willow is almost as good.

SECTION III.—EXECUTION OF THE WORK.   FIRST THINNING.

Assuming that the man appointed to the work of thinning fully comprehends what is wanted, he should first mark the trees that are to be removed, beginning at the northern boundary of the plantation and working southwards so that the sun will not be in his eyes. Entering at one side, and taking a strip or section of convenient width next the aforesaid boundary, he should, with a slash from a billhook, mark all the trees to come out on their south side, and as high up as he can reach, so that the man who follows him with the axe will be able to find them readily in the plantation. Only the dead, diseased, weakly, or dominated trees should be marked, and nowhere should a gap be made so wide as to admit the light to the ground between the trees, and the branches of the trees left should much more than meet to prevent that. Of course, in practice, the work cannot always be carried out exactly according to theory, and the marker has to use his discretion; but, as a rule, when he has any doubt he should leave the tree. When he has finished one strip he should wheel round and take up another, and the marked trees of the first line will be his guide, and so on till he has gone through the plantation. The man whose duty it is to fell the marked trees will then begin where the marker left off, and the marked trees will face him and be easily seen. The thinnings should be cleaned and sorted according to size and quality, and removed to spots where they can be seen and disposed of. First thinnings at this stage will not be very valuable, but of the length of from twenty to thirty feet, from a dense plantation such as is here contemplated, they ought to be of more useful dimensions than can be expected from plantations thinned often and severely on the system hitherto practised. Such thinnings, according to general testimony, seldom pay for the cost of removal, being short, tapering, and rough. A reference to Plate No. 2 will show what these rails are like in a forest of Scotch fir. Being branchless almost to the top, smooth, of almost uniform thickness throughout, from two to three inches in diameter and from twenty to thirty feet long, they are useful for fencing and other purposes, and are in good demand in that way. In parks surrounding some of the most palatial castles in Germany, the fences along the avenues are often of spruce rails joined neatly together. As to the small brush-wood and tops, unless disease is feared, or it can be sold for firewood, it may be left to decay where it lies. This ends the first thinning, and if it has been properly executed the tops of the trees all over the plantation will have an even and regular appearance, and there will be no gaps anywhere.

The second thinning should be conducted on the same principle as the first, and, if practicable, it should be delayed until the trees have reached measurable pole dimensions of from two-and-a-half to four feet or thereabout. It is the general custom in timber sales in this country to value all poles above one cubic foot and upwards as " timber " at so much per foot, and as the price per foot is usually a great advance on that received for rails and stakes below that size, it is prefer-able to delay thinning until the measurable size is reached. Spruce and Scotch fir poles of small size are of least value, but ash, sycamore, birch, oak, alder, and larch are readily disposed of when they exceed one cubic foot; and under ordinary con-ditions the cubic contents of the trees in a young plantation should average from two to three feet at the age of thirty-five years, before which time the second thinning should hardly be necessary. The subject of thinning, from this point of view, is most important. In evidence given before the Forestry Committee some years ago, it was plainly shown that one of the mistakes made in estimating returns from woods, conducted on Brown's system of early and frequent thinnings, was that far too high a value was put on the thinnings and that they were almost worthless, being under measurable size, rough, and useless. In the system of thinning proposed here, and practised on the Continent, the numerous thinnings conducted every few years on Brown's system are embraced in one or two thinnings. This gets rid of the expense of frequent and useless repetitions and allows time for the trees to reach a useful size, when thinning becomes really necessary. What the value of the thinnings might be under the dense system of culture we have had no means of knowing in this country, but judging by what we have seen in Germany of examples that could be easily repeated in Britain, and by the fact that the nearly four thousand trees per acre, at the twentieth year, are reduced in number by nearly three thousand, by the fortieth year, in about two thinnings, we can certainly conceive of crops in which the thinnings would pay well in the time specified, at prices such as have long been common. The disposal of three thousand poles, however small, between the twentieth and fortieth years, as shown in Schlich's table, means bulk, and a transaction of considerable value, as timber sales go, and takes no account of subsequent thinnings or of the ultimate crop.

Coming to the third and subsequent thinnings, or rather falls of timber, the same rules should be observed as before in maintaining the overhead canopy, removing the worst trees, and reserving the finest and largest. By middle-age, growth will have become less vigorous and the overhead canopy will not be so soon restored where interrupted by the removal of any trees; but by this time the effects of judicious crowding in the earlier stages will have been to a great extent secured in a clean height-growth, and if a little more room is afforded to the tops it will help to promote girth without encouraging side growth, the stage being passed at which lateral growth may be feared. Oaks and some other broad-leaved species do sometimes push out a twiggy growth from their trunks in old age, when the forest becomes thin, but they hardly affect the quality of the timber. In conclusion, it may just be added that much will depend on general management and a proper comprehension of his duties by the forester. The lines of management are easily understood and should not be departed from. The foundation of the crop is laid at the beginning. The aim should be not so much a crop of mature timber at some indefinite period, but a remunerative return from the plantation as soon as possible.

In thinning established plantations care should be taken not to thin too severely at any one time. Sudden and severe thinnings check increment in a marked degree in the trees left. Plate 13 shows this very plainly. It represents a section of a larch tree, and is an example of all the trees in part of a mixed wood that was severely thinned and from which the underwood and the fences were removed when the trees were taken into the park in the form of a clump. The broad rings from the centre to the letter A show the rate of increment while the trees were sheltered, and the rings above the letter A show the decreased rate of increment after the shelter was removed. This group was under the author's observation for many years, both before and after the thinning. The larches becoming stunted were felled, and the section was then photographed.

SECTION IV.—PRUNING.

The pruning of forest trees is not necessary, except in mixtures of ill-matched species, in which the weaker subjects have to be preserved at the stronger ones' expense, and such mixtures are condemned, for these reasons, in another chapter. Pruning is only required in the case of park and ornamental trees from which limbs have to be removed because of injury to them, or for some other reason. In pruning such trees, projecting stumps should not be left. The limb to be removed should be cut back to the next main limb or growing point, and whether that point be at another limb or at the main trunk, the cut should not be made flush with the bark of either, but at the swell or ring of bark which is usually found at the junction of a limb with the limb from which it springs. This leaves a slight knob, the cut is of less diameter, occlusion sets in sooner, and the wound is soon healed. Wounds soon heal up in growing trees, but much depends on their size and the age of the tree. Decay sets in where limbs have been broken off, and often extends several feet down the limb or bole, reducing the value of the tree. Purchasers probe such wounds with flexible steel probes to ascertain their extent. In treating wounds caused by pruning, or anything else, care should be taken to seal them up with some kind of styptic, like wood pitch, black varnish, or white lead. If pruning is done in early winter, when the sap is down, wounds soon dry and may be painted over or plugged to exclude air or water. The margin of bark round the wound must not, however, be touched by the paint, but just smoothed by the knife and so left. A roll of new tissue soon begins to form round the edges of the wound, which in time is quite covered over.

CHAPTER XIII.

SHELTER BELTS AND HEDGE-ROW TREES.

SECTION I.—BELTS.

IN an earlier chapter we have alluded to the importance of combining shelter to adjoining lands with the laying out and distribution of the wooded areas, but the subject of tree belts planted with the special object of shelter to farm stock and crops demands separate notice. No doubt belts, when judiciously laid out, do afford shelter from cold cutting winds during winter and shade in summer; but from a special acquaintance with the subject on high-lying inland situations we believe that the value of single shelter belts has been much exaggerated. They are non-productive, so far as timber is concerned, for they have to be kept dense, and if the advantages they are supposed to afford in the way of shelter are not equivalent to their cost of maintenance there must be loss instead of gain. Belts are usually planted on north-west, north, and north-east exposures, and consequently, like a north wall in a garden, they have a cold and a warm side, but unlike the wall the cold side is of little utility, for the influence of its cold shade extends just about as far as does its protection on the other side. A belt running east and west on level ground has a distinctly injurious effect on all crops on its northern side, and this is particularly noticeable on grain, turnip, and potato crops. Besides, it is mainly from winds that belts afford protection, as in calm weather their influence is nil. In addition to this, belts occupy land often as good as that which they are planted to shelter. In England belts from thirty to fifty yards wide, and even much wider, are common on estates, often taking up many acres of good land. Strange to say, too, these belts often consist almost wholly of deciduous species, which afford least shelter when it is most needed, viz., in winter. These are some of the merits and demerits of belts, and should be considered in planting. In any case, in order that such belts should cost as little as possible, and at the same time be effective, they should occupy as little land as possible and be dense enough to stop winds. A width of from twenty to thirty yards is enough, and the tall-growing species should be in the middle, and on the sheltered side, and the dense-growing species on the exposed side. The Douglas fir and other spruces are good for the sheltered sides and are tall, and the Austrian and Scotch firs can hardly be beaten for cold exposures—especially the first. Among deciduous species none surpass the beech for standing either exposure or shade, hence it may be planted freely on the cold side of belts, and during almost any period of a plantation's existence it may be planted under the shade of the other trees in order to thicken the covert. No thinning is needed in belts, which should be planted thickly at the beginning and encouraged to grow up as soon as possible. Double belts are strips twice the width of single belts, and which, in addition to affording shelter, provide a crop of timber by being cut down alternately, so that the shelter always exists. The rotation period is regulated by the age and height of the trees, and while one half of the belt is growing and dense the other half is treated like any other plantation, and finally cleared off and re-planted, the other half being subjected to the same treatment in its turn. There is not much economy in the plan.

SECTION II.—HEDGE-ROW TREES.

Hedge-row trees are a device of the old planter. Once upon a time, before the principles of timber culture were understood, it was thought that a crop of timber was filched from the land for which the tenant paid a rent, and even yet farm agreements provide for the preservation and care of the hedge-row trees for the landlord. We have often known tenants complain to agents and landlords against hedge-row trees, but never knew of any farmer proposing to plant them. They are of no value whatever to the farmer as shelter, because the cattle invariably destroy the branches up to the shelter line, and the trees destroy all live fences, except beech, wherever they grow. They also hurt crops by their shade, and they rob the soil by their roots. To the landlord they are equally valueless because there is little demand for the timber, which is too rough, and often full of nails driven in in mending fences by the tenants; and lastly, an excessive quantity of hedge-row timber has been often pleaded as a good reason for a less rent.   Wherever the farming is of a high order the fields are largest and the hedge-row trees fewest in number, and the Lothians, the finely-farmed districts of east Yorkshire, Lincoln, and Surrey, and elsewhere may be cited as examples. On the great cultivated plains of the Continent there are practically no hedge-row trees, which are considered an unmixed evil.   It has been maintained that hedge-row trees are ornamental in the landscape.   To those who plead this for what is a nuisance in almost every other way we have nothing to say except that trees dotted in straight lines along fences do not consort with the landscape gardener's ideas of good taste.   To the existence of trees along the highways, bye-ways, and lanes there are fewer objections, and when these are furnished the landscape lacks nothing in the shape of trees on a land otherwise fairly well wooded.   There is no excuse for growing valueless trees on good land on any estate on which any land exists that ought to be planted.   Trees for shade are another thing, but very few of these suffice on any farm.

CHAPTER XIV.

CROPS FROM OLD STOOLS.

Poles. – Coppice. – Underwood.

SECTION I.—POLES.

NEARLY all the broad-leaved species of forest trees produce shoots or suckers from old stools—notably the oak, elm, ash, sycamore, alder, and Spanish chestnut; but the reproductive power depends upon the age and vigour of the stool. Taking the oak, for example, one of the most productive from the stool, old trees in which the annual growth has become feeble, and the heart-wood extends nearly to the bark, leaving the sap-wood layer thin, rarely push strongly from the stool, and many·such stools never push at all. Reproduction in such cases should be made by sowing or planting, and no dependence placed on the stools. On the other hand, stools of trees that have been felled in the flush of vigour, always indicated by a broad layer of white sap-wood, reproduce strong shoots quickly that form a plantation much quicker than plants do under the most favourable circumstances. Timber crops that are thriving are, however, better left than felled, because they are laying on timber and value much quicker than a second crop of trees from the stools would do for a long time to come, the increment in all plantations increasing with the size and age of the trees. These remarks refer chiefly to crops that are clear cut. In mixed woods which have to be thinned there are always crops of suckers coming up more or less from the old stools, and these, if looked after and properly regulated, soon re-stock a wood, but, as a rule, the stools are neglected or the young shoots are eaten down by rabbits as fast as they grow up, and the crop is lost. We have, however, occasionally seen fine crops of poles from stools, the number of poles to a stool averaging from three to four. When a stool crop is expected the trees should be cleanly felled close to the ground when the sap is down in winter, as if felled in spring some species bleed freely. Tending and thinning of stool crops is the same as in young plantations. See Plate No. 7.

SECTION II.—COPPICE.

Since the first edition of this book was written I have inspected many crops of coppice in the southern and western counties, and if the reports of owners are anywhere near the mark, coppice is now one of the most unprofitable wood crops that can be grown. The demand has subsided, but the decline in value has been mainly due to over-production. Twenty shillings per acre rent induced owners, at one time, to grow more coppice than timber, and the price has gone down about 70 per cent.—unless it be of first-class stuff. Where ash, oak, birch, Spanish chestnut, and alder have been mixed with the hazel, which usually constituted the main crop, the plan of converting the coppice into timber has been successfully adopted in some places. This is done by gradually doing away with the underwood and leaving the strongest shoots of the species named to grow into trees. In such cases the main point is to thin the shoots on the stools early, leaving plenty, and taking care to leave those suckers or shoots that spring from near the soil, as these make independent roots and always produce the soundest trees.

Where the crop consists of hazel exclusively nothing can be done, and on some estates owners would be glad to get rid of the stools if that were practicable at a reasonable expense. I have noted a fact bearing on this head which is worth mentioning. Rabbits are very fond of hazel underwood when young, and, if allowed, they will attack and completely destroy the young shoots after a clear cut, and in two or three years the stools will rot and die out. I have seen acres of hazel stools quite killed in that way, and where stools that had produced a dense crop before could be kicked out by the foot. Ash and other species succumb in the same way, but not as soon as the hazel, which does not seem to long survive the close cropping of the young shoots.

The general management of coppice consists in growing the most useful species, and such as grow up quickly, like the ash, sweet chestnut, larch, and hazel, and in regulating the crop at an early stage so as to produce useful small poles or rails as soon as possible. The area devoted to coppice should be divided into sections, which may be cut in succession, so that when the last section is cut the first may be ready to go down again. Where coppice is specially planted for stakes and very small poles, there are no species equal to the larch, ash, and Spanish chestnut, and these should be sown or planted thickly.

SECTION III.—UNDERWOOD SHADE BEARERS.

It has been stated in Chapter III. that underwood, in the old sense of the word, is incompatible with dense forest-tree culture; and so it is. It is an advantage, however, to have over-thinned woods stocked with good underwood, because of its sheltering influence to the trees and soil, but in dense timber it is inadmissible except as covert for game, and then only the few shade-bearers will succeed that are named in the list given elsewhere. It is not sufficiently understood by owners of game preserves, who are constantly making enquiries on this subject, that there are few if any species of shrub or low tree that naturally prefer the shade of other trees; they all love the light, and what destroys underwood so frequently in woods is shade. For planting as under-cover, therefore, those species that bear shade best should be planted, and no other. If this was done in a systematic way, in conjunction with the scheme suggested in Chapter II., we can conceive of thoroughly well timber-stocked areas on private estates combined with game covert far superior to anything yet attempted in that way.

The shade-bearers for under-planting are the spruce, beech, hornbeam, holly, yew, rhododendron, and snowberry. These are the best shade-bearers we have, and the beech is the best in the list. Young beech trees have the advantage that although the leaves die and turn brown in autumn, they are not shed, but remain upon the branches during winter, thus providing a warm shelter. We have often seen the beech growing freely under the dense shade of deciduous trees, and German foresters often take advantage of it for under-planting. The hornbeam ranks next to the beech, and the other species mentioned are well known. The snow-berry is perhaps not so well known as a shade-bearer, but we can testify that it is one of the best for either fox or game covert. It grows about seven feet high, extends by suckers, which are thrown out freely, and owing to its erect habit and close way of growing it collects the dead leaves of other trees between its leafless stems until quite a thicket is formed that pheasants and other game birds and animals resort to during winter. But our own inclination in planting an under-covert of the kind here described would be to use the beech in a proportion equal to all the others, and to plant thick either over the whole area or in patches here and there.

CHAPTER XV.

THE BARK CROP.

SECTION I.—STRIPPING AND DRYING.

THE bark crop is not now of nearly so much importance as it once was.   Larch bark has practically gone out of demand, and oak bark, though still extensively used for tanning purposes, is hardly worth the harvesting for its own value. Peeled oak timber, however, fetches a better price than that which is not peeled, and the removal of the bark reduces weight and the cost of haulage very considerably.   For these reasons alone purchasers still strip the bark, going even to the expense, in some parts of Yorkshire, of stripping the trees standing at a cost of thirty-five shillings per ton.   The causes of the decline in the value of oak bark are that substitutes for tanning purposes are now in more common use, if not by themselves, in conjunction with oak bark to accelerate the process and reduce the cost, and that much good bark is sent over to this country from the Continent.

The barking season depends upon the ascent of the sap, which, in its turn, depends on the weather, or rather the temperature.   The bark cannot be detached before the sap is fully on the move, nor after the leaves have expanded, and attention is therefore needed to catch the crop at the right time.   Whether owing to the sudden thickening of the sap, or some other cause, the work of stripping may be completely arrested by a sudden change from mild to cold weather, and quite frequently in peeling standing trees one side of a tree will peel when the other side will not.   Neither do all the trees in a lot come on at the same time, hence, when a lot is felled straight off and peeled down, the mallet has to be used oftener than is desirable to loosen the bark, which is best got without such assistance.   Stripping the bark from the trees standing is probably the best way to get most bark and preserve the timber, but the rule is to fell and strip afterwards.   The trees may be tried with the chisel while standing, and such as are found to be ready should be felled and stripped forthwith, and so on till the lot is finished.   It is of much importance to get the bark off quickly, dried, and away, or stacked in the wood until it can be removed.   In drying the bark it should be laid out so as to allow the air to play around it. For this purpose gantries should be erected in the wood in open, airy spots conveniently near, and on these the bark should be laid thinly and be frequently turned, always keeping the outer side of the bark uppermost. The gantries, or drying stages, consist simply of two stout rails laid parallel, about two feet apart, on forked sticks driven into the ground about three feet apart, and standing up about a yard from the ground so as to allow the air to circulate freely underneath. Sometimes only two rails are required, but more may be used by laying cross pieces on the forked supports and laying the rails in these. In stacking bark large quantities should not be put together unless it has been well dried, and the stacks, which should be round, should be thatched with the best pieces of bark or covered with tarpaulin. On all large estates there are always woodmen who understand the work of stripping and drying, and on most estates in the north of England it is the custom to let the getting of the crop by contract to such men, who employ assistants. This plan usually works well for both sides provided the conditions are made clear, viz., that the work is to be proceeded with diligently with a sufficient number of hands, while the season is on, the bark to be properly dried and stacked, or loaded off by road or rail to the consumer. Should the season be warm and favourable it is of much importance to have everything ready and a sufficient number of hands for the work, otherwise it may not be possible to secure half a crop before the leaves are out and the work has to cease. Barking tools consist of an axe, bill-hook, barking iron, and mallet, which are described in the chapter on tools.

CHAPTER XVI.

VALUING AND SELLING TIMBER.

Timber Valuers.—Standing Timber.--Fallen Timber.—Cordwood.
Conditions of Sale.—Felling Timber.

SECTION I.—TIMBER VALUERS.

IT will be granted, we think, that unless the owner succeeds
in getting his timber valued and sold to advantage he cannot
be said to have fully realised the object of growing it. Whatever system of forestry may be adopted the methods of
valuing and selling the timber are much the same in all cases,
but we strongly advise owners who value the future of their
woods to employ either their own or some other competent
forester to set out the lots for sale and ascertain the quality of
the timber and the number of cubic feet in each lot. The last
is the main object, as when the quality is known the vendor
may safely hold out for a fair price, and will usually get it.
We are here referring to standing timber; fallen timber can
be measured, but more is sold standing than fallen in England
at present.

In setting out standing timber for sale, where a clear cut is
not desired, only the trees that ought to come out should be
marked, and these will usually be a portion of the oldest trees,
and such as show signs of decay, or such as need to be
removed in thinning, the healthiest growing trees being left in
a regular way throughout the wood. No one can do this but
a forester—and his employer's interests are his own. This
advice is offered because there are persons calling themselves
estate and timber valuers, or surveyors and auctioneers, who
profess to conduct timber sales to far better advantage than
those on the spot can do, and who seek for engagements of
that kind over the heads of resident agents and foresters.
They set forth to owners of woods that their extensive connection with the timber trade and the facilities they possess give
them advantages not possessed by others, and not unfrequently
secure important engagements, particularly among proprietors
who happen to have considerable quantities of timber but who
do not employ a regular forester. We dare say such agents
may occasionally be able to value timber and sell it too, but
their woodcraft ends there. Some recognise this, and employ
foresters to do the work for them, in which case the vendor

has to pay both. The agents we speak of have usually their head-quarters in London and in a few other large towns. They do not care to trouble with small or poor lots, but prefer to deal with large trees and large quantities of undoubted quality that anybody can sell, and they set the lots out themselves. Gentlemen are written to by such firms that they have been engaged to dispose of the valuable lots on Mr. So-and-So's estate, in the neighbourhood of the party addressed, on a certain date, and their patronage is solicited at the same time, the plea being urged that their extensive acquaintance with timber buyers enabled them to bring noted buyers to the sales that would not otherwise attend, and that the result was sure to be advantageous to the vendor. With the phraseology slightly altered, the above is a copy of a communication of this kind. We have looked into sales of this description conducted by well-known London firms, two hundred miles from London, seen the lots after they were set out, and been present at the sales, and our opinion is that a loss may be sustained by employing such agents, but no advantage gained. One example may suffice. A London surveyor and auctioneer was appointed to sell several thousand pounds' worth of oak timber on two different estates. His charge was seven-and-a-half per cent. on the sales, and with the aid of his men, who came with him, the lots were set out over the heads of those in charge, and the sale was transferred from the usual place to an hotel in another town. We went, previous to the sale, to every tree marked, and found that the process of valuing and setting out consisted in simply marking the best and biggest trees in the wood—a mere timber merchant's device—without regard to the future crop. At the sale the old faces were present—all local men—and every lot went to the same purchasers as before ; the finest lot going to a timber merchant who resided about four miles from the wood. The fact is, as every forester and timber merchant knows, that timber in the rough is one of the most expensive commodities to move about, and those purchasers and consumers who live near the spot where the timber is can, as a rule, afford to give the best prices and do give them. There are buyers in or near all towns of any importance, and they will buy near home if they can, to save carriage, and the difference goes into their pocket and that of the vendor. We have known purchasers to encumber themselves with lots they did not need at the time because they happened to be near. We are here speaking of general lots of timber. Trees of special quality are often bought and carried long distances, but such cases are the exception. No auctioneer or other agent can draw purchasers to a sale as surely as a properly worded advertisement in any of the timber trade journals and local papers can do, and it may be accepted as a rule that, all other things being equal, the further the purchaser has to come the less he can afford to pay, unless he can enter the lists in the local market, which he cannot easily do with advantage.

<h2 style="text-align:center">SECTION II.—STANDING TIMBER.</h2>

On estates where considerable quantities are sold annually it is a common practice to sell the lots standing in quantities to suit purchasers, who take all the risks of felling and removal, subject to the usual conditions in such cases. This is the cheapest and most convenient method for the proprietor, and the best, provided the lots are accurately valued before they are offered for sale, and experienced men only can do that. The contents of standing trees have to be estimated by sight principally, much as butchers judge the weight of fat cattle, and foresters who have had much experience in felling and measuring timber can estimate the contents of standing trees very closely when they go methodically to work, beginning with the trunk and most valuable portion of the tree and finishing up with the main limbs and branches of measurable dimensions one by one. No expert can pretend to get at the contents of a tree in any other way. As a rule, the greater the average girth of the trunk of a tree and the longer and straighter it is the greater the value per cubic foot it should be. This applies especially to oak, sycamore, beech, elm, and ash. Oak of fine quality, flowery texture, and good dark colour, fit for making furniture or sawing up into thin veneers and such like purposes, should not be sold standing, but felled and sold for what it is worth. What a fine tree of this kind might fetch standing in a lot would in all probability be far below its real value. One cubic foot of oak sawn into veneers about one-sixteenth of an inch thick or less would produce nearly two hundred superficial feet, and each square foot would fetch a good price. The vendor could not expect this price in the wood, but the trees should bring a much higher figure than oak of ordinary quality. Much fine English pollard oak is sent from Liverpool to America, a great proportion coming from the south of England.

In proceeding to value a lot of standing timber the valuer should provide himself with a pass book, a telescope measuring rod, in five feet lengths, marked in feet and half feet, a woodman's measuring tape, and a Hoppus's timber measurer or ready reckoner, which is in universal use, and almost the only guide purchasers will accept, and near enough for all practical purposes as long as both vendor and purchaser agree to its use. As shown in accompanying example, on pages 184 and 185, the valuer's pass-book is ruled on the left-hand page for "trees," by which is meant all trees in any lot containing ten cubic feet and upwards; all below that figure down to one cubic foot being reckoned as "poles," which are entered on the right-hand page in fives, as shown, their cubic contents to be averaged and summed up afterwards.

Provided thus, the valuer, with his assistants, beginning at one side of the wood, should set out the lot in sections or strips as directed in setting out thinnings in another chapter. The trees and poles should all be marked on the same side with white paint, the trees being numbered in consecutive order and the poles dotted. Some use a scribe only, but paint is better, being easily seen and not so easily tampered with. The trees and poles should be taken as they come, and those that are to be left need not be marked at all. Any experienced woodman can distinguish the trees from the poles at sight, and the valuer's assistants should mark those that he points out to come down.

Many of the hard-wood trees in our woods and parks consist of a not very tall trunk and numerous limbs, all of which should be estimated separately as "timber" down to six inches quarter-girth, the smaller branches and top-wood being reckoned as cord-wood. The telescope measuring rod may be used to find the height of a tree, and the girth of the trunk may be taken as high up as a man can reach, in order to ascertain approximately what the girth half way up may be; but for that, and the length and girth of the upper limbs, the valuer has to depend on his judgment and sight. All trees are, generally, measured above the bark, except the oak, in which an allowance at the rate of one inch in twelve of the girth is made. Sometimes the bark is allowed for in larch, but that depends on the agreement between the vendor and the buyer. In the case of the oak the quantity of bark is calculated, in standing timber, at the rate of a ton to every one hundred and sixty to two hundred feet of timber, according to its thickness, and the value is added to that of the timber in the lot.

In proceeding to work, the valuer first ascertains the height and middle-girth of the trunk, or sections of it, between main limbs, and sets the cubic contents, which he will find in his " Hoppus," down on his slate. Next he counts the number of measureable limbs, notes their length and girth separately, and puts the contents down beside those of the trunk, prices both separately, according to size and quality,

LOT 1

TREES.

No. of each Tree.	Kind of Tree.	Contents in Cubic Feet.	Value. £ s. d.
	Oak.	40	3 0 0
2	Ash.	30	1 7 6
3	Sycamore.	80	8
Totals ...			

Carried forward...

adds all up, and, lastly, enters the number of the tree, its kind, the feet, and the total value, in their respective columns, and proceeds to the next tree, carrying the count of poles in the strip along with him, and so on till the lot is finished. Tapering fir trees are easily estimated, as the run off in the taper is regular, but hard-woods should be measured in sections or lengths between main limbs. In all spreading,

HAGG WOOD.

POLES.

Oak.	Ash.	Sycamore.	Beech.	Elm.	Birch.	Alder.
I I I I I	I I I I I	I I I I I	I I I I I	I I I I I	I I I I I	I I I I I
I I I I I	I I I I I	I I I I I	I I I I I	I I I I I	I I I I I	I I I I I

Carried forward ...

large-limbed hard-woods the main trunk decreases in girth beyond every "break," that is to say, where limbs diverge from the trunk. Hence every break should be measured separately to get the true contents of the tree—first, its length from the upper side of the limb below to the upper side of the limb above, where the girth drops off, and next the quarter-girth half-way between these two points. This will give the solid contents. It is generally in park trees where this kind of work has to be done, and as a rule the best plan is to fell these and measure them afterwards. In any case, no novice nor beginner should be allowed to measure timber standing or felled, as he is sure to be far out one way or the other. The next business is the averaging of the poles. This is done by measuring carefully a score or more of poles on one spot, and all on the spot, at regular distances apart, in every part of the wood, so as to get as fair an average as possible. These measurements in cubic feet are then added together and divided by the number of poles which they represent, and the result will be the average to be applied to all the poles in the lot. Thus: supposing there are three thousand poles in the lot, and that three hundred poles have been measured, giving an average of five feet, the total quantity of feet in the lot would be fifteen thousand feet, and the price per foot would give the total value. This should be added to the trees, etc., and all particulars entered in the timber book fully worked out, and the lot is ready to be offered.

SECTION III.—FALLEN TIMBER.

Wherever the proprietor has any doubts about selling his standing timber to advantage, he should sell it down. This will cause an expense of from one penny to twopence per foot in felling, hauling, and lotting, which must be added to the standing price. The lots should be felled between November and March, and every tree and pole should have its contents marked with a scribe on the thick end where they can be seen when the trees are lotted. The different kinds should be lotted in quantities of one hundred feet or thereabout, and arranged according to quality, not mixing the good with the bad, in the false expectation of making the one sell the other, as is sometimes done. The best price is obtained when the lots are arranged to suit all sorts of purchasers and consumers. Small local consumers do not buy large lots of timber: they do not need them, and will often pick out and buy what they want from a larger purchaser after the sale is over, the vendor thus losing by the transaction, for the merchant must sell at a profit. The lots should be laid conveniently near to roads or drives, and the trees should be nicely trimmed with the axe and laid with their thick ends evenly to the road. Very large and valuable trees may form single lots, and such trees are better sold where they fall, as hauling out of the wood is expensive work. Small timber is different, and must be presented in lots.

SECTION IV.—CORD-WOOD AND UNDERWOOD.

No precise rule can be laid down for the disposal of these. The cord-wood is valued by the ton or cord, either ranked or as it lies, about four shillings and sixpence being allowed for ranking, the value of the cord-wood itself varying from two shillings and sixpence to five shillings per ton; cut and ranked, seven shillings and sixpence to nine shillings and sixpence per ton or cord. In many localities now-a-days, however, the cord-wood cannot be given away; while in some cases, when it included a good deal of thick wood from old park trees, we have seen it fetch ten shillings per cord.

Underwood is sold by the acre or lot, according to the quantity, as much as from £10 to £20 per acre being got for a good thick crop consisting principally of hazel and good crate wood, but such prices are rare now.

SECTION V.—CONDITIONS OF SALE.

Whether the lots are sold standing or felled, they should be offered for sale early in the autumn, to enable purchasers to have the timber got at the right season of the year. Printed circulars containing particulars of the number of the trees and poles, the different kinds, etc., date and conditions of sale, should be sent to likely purchasers, and the lots should also be advertised in the local papers in good time. The vendor may sell by private bargain, by tender, or by auction; each plan being good in its way, provided the lots have been fairly valued and the vendor knows about what they are really worth. He is not bound to accept the highest or any offer, and he should make that clear in the conditions of sale. Purchasers

should sign an agreement like the following, which is usually
sufficient; as, however stringent the conditions may be, everything depends on them being carried out, and that depends
more upon the vendor's agents and the purchaser's workmen
than anyone else.

The following form is shown filled in, but the words in
italics should be left out and the spaces blank to be filled in
according to the conditions and circumstances, and both pages
should be on the opposite sides of one sheet.

FORM OF AGREEMENT FOR THE SALE OF TIMBER.

CONDITIONS OF SALE

OF TIMBER AND WOOD, THE PROPERTY OF *A.   B.*, ON
THE ESTATE OF *W———*, IN THE COUNTY OF *YORK*.

1.—That the purchase money shall be paid on completion of
purchase, or on or before the *twenty-ninth day of
September, eighteen hundred and ninety-nine.*

2.—That the timber shall be at the purchaser's risk on completion of the purchase agreement.

3.—That the various lots are believed to be correctly described,
but the vendor shall not be responsible for any errors or
mistakes that may have been made.

4.—That the timber or wood shall be removed by the
purchaser on or before the *first day of November,
nineteen hundred.*

5.—That the timber shall be removed subject to the wood
agent's directions, and any unnecessary damages to
gates, fences, standing trees, coppice wood, or farm
crops, shall be made good by the purchaser to the
vendor's satisfaction.

6.—That the lots shall be felled and removed at the purchaser's
expense and risk.

DESCRIPTION OF LOTS REFERRED TO.

Where situated—*in Hagg Wood.*

Lot 1.—*Consisting of*

240 Oak Trees.
400 Oak Poles.
40 Ash Trees.
8 Ash Poles.
5 Elm Trees.
30 Mixed Poles.
With Top-wood and Underwood.

AGREEMENT.

I, *Thomas Jones, of*   *Yorkshire,*
do hereby acknowledge that *I* have become the purchaser
of the Lots described in the annexed particulars, at the sum of
three hundred and fifty pounds, ten shillings net, on the
terms of the foregoing conditions, which I hereby engage to
abide by and perform in every respect, *as*

Witness *my* hand this *first* day of *March,* 1899.

Purchase Money ... *£350 : 10 : 0 net.*

Witness to signature,

STAMP.

SECTION VI.—FELLING TIMBER.

Whether the trees are felled by the proprietor of the woods or by the purchasers of the timber, the men employed should be the workmen belonging to the estate, or such as are approved of by the forester.   This is a common custom, and the reason of it is that the regular woodmen on the estate are likely to be more trustworthy and careful than strangers.

There are probably no axe-men in the world who surpass the English woodmen accustomed to fell hard-woods. Canadian woodmen are often spoken of as experts with the axe, but their work is roughly executed.   Even the German woodman, so careful, as a rule, is a slovenly axe-man compared to the regular timber feller in England, often leaving the stumps of the trees standing above ground and not cleanly cut, the hand-saw being commonly used for poles.   The English woodman uses both the double-handed saw and the axe, but many woodmen prefer the axe alone, with which they fell the largest trees with very little waste.   It is, however, preferable to use the saw after the tree has been prepared by the axe, so that the saw can be effectually got to work.   There are several kinds of axes in use for felling, but the English and American axes are now mainly used.   For hard-woods the long, narrow English axe is by far the best.   This axe weighs fully seven pounds, and has a face not exceeding three-and-a-quarter inches, and a much curved edge.   With a tool of this size and weight the workman can deliver a deeper stroke, in a hard oak for example, than he could with the broad, square-faced American axe, which is no doubt suitable for soft fir and the axe, but next to useless in felling hard-woods. The good axe-man fells his trees low, without waste, and smoothly, off by the surface of the soil.   He prefers to do his work by contract at so much per ton of forty cubic feet. From two shillings to two shillings and ninepence per ton are common prices in the Midlands, the lowest prices being given for soft woods and the highest price for hard-woods.   As a rule, the expert axe-man, with the aid of wedges, can lay his tree where he chooses if he takes his bearings beforehand, and so avoid damaging standing trees.   All is reckoned measureable timber down to six inches quarter-girth in hard-woods and three inches in larch, whether trunk or limbs, and the feller's contract includes the cutting off from the trunk the limbs, where necessary, and trimming the tree in a workman-like manner ready for removal to the saw mill.

CHAPTER XVII.

OSIER CULTIVATION.

SECTION I.

OSIER cultivation is a subject more allied to market gardening than to forestry, as carried on at present, but there is no reason why osiers should not be grown on private estates where a market can be found for the produce. The demand, however, is not very great, and the trade is mainly in the hands of growers in the Thames and Severn valleys and in Cambridgeshire and Huntingdonshire. In addition to the home supply, about three hundred thousand bundles are imported annually from Holland and France. Osiers (willows) are used for tying purposes by nurserymen and others, in hurdle making, and extensively for making chairs, baskets, etc. No great capital is required to go into osier culture, and the profits are said to be large, as after the beds are established very little cultural attention is required, and the beds last for more than twenty years. Osiers require a very moist or wet soil, and do not suffer by flooding in summer, but means should be provided to drain the water off in winter or when required. Thick planting and dense culture is essential in order to prevent the stems from producing side-shoots, clean, single wands being the aim. The French pay much attention to this, using varieties of the willow and methods of culture that produce wands of suitable size for all purposes, the thicker and coarser ones going for common purposes, and the slender ones for the manufacture of neat baskets and other useful articles. The ground having been selected, deeply dug, and thrown into beds about ten feet wide, with alleys between, it should be planted about February, or earlier, by inserting short pieces of mature shoots into the soil from fifteen inches to three feet apart, according to the variety and the purpose for which the osiers are intended, strong-growing varieties being given most room, and vice versa. Some recommend the beds to be frequently hoed and dug to prevent weeds growing; but given a good soil to begin with, very little attention of that kind is needed. Most good osier plantations that we have seen were so dense that no weeds could grow under them, and the surface of the beds were covered with a layer of black mould produced by the dead foliage. Top-dressing with manure is not objectionable, but in producing slender wands no manure is applied. The crop is cut during winter months, and in cutting care is taken to cut close to the stools to keep these near the ground. The sorting, preparing, and peeling of the osiers for the market and for various purposes is a business that can only be properly learned on the spot, and those who contemplate osier culture should seek information on this subject from experienced osier growers when the crop is being cut and stored. The varieties of willow in cultivation for osiers are not numerous, and they are the same now as they were half-a-century ago or more; strength, slenderness, and toughness being the qualities most desired, and in which respect varieties differ considerably. We take the liberty to add the following notes from the "Gardener's Chronicle" of November 19th, 1898, on this subject:—

"*Species.*—There are two species of osier here—

"(1.) *Salix viminalis* (common osier). The leaves are elongated, the bark grey. This species does well for coarse wicker-work, and is the more prolific of the two.

"(2.) *Salix purpurea* (Spanish osier). The leaves somewhat resemble those of the peach, and easily distinguish it from the common osier. The bark is reddish-purple. This species is better adapted for fine wicker-work.

"*Dangers to which the crop is exposed.*—Insects constitute the chief danger. A destructive leaf-roller—*Earias hlorana*—is found, which often eats into the centre of the leading shoots, and destroys the growth of the willows.

"*Yield.*—The slips are planted $2\frac{1}{2}$ feet by $2\frac{1}{2}$ feet apart, so that we get $\dfrac{43,560}{2\frac{1}{2} \times 2\frac{1}{2}} = 6969$ (say 7000) stools in an acre. If the stools give an average of ten wands apiece, we shall get 70,000 wands per acre. In France they are often grown much closer than this. These shoots or wands are tied up in bundles called "bolts." Each bolt contains about one hundred wands, and is worth 2s. This gives us about £70 gross return per acre.

"This cultivating of osier coppice is a good, sensible way of utilising what would otherwise be practically useless ground, and is certainly to be recommended."

CHAPTER XVIII.

CONVERSION OF TIMBER ON ESTATES.

Sawn Timber.—Transport of Timber.—Creosoting.

SECTION I.—SAWN TIMBER.

A SUGGESTIVE feature in one branch of the timber trade in Germany, that travellers notice, is that on the railway and canal wharves, etc., the timber for transport anywhere is generally in the sawn state, in the shape of boards, battens and other scantlings, in net bulk, so to speak; whereas in this country it is almost always in the round or rough state as it is felled in the wood, representing an enormously greater expense in haulage as well as loss in other ways. And this partly converted timber from the German forests represents only a portion of the produce, much of it being worked up in factories in or near the forests, all the small wood and waste being left behind for firewood and other purposes. On the Continent, however, the supply is regular, and employment for saw-mills, driven by steam or water, is constant. In Britain that is not the case, even on the largest estates, and saw-mills, except in a small way for estate purposes, are costly to erect and maintain of a capacity to deal with all sizes of timber, otherwise it would certainly pay the owners of timber, when felled in considerable quantities, to partly convert their timber at home before offering it to purchasers. The portable saw-mill offers some facilities in that respect, whether hired or kept on the estate, but travelling saw-mills are not as yet common. The extensive windfalls of recent times in Scotland has, to some extent, brought them into use, but in England they are not readily available. With a saw-mill near to the timber, battens, boards for flooring and other purposes, scantlings of various kinds, railway materials, fencing rails and posts, pit-props, telegraph poles, etc., all of which are now either imported or sawn up at local saw-mills, could be easily manufactured and as readily sold. Railways and waggon builders alone provide a very ready market for large quantities of our best timber. For one oak waggon sole,

13

free from flaws, about eighteen feet long and about ten
inches by six inches, a price can be got sometimes exceeding
the price of a whole tree, sold standing, that might probably
contain several such pieces of timber.   The same remarks
apply to the other timbers required for the frame work of
waggons, and also to good butts of sycamore, ash, and beech,
etc.   In short, the home saw-mill could cut up a great variety
of materials in constant demand by different trades.   The
disadvantage would be, on most estates, that the supply
would not be regular, and orders could not be always
accepted to suit purchasers.   A partly idle saw-mill is not
a profitable concern, and such workshops require trained men,
and come within the scope of the Workmen's Compensation
Act.   Where water-power can be had, a saw-mill for
ordinary estate purposes does not cost a great deal, but to be
of sufficient capacity for general purposes the plant would
have to be on a scale such as few private estates could
profitably maintain.

SECTION II.—TRANSPORT OF TIMBER.

In regard to this subject it need only be stated that horse
labour is the most expensive method by far of hauling timber.
Traction engines can be employed on almost any wood road
or drive, provided the wheels are about two-and-a-half feet
broad, and the engines do not much exceed ten tons, and they
are much cheaper than horses where much work has to be
done.   Fifty per cent. or more is said to have been saved by
their use.   Tramways are cheaper still when the timber has to
be transported a good distance, and are much employed in
the colonies.

SECTION III.—CREOSOTING TIMBER.

Considering how cheaply creosoted fencing materials can
now be bought from Hartlepool and elsewhere, we cannot here
recommend creosoting plant, generally (usually involving a
saw-mill), for private estates, except where many miles of
wood fencing have to be kept up.   Spruce and Scotch fir
posts and rails can also be made, seasoned and dipped in
black varnish or gas tar, at the rate of about 6d. per cubic foot,
including the price of the timber ; and a creosoted cubic foot

costs nearly twice that sum. A fair-sized creosoting boiler costs from £150 to £200 exclusive of fixing, the oil costs from 4d. to 5d. per gallon, and about one-and-a-half gallons are required to soak one cubic foot of timber. Spruce and Scotch fir ought to be chiefly used for creosoting, as they are worth least to the owner, and save the use of larch and oak.

The following abridged extract from the "Land Agent's Record," April 7th, 1900, refers to an estate where an extensive creosoting apparatus is in operation:—"Since 1895 we have used scarcely any fencing but creosoted home-grown spruce, Scotch and silver fir for fencing purposes, and find that the spruce posts put down in 1895 are to-day apparently as sound as ever. The posts are bored and morticed, and all the bark (if any) removed, and then piled up to dry for some time before creosoting. We generally give them about three hours at a pressure of from 60 to 70 lbs. per square inch, and find that as a rule is enough. But, of course, the drier the timber the more oil it absorbs, and the larger the posts, etc., are, the longer pressure they require. When practicable, rails, pales, boards, etc., are done by themselves, and fence posts, etc., and similar sized pieces likewise. The cost of creosoting depends chiefly on two things, viz., the price of the oil and the amount injected per foot. At present I am getting a good oil, 1040 specific gravity, delivered at our nearest station, at 4⅛d. per gallon. To cart and empty forty casks (two trucks) and return the empties takes an engine and three men two days, loading back the second day with coals. As to the cost, the following are the results of some tests made in 1899:—Thirty-nine posts (morticed for four rails), 6½ ft. long × 6 in. × 4½ in., weighed 35⅕ lbs. each before creosoting, and 48½ lbs. after—that is, 13 $\frac{3}{10}$ lbs., or 1·28 gallons of oil per post, was used. This would be at the rate of about 5¼d. each. The posts were naturally dried and were subjected to a pressure of 65 to 70 lbs. for 3½ hours. One hundred and twenty Scotch, silver, and spruce rails, 8 ft. long × 4 in. × 2 in., absorbed 5lbs., or ½ gallon each, costing 2½d. per rail. Generally we use 1 to 1½ gallons of oil per cubic foot, and creosote gates, hurdles, scantlings, posts of all sizes, rails, pales, boards, etc.—in fact, anything that will go into the cylinder. The cylinder is 25½ ft. long, the diameter of doorways is 6 ft., and of the main portion 7 ft. It is made of mild steel and steam jacketed, and costs about £200."

CHAPTER XIX.

DISEASES AND ENEMIES OF FOREST TREES.

General Remarks—Four-footed Enemies of Forest
Trees.—Insects and Diseases.

SECTION I.—GENERAL REMARKS.

BOOKS have been written on this subject by such authorities as Hartig, Marshall Ward, Schlich, and others, to whose works we must refer the reader for a full account of the almost endless list of plagues that attack trees. Here we propose only to give prominence to those diseases and insect pests, etc., that do most damage to the timber trees recommended for planting in this work; and for the names and descriptions of some of these we are indebted to the authorities named.

We hope we shall not be considered as under-rating the services of able and patient investigators of forest tree enemies and diseases if we say that the subject looks much more formidable on paper than it does to the practical forester, either in this country or on the Continent. The name of the plagues that are now described as enemies of forest trees is " legion," but in this country the number the forester has reason to fear and be really anxious about might almost be counted on the fingers of the two hands, and these few, rabbits and the like excepted, he has hardly any practical means of combating except by giving effect, as far as he can, to those conditions relating to climate, soil, exposure, and choice of species, etc., that control tree life. Preventive measures of a practical kind are not likely to ever extend further, and such authorities as Hartig and Marshall Ward seem to realise that. The latter, in his preface to the English edition of Hartig's " Diseases of Trees," says, that the practical forester may object that the author gives too little information as to the details of combative or therapeutic treatment of the special diseases, but that it is not necessarily the duty of the scientific pathologist to devise plans of remedial treatment, which may or may not be true ; but it might be replied that a mere list of names is of no service to the forester who is not a scientific pathologist, and we always thought that the investigation of disease and its prevention or cure went hand in hand, and at least endeavoured to keep pace with each other.

The diseases and parasites, of one kind or another, that attack trees are, according to investigators, so hopelessly overwhelming in number that one is almost tempted to think they are but a part of the "universal plan" in the economy of nature, and need not be regarded in all cases as seriously destructive agents.

A list of the pests that beset but two of the best known species, the oak and the Scotch fir, for example, will afford some idea of the nature of the task anyone has before him who regards them as troubles calling for practical measures of prevention or cure over large areas   The oak and Scotch fir happen to be among the worst afflicted, it is true, but their case is suggestive.   According to Schlich, Kallenbach, in an incomplete list, enumerates five hundred species of insects alone that attack the oak; while Hartig, in his "Classified List of Diseases," resulting from cryptogams, phanerogams, bacteria, and fungi, puts the number for the oak at fifteen.   Nearly a score of grubs and insects, etc., attack the Scotch fir, and Hartig's number of diseases for the same tree is thirty, and so on, Hartig's general list occupying twelve pages; while he states elsewhere that the predisposing causes, alone, of disease are "endless."   Another emphatic statement. of Hartig's, p. 16, will bewilder those writers on forestry and gardening who have so confidently held that disease is transmitted by seed, and that, hence, seed should not be collected from diseased trees and plants.   Hartig writes, " a transmission by inheritance of disease to descendants is unknown in the vegetable kingdom.   One may without hesitation make use of the seeds of plants suffering from any conceivable disease for the propagation of new plants."   Hartig's definition of actual disease is a "sickly condition leading to the death of some part of the plant."   A diminution of growth may not be disease, but disease may result from it.   According to the general definition, disease is anything, excepting accidents, that causes "a diminution of the functional power," and Dr. Lindley, in his "Theory and Practice of Horticulture," says the assertion that seeds in all cases produce healthy plants will not bear exact investigation, and most foresters and gardeners will agree with him.   It is a general rule, says Dr. Lindley, that seedlings take after their parents, an unhealthy mother producing a diseased offspring, and vice versa.   There cannot be found a gardener of any large experience, he adds, who does not know that seedlings will exhibit every diversity of constitution from health to decrepitude.

Perhaps the safest plan for the forester is to act in practice on Dr. Lindley's opinions, and collect seeds from healthy subjects only.

SECTION II.—FOUR-FOOTED ENEMIES OF FOREST TREES.

These include rabbits, hares, squirrels, mice, and deer, and it may be taken for granted that these animals damage and destroy all forest trees more or less if they have the chance, and the only means of preventing their ravages is to destroy them or shut them out of plantations. Rabbits bark both young and old trees to a destructive extent. Hares nibble the shoots and leaders of young trees, especially of the larch. Deer bark trees and also injure them with their horns. Where squirrels abound they do almost as much harm as rabbits by nibbling the buds and shoots. The proprietor of one Highland estate writes us that he had lost thousands of pounds through their depredations although he killed hundreds every year. Voles and mice gnaw the bark like rabbits, but their ravages can be told by their teeth marks and by their usually attacking young trees close to the soil under the grass, while rabbits usually eat above the grass. In hard weather mice also climb trees and eat the bark on the branches and small twigs. There is one thing connected with the attacks of rabbits upon young trees that woodmen have often noticed, viz., that planted trees are more frequently attacked and more severely injured than trees that spring up naturally from seed. This we have noticed often, especially in reference to the sycamore and ash. Patches and single trees of these spring up naturally and escape, but fill up the vacant patches in the same wood with the same species, and the chances are they will be destroyed if the rabbits are there. We have known such cases often, and could point to nice groups of self-sown sycamore, of considerable extent, twenty years of age and upwards, that have never been seriously injured, where scarcely a planted tree in the same wood escaped. We cannot explain the fact, but probably the rankness with which seedlings spring up may have something to do with it, for there can be no doubt that when thick planting is resorted to, and two or three plants are put into each hole, the crop suffers less from rabbits. Sheep bark some kinds of trees very badly, and also eat the leaves and shoots of many species indiscriminately. Cattle and horses also browse on many kinds of trees, as may often be seen in parks where the trees are usually cropped as high as the cattle can reach. Cattle and sheep are not, however, expected to be admitted into young plantations.

SECTION III.—INSECTS AND DISEASES.

In the following list the species are taken in the order in which they are given in Chapter VII., and those species that do not suffer seriously from disease and insects are grouped together.

THE OAK.—The foliage of the oak is often destroyed about midsummer by the oak caterpillars—*Tortrix viridana* and *Liparis monacha*. Whole tracts are frequently quite defoliated, not a tree escaping. The consequence is a severe check to growth and a weak, ill-matured second growth of leaves after the caterpillars have gone. Caterpillars are always worst on poor, slow-growing trees, the growth of which they quickly overtake.* They are always present in oak woods to a greater or less extent, and are worse in some places than others. The grubs also drop from the oaks upon the underwood beneath, which they also defoliate, so that an oak wood, badly attacked, presents a very miserable spectacle. Drought and poverty in the soil seem to be the main predisposing causes. Flocks of rooks, starlings, and other birds follow the caterpillars and destroy immense numbers, the rooks gorging themselves to such an extent that they can scarcely be made to rise.

RING-SHAKE AND STAR-SHAKE.—Whatever the cause of this evil or disease may be, it affects the timber of the oak on many estates and destroys its value. In a ring-shaken tree the annual rings of the trunk and main limbs are shaken loose, so to speak, become detached from each other round their whole circumference, hence the word "ring-shake." There may be several shakes in the trunk, but there are seldom two close together. Ring-shake ruptures the timber, and when the tree is sawn up it falls to pieces and is worthless. A badly-shaken tree is said by timber merchants to be "shaken like a besom," and where ring-shake is known to exist to a serious extent the timber cannot be sold standing,

---

* The geometer moth caterpillar, similar to the oak caterpillar, is also invariably most destructive to pine plantations on poor, dry soils. ("Highland Society's Transactions," 1897, p. 119.)

as the shakes cannot be seen till the tree is felled.   This
disease, or whatever it may be called, is much dreaded, and
is, we believe, worse in Scotland than in England, and in thin,
exposed woods, the probable reason of which will be shortly
explained.   The extent of the losses sustained by ring-shake
in oak woods may be gathered from a report of a sale of
timber on the Haystoun estate, near Peebles, which appeared
in the " Scottish Farmer " of November 5th, 1898, and which
states that:—"Oaks have become almost an impossibility
on the Haystoun estate on account of the prevalence of ring-
shake.   A considerable number of what would otherwise
have been valuable timber trees were seen to be badly
affected, and are thus reduced to very little over firewood
value."

In " star-shake " the cracks radiate from the centre to the
outside of the stem, or nearly so, but in shakes produced by
frost the cracks extend inwards from the outside, always
leaving a seam in the bark where it has healed over.   These
outside cracks are well-known to be due to frost, and so
probably are those found radiating from the centre.   Both
ring-shake and star-shake may be found in the same tree, and
when that is the case the tree is perfectly useless except for
firewood.

As regards ring-shake, the following case, which came
under our own observation, points strongly to frost and exposure, from sudden over-thinning at mature age, as the cause of
the evil.   In 1868, a heavy fall of oak timber was taken out
of a fairly dense wood, which was also well-furnished with tall·
underwood that was sold at the same time.   The timber was
sold standing, and was sound when felled, there being very
few shaken trees in the lot.   About twenty-five years later
another fall was bought by the same purchaser, from the
same ground, and so many of the trees were ring-shaken as to
cause serious disappointment to both vendor and buyer, the
latter having felt confident that the trees would fall as sound
as before.   The only explanation of this we can think of is
that the removal of the underwood and the thinning, in the
first fall of 1868, deprived the trees of the shelter they had
been accustomed to and permitted the cold and frost to reach
the trunks.   Owing to rabbits and the dense crop of bracken
that had overspread the wood before 1868, the underwood
never grew up again, and its removal, together with the
thinning of the oaks, probably affected the trees left.   Hartig
draws attention to the fact that the bark and tissues of a tree

that has grown up in a dense wood will not stand vicissitudes of weather like a hedge-row tree that has long grown accustomed to exposure. Hartig's ring-shake, p. 191, caused in spruce trees by *Trametes pini*, is not the ring-shake of hard-woods in this country. At page 285 he just alludes to radial and peripheral cracks that he had "sometimes noticed" in old oaks, but gives no satisfactory explanation as to their cause.

THE ASH.—This species is not troubled seriously with very destructive pests. The bark-boring beetle, *Hylesinus fraxinus*, is often found on old decaying trees, on which it makes fantastic tracings under the bark; and the blister beetle, or one of the wasps, causes large blisters to form on the trunk and branches, which finally kill the tree. These blisters are common upon single trees here and there in a wood, some trees being a mass of blister from top to bottom. A puncture is apparently made through the bark in the first instance, and never heals over like other wounds. A ring of new bark is formed round the puncture, and other rings inside of that, until a large, rugged, round blister, perhaps nine inches in diameter and depressed in the centre, where the original wound will be found still open, is formed, such blisters often being many years of age. A kind of scale also attacks young trees, especially weak saplings, and does some damage. The ash is not subject to any other serious complaints.

THE ELM.—This tree, at any age above thirty years, often dies off at the top by slow degrees. We have had to cut many Scotch elms down in mixed woods that were dead or dying from this complaint. The symptoms seem to indicate the presence of the *scolytus destructor* mentioned by Schlich and others as doing much harm to the elm. Otherwise the tree is generally a good grower either in the forest or open country.

THE BEECH.—Old trees of the beech are often attacked by the beech blight *Chermes fagi*, which attacks the bark of the trunks, generally near the bottom, and travels upwards, either following decay in the bark or causing it. The bark becomes broken and ruptured and easily detached. "Damping off," caused by a fungi *(Phytophthora omnivora)*, is very destructive among young seedlings, and where it is troublesome there is no sure preventive of its attacks but a complete change of ground.

SYCAMORE, BIRCH, ALDER, MOUNTAIN ASH, POPLAR, WILLOW, LIME, CHESTNUT, HORNBEAM, CHERRY, WALNUT. —We class these together. All of them suffer more or less from insects and diseases, but not to an extent to cause anxiety, and so far as we are aware no complaints of serious injury have been made by foresters in this country when the trees have been planted in suitable situations and tended with ordinary care The fungus, *Nectria cinnabarina*, frequently kills young sycamores, and is easily known by the eruption of red, coral-like dots which appear on the dead bark.

SCOTCH FIR, CORSICAN FIR, CLUSTER FIR, AUSTRIAN FIR, WEYMOUTH PINE.—These species are also classed together because the same diseases and enemies are common to them all. Numerous beetles and other insects attack all the species, but the four most feared, although seldom extensively destructive in this country, are the fir weevil, *Hylobius abietis;* the pine beetle, *Hylurgus pineperda;* the pine sawfly, *Lophyrus pini;* and the pine geometer moth, *Fidonia piniaria.* The first is about half-an-inch long, dark-coloured, with dull yellow bands. It begins its ravages in summer, attacking the young shoots and killing or greatly injuring the trees. The pine beetle is very small, slender, and dark. It bores into the young shoots and along the pith, and shoots die and fall off or wither on the tree. The saw-fly devours the leaves in the caterpillar state, denuding the trees completely in bad cases. We have known it attack the Austrian fir badly where the Scotch fir escaped with little damage. This was on a hillside in North Yorkshire. The geometer moth's ravages are similar to those of the saw-fly and are much dreaded in Germany.

Of fungus that attack the Scotch fir and others named, *Agaricus melleus* and *Trametes radiciperda* are the worst. We have had no experience of the last, but the first has been very troublesome on the Wortley estate, where it has caused gaps in young plantations. The presence of the fungus is often not detected till a tree in some spot loses colour, and droops and dies. Another and another follows next to the first one, and so on till in the course of a couple of years or so a complete clearing is made in the plantation. Corsican, Scotch, Austrian firs and larch all went with us at the same spots. The fungus attacks the roots and collar of the tree, and if a slice of bark be removed at the collar the fungus will be seen under the bark enveloping the stem in a sheet of white fungi, and in October and November the stools will be found growing at the collar of the affected trees and away from them as well. Hartig gives a very correct description of this fungus, and also of *Trametes radiciperda*, which he describes as being, if anything, worse than the *Agaricus*, affecting the trees in a similar way. The only preventive he suggests is digging a deep trench round the affected spots to prevent the fungus extending, which it can only do through the soil, but in our own case that is impracticable, as the stools are everywhere in autumn, and the surprising thing is that so few trees comparatively are attacked.

Reverting to the beetle plagues mentioned, we 'have come to think that some trees are more predisposed to their attacks than others. It is certain, at all events, that the pine beetle and fir weevil are rarely or never absent from pine woods, and are often tolerably abundant where no damage to anything approaching the extent described by Miss E. A. Omerod is ever seen. The only preventive measures suggested by experts in these matters is the removal of all debris in the shape of decaying stumps and branches from the woods, as the insects shelter and breed among these in winter and spring and come out to feed on the trees in summer.

COMMON SPRUCE FIR, SILVER FIR, AND OTHERS.—With these are included the later introduced species like the Douglas fir, *Abies noblis*, and others named in Chapter VII. The common spruce and silver fir suffer more from diseases and insects than any of the other spruces, the same beetles, weevils, and fungus attacking them that attack the Scotch fir. The spruce gall aphis crimps the shoots of weak trees but does not hinder trunk development seriously. What seems to hurt all the *abies* family most and predispose them to disease are cold keen winds. Western gales blow the trees down, but keen, cutting east winds kill the trees eventually wherever they are exposed, and none are more sensitive than the common spruce. Planted in gullies, or in plantations well sheltered at their margins, the trees grow fast and are not seriously affected by disease unless the soil is very thin and dry, and then they make little headway anywhere. Removal of the debris from the wood is the only preventive of the ravages of insects.

THE LARCH.—Among forest trees no disease has caused so much trouble and disappointment to planters as that commonly known as the "larch disease," viz., ulcer or cancerous blister. This disease attacks the tree in all soils and situations, and it is doubtful if any of the explanations offered regarding the cause of its development and virulence under various conditions are correct.   There seems to be no doubt now that the disease is caused primarily by a fungus, *Peziza wilkommii*, because experts claim to have proved that the disease can be produced anywhere by innoculation.   Granting this, Hartig's theory of the spread of disease throughout Europe is probably the right one.   This theory, put shortly, is, first, that the disease has always existed, but not to a destructive extent, in the native habitat of the larch in high Alpine regions ; second, that when the tree was first distributed throughout Germany, Britain and elsewhere, the disease (not being propagated by the seeds) was left behind in its native habitat and the trees distributed flourished to perfection ; third, that after larch woods of all sizes had been established, from the foot of the Alps to the coasts of the North Sea and the Baltic, affording a continuous line of communication, the fungus spread downwards from the Alps to find everywhere the most favourable conditions for its development.   These consisted of dense pure woods and groups, moist, stagnant air, and wounds from various causes at which the disease entered.   Preventive measures, it is held, should consist in planting the tree, not in pure woods, but in small proportion in mixed woods, and in open airy situations (see Hartig's " Diseases of Trees "—the larch). Hartig, arguing that fungi require much moisture in the air to assist their development, thinks that the larch fungus is almost certain to be worst in low-lying, damp situations, an opinion shared by some foresters, but open to doubt.   It is known, for example, that the conditons as regards rainfall, moisture, and sunlight vary greatly in this country, and according to Hartig's theory we would expect the disease to be most virulent in wet districts and situations ; but that is not the case, for in very dry localities the disease is found in its worst form, and not always bad in wet ones.   We have seen many diseased plantations in England and Scotland, and the very worst case we ever saw was in Norfolk, near the mouth of the Wash, where the rainfall is about the lowest in England, the situation dry, and the soil favourable, as indicated by the health of older larch crops at the same place.   A plantation about seven years of age, that had grown in that time to a height of fifteen feet or more, was a mass of disease.   The stem of every tree was almost covered with blisters, which also extended to the side branches up almost to the base of the current year's growth.   On branches four-and-a-half feet long, as many as ten blisters, most of them well developed, might be seen. In another and opposite case, in the north of Yorkshire, in a plantation about the same age as the above, and in a valley beside a stream, the disease had begun in good time but had not made nearly so much progress as in the Norfolk plantation. Such puzzling examples are common. What struck one in the Norfolk case, moreover, was the enormous number of bark wounds which the trees must have received if, as experts say, the larch fungus can enter at a wound only. Hartig says that slow-growing trees are soonest overtaken by the disease and soonest succumb; but we venture the opinion that the disease makes most progress on gross, luxuriantly growing trees, and least progress on those that are well ripened and hard in the texture of their wood. Gumming, or canker, in peach trees, is caused by a fungus, and is so like larch blister in its general appearance and effects that the one might almost be mistaken for the other but for the smell of the resin in the larch and the bark, and all gardeners know that gumming is never bad on well-ripened trees, but only on trees with gross, ill-ripened growth. Gumming is quite under control under glass, but is often destructive out of doors. We believe that the larch disease is likely to be least troublesome on high and dry slopes where the soil is, if anything, rather thin and poor and the annual growth is likely to be well-matured.

Beetles and insects named as attacking the Scotch and other firs also attack the larch, but the worst plague is the *Chermes larcis*, or larch bug. It is worst in dry summers and on poor trees, which it soon covers, but one bad attack does not indicate another attack the following season. The attacks come and go, the trees being, as a rule, comparatively free from attacks where the conditions are favourable to its growth.

DEODAR AND WELLINGTONIA.—Neither of these species suffer noticeably from diseases or insects, but the wellingtonia does not stand cold, keen winds in open situations, where it should be grown as a plantation tree.

CHAPTER XX.

FORESTRY · EDUCATION.

SECTION I.—SCHOOLS.

WHILE not disputing the need of forestry education in this country, we have long regarded comparatively recent agitation on the subject as to some extent unreal. One might suppose, from much that has been said and written, that sylvicultural operations in this country would have to be almost suspended, and that we must sit with our hands folded until a new generation of foresters had arisen and set to work ; whereas, on almost any estate in Great Britain owners might start the newer and better system at once with the men and materials at their disposal; and some enterprising owners, like Mr. Monro Ferguson, of Raith, have already begun and reorganised their woods on the Continental system. In this book we have carefully confined ourselves to the production of timber. We know that British foresters and gardeners cannot be matched as growers of fine trees, and expert Continental foresters have admitted as much. The man who can grow fine trees can grow timber by simply changing his plan. M. Boppe, inspector of French forests, in his report of English and Scotch forests, speaking of learned treatises on forestry, says, foresters " may very well neglect the text if only they will adopt some of the principles which they contain," and that " ten years of systematic treatment (of woods) would form in itself the basis of a regular forest working plan, and the doctor's prescriptions would no longer frighten the patient."

Regarding forestry education in the abstract, and without prejudice, the problem is how to afford the best to those who have to plan and superintend the work in our woods. Owners of woods rarely profess to understand the practical duties of the forester, leaving the business to their agents and foresters. But experience has shown that agents usually know as little about the subject as their employers, and the evidence given before the Forestry Parliamentary Committee was strongly to that effect. They were said to depend upon the woodmen under them, who were also ignorant. A witness, Mr. Britton, who had much experience in the home timber trade on estates,

was satisfied that very few estate agents had a capable knowledge of forestry. He thought he could count all the
exceptions he had ever come across "upon his finger-ends."
The evidence of another witness illustrated the vagaries to
which a systemless forestry lends itself, and the extravagant
schemes to which owners of woods may be committed by their
agents. According to the Blue Book, this witness described
himself as having "had more practical experience than most
men," as a landscape gardener, and as having at one time had
the control of some of the most extensive woods in England,
with foresters under him, whom he taught. His system
of planting forest trees generally was to prepare the trees in
a nursery till they were at least four or five feet high, seven or
eight years of age, and plant them out finally twelve feet
apart, so that they would stand without thinning till they
became adult trees. After the trees were established, pines
for example, he proposed to go over the plantations every two
or three years and pinch in the side shoots in order to produce
straight trees like the columnar cypress, we presume. The
labour involved in growing timber-trees in this way struck the
examiners, as well it might. The cost of the trees of the
above age and size, in the first instance, would probably equal
or exceed the value of the ultimate crop of timber, to say
nothing of rents, rates, taxes, capital invested, and incidental
expenses. Yet the scheme was seriously proposed by one
who has been much employed by owners of estates in planting.
A knowledge of forestry conducted on rational principles
would soon dispose of foresters of this stamp, but that they
should exist is significant. A well-known owner of woods
in Scotland, who gave evidence before the Forestry Committee, lamented the differences of opinion that existed
between foresters, as illustrated by discussion amongst them,
but the foregoing views on the subject are probably unique.

Continental forestry schools have been pointed to as
examples to be copied in this country, but there is hardly any
parallel between Continental and British forestry, and the
same arguments do not apply in both cases. It is the extent
and importance of the forests, the system of forestry adopted,
and the prospect of desirable posts and promotion held out
to foresters that have brought the schools into existence on
the Continent, and made a good forestry education worth
trying for, conditions that hardly exist in this country. If we
consider the vastly greater extent of the German forests, for
example, compared to our own, that the proportion of land

under forests in Germany is as twenty-six or thereabout against two in Britain, reckoning density, and that German forests find well-paid posts for a whole army of officers, the relation of schools to forestry there will be better understood. The German forester has an important and well-defined charge, a good salary and position, and a number of privileges. The young German forestry candidate is also encouraged to go forward. After he has passed his two principal examinations —the first to test his theoretical knowledge of forestry, and the second to test his ability to apply what he has learned and capability for employment as a forester—he is employed in some probationary work, for which he receives a certain weekly or daily allowance, and may look forward to a permanent post within a reasonable period. The British forester has not these advantages, nor anything like them, and to expect him to seek a German forestry education for a situation in England or Scotland is absurd. It is not worth his while. In Germany it is the men who are to work in the forests that go to school, and it should be the same in this country when we possess schools of the right kind. If by some kind of reorganisation the forester's charge in our own country could be extended so as to include whole districts, better men would soon be found. Colonel Pearson, of the Indian forests, in his evidence before the Select Committee on Forestry, said that, "at present there is no field in Great Britain in which an educated forest officer, such as we find on the Continent, might gain a livelihood." The Indian Forest Department is the field that attracts men of the better class, and it is difficult to see, while present conditions and uncontrolled private ownership in woods exist in this country, where a better paid class of foresters could find posts. Reorganisation of our woods and forests is wanted first; and the conviction has to be borne in upon the minds of estate owners that planting for timber might be made remunerative before they will pay high salaries to foresters. As private estates are conducted at present, the only persons worth whose while is is to learn forestry on the higher scale and combine it with their other duties are estate agents, and at present they do not even profess, as a rule, to understand the business, although the woods usually represent a large portion of the value of an estate, and the most interesting portion of it as well. Carelessness on the part of owners, and indifference on the part of their agents, correctly describes the state of affairs on most estates at present, so far as general management is concerned.

Our agricultural schools profess to teach forestry, and employ "professors" of the art as teachers, but their pupils belong almost exclusively to a class who never become practical foresters, and the fees charged are prohibitive to those who seek foresters' situations. Besides, the practical element is wanting in such schools, if one may judge by the examples they turn out, and we have had rather exceptional means of knowing. Such pupils talk intelligently and glibly about the science of forestry, and often pass examinations successfully, but they are usually ignorant of the most elementary practical duties of the forester, incapable of organising work, do not know when it is properly executed, and are frequently so unfamiliar with our forest trees as not to know many common species when they see them. The general course of instruction pursued at agricultural schools is too lengthy and varied for those who desire to master one subject in a reasonable time, and special attention cannot be given. The forester does not require so many scientific attainments as has been prescribed for him. He requires very little chemistry, no more geology than relates to the surface soils and the name of the formation they overlie, and his entomology and plant pathology need not extend beyond narrow limits. It is not from want of any of these that he cannot grow good crops of timber of the right quality. Such subjects as climate, rainfall, heat, light, air, moisture, soils, in their relation to forestry, and vegetable physiology, he should understand fairly well; and in a business capacity he should understand land surveying, valuing, timber measuring, labour, and the timber trade. This is not as formidable a list as it looks. Even in Germany, we are told, although the school course is long and hard, much of the cramming that the pupil undergoes is afterwards lost or neglected in practical work, and it is interesting to note how well managed many extensive forest areas are on few and simple lines. A rigid system, strict rotation periods, few species to care for, and careful inspection by superior officers, keeps the regular German forester in a pretty safe groove.

Theory and practice are best taught in conjunction, and there are plenty of well-wooded estates in England and Scotland where this could be done, under competent teachers, for all the conditions that regulate the production of timber-trees are present in our own woods (no matter whether the system practised be right or wrong), provided they are sought out and properly studied. It is not necessary to see a whole forest in

14

order to understand how an oak or a fir tree ought to be grown.   Provided the physiological and other conditions are understood, and a few examples can be found, that can be demonstrated anywhere.

In order to teach foresters their duties quickly and cheaply a " school station " on a well-wooded estate would provide all the essentials. Here, if an agricultural college, like Cirencester, for example, was to establish an out-station, a dozen or score of pupils at a moderate fee would make it worth while.   More than a class room would hardly be needed if the pupils lodged out, as many of the University lads in Scotland do now, and they could provide their own books, etc.   A forestry education of this kind is as much as the intending forester can afford, and as much as he needs, as forestry goes at present, and plenty of owners of woods would, we have no doubt, be glad to let their woods be used for such a purpose, and be willing to adapt their management to any system that promised to be advantageous.   Given a good teacher, a system, and the right text books, the wood should furnish the rest.   A good theoretical training is absolutely necessary, but without the practical part the pupil has no confidence in himself.   He must see and handle things and become familiar with woodcraft in all its branches ; but he need not become a mere wood labourer for that purpose, although he will be much benefited by being brought into frequent contact with the ordinary wood hands at their daily work.

We do not under-rate the value of special schools on a large scale with woods attached (but not yet created), as seems to be the idea of some.   What is here suggested is a practicable scheme likely to meet present wants, and we have the materials at home for that purpose if properly utilised.   There are foresters now who have never been far beyond their own neighbourhood, who have a perfectly clear conception of the Continental forestry system, gained by reading and by observation in the wood, and who could carry the same system out perfectly well if called upon.   As yet the educated forester has no scope.   The first thing to be done, where a Government has no control of the forests, is to convince proprietors of the need of a change and of a recognised system of wood management, and the men would then be forthcoming.   We have faith that the owners of estates in Great Britain and Ireland, who have undoubtedly planted extensively and with praiseworthy motives in times past, will soon come to see the necessity of taking better care of their plantations than has been the case hitherto, although the mismanagement has not been due so much to the neglect of owners themselves as to the ignorance of those who professed to understand the business and who advised them. The only men fitted to engage in scientific forestry at present are those who have had a gardener's education to begin with. That, the ordinary woodman of the past has seldom had. It might have been supposed that two professions so closely connected as forestry and gardening would have progressed hand-in-hand. But they have not done so, for horticulture has gone ahead, while forestry has almost stood still. On many estates not a few of the more important duties of the forester have devolved upon the gardener, and it is an indisputable fact that with the exception of some recent works nearly all that has been written on forestry and allied subjects has been written by gardeners, while the horticultural press has served as the organ of forestry, every attempt of the latter to establish a paper of its own having failed from want of support from owners of woods and their foresters. Arboricultural societies have, as is well known, been next to impotent institutions, and have had little or no hand in the present revival of forestry, which originated from outside sources, including the horticultural and agricultural press. The Continental system of forestry, now recommended for adoption in this country, was in operation long before our arboricultural societies were founded—has been in force for over a quarter-of-a-century in our Indian forests; and our arboricultural societies, with means and influence at their disposal, might have been expected to introduce an improved system at home to which general practice might conform, but their "transactions" show few or no signs of their having ever realised the necessity of moving in a practical direction, or of having had any real acquaintance with any other system of forestry than that practised by the mistaken followers of Brown, among whom their awards and commendations have been somewhat promiscuously distributed from time to time. And this has been going on while a system of forestry, reduced almost to an exact science, has been in operation at our door, so to speak, and the products of which have been a constantly standing evidence of our own mistaken practice.

This is not the first time it has been pointed out that a mere labourer's experience in woods for a few years is insufficient to qualify a man to have charge of woods and plantations on estates. The young intending forester should serve a joint apprenticeship to both gardening and forestry as the first preparation for the post of forester, unless he can afford to go to a forestry school.   Even Brown has admitted in his " Forester " that, with a few exceptions, many foresters in this country are mere workmen whose only qualification is that they can plant trees in the usual way and cut them down when they are ready for the axe.   Sir Henry Stewart, in his " Planter's Guide," dedicated to the King, 1828, describes foresters, even in Scotland, as " mere loppers and cutters of wood," and declared that gentlemen saw with the eyes and heard with the ears of their gardeners, who were a class of men of superior intelligence.

What gives the gardener the advantage of the forester, whose experience has been confined to woods alone, is the far more extensive and varied nature of his experience and knowledge in plant and tree culture, derived from experience in the garden, in public nurseries, and from books, sources of which the young forester has hitherto rarely availed himself.

The gardener is already an accomplished arboriculturist, or tree grower, and he has only to reverse the process to become a sylviculturist or timber grower.   There are a few things in forestry his education does not prepare him for, such as planting and thinning for timber, and valuing standing timber, etc., but these may soon be learned, and the time will probably soon come when all timber will be felled by the vendor and measured and sold down, instead of standing, when valuing becomes an easy task.

We strongly advise young gardeners to learn forestry. On many large estates gardeners already have control of the woods, and on estates where no regular forester is employed they have long performed all the chief duties of the forester. It is not suggested that the gardeners should usurp the forester's place, but it would certainly often be an advantage to both the employer and the employed if the gardens and woods could be worked in conjunction on estates of moderate extent.   .

CHAPTER XXI.

FORESTRY TOOLS AND APPLIANCES.

IT is not needful to give more than a list of these, as they are for the most part familiar to woodmen, and nearly all seedsmen keep a stock on hand from which selections can be made. Here we shall only name such tools as are in general use in woods.

PLANTING TOOLS.

Garden Spades, 1st and 2nd sizes.
Narrow Planting Spades, 1st and 2nd sizes.
Steel Forks, 1st and 2nd sizes.
Trowels, largest size.
Dibbers, Planting, shod with iron.
Hacks, Planting.
Mattocks.
Picks.

PRUNING TOOLS.

Axes.
Bill Hooks, short and long-shafted.
Hedge Bills.
Hand Saws.
Pruning Saws.
Knives.
Chisels, on shafts.
Secateurs of several sizes, French.
Hedge Shears.

FELLING TOOLS.

Axes, English and American.
Double-handed Saws, large and small.
Wedges.
Barking Irons.

Tools for Marking and Measuring Timber for Sale.

Measuring Rods, in five feet lengths, socketed.
Measuring Tapes, Woodman's quarter-girth.
Marking Scribes.
Spokeshaves.
Paint Brushes.
Paint Pots.
Ladders.

Sundry Tools and Appliances

Trolleys.
Wheelbarrows.
Hand-barrows.
Crowbars.
Hammers, for driving and nailing.
Mallets.
Augers.
Scythes.
Chisels.
Dutch Hoes.
Draw Hoes.
Rakes, Wood and Iron.
Lines.
Edging Cutters.
Measuring Tapes.
Measuring and Levelling Rods.
Garden Lines.
Rollers.
Watering Cans.
Sieves and Riddles.

INDEX.

—

A

B

C

S

T